T0247541

'This book is the result of rigorous text [illegible] valued not only by the academic comm[illegible] practitioners. This book serves as an imp[illegible] who wish to learn *about* Buddhist thoug[illegible] and those who wish to learn *from* it.... As a monk engaging himself in Buddhist meditation as well as a professor applying a historical-critical methodology, Bhikkhu Anālayo is well positioned to bridge these two communities who both seek to deepen their understanding of these texts.' – **from the Foreword, 17th Karmapa Ogyen Trinley Dorje**

'In this study, Venerable Anālayo Bhikkhu brings a meticulous textual analysis of Pali texts, the Chinese Āgamas and related material from Sanskrit and Tibetan to the foundational topics of compassion and emptiness. While his analysis is grounded in a scholarly approach, he has written this study as a helpful guide for meditation practice. The topics of compassion and emptiness are often associated with Tibetan Buddhism but here Venerable Anālayo makes clear their importance in the early Pali texts and the original schools.' – **Jetsunma Tenzin Palmo**

'This is an intriguing and delightful book that presents these topics from the viewpoint of the early suttas as well as from other perspectives, and grounds them in both theory and meditative practice.' – **Bhikshuni Thubten Chodron**

'A gift of visionary scholarship and practice. Anālayo holds a lamp to illuminate how the earliest teachings wed the great heart of compassion and the liberating heart of emptiness and invites us to join in this profound training.' – **Jack Kornfield**

'Arising from the author's long-term, dedicated practice and study, *Compassion and Emptiness in Early Buddhist Meditation* provides a window into the depth and beauty of the Buddha's liberating teachings. Serious meditation students will benefit tremendously from the clarity of understanding that Venerable Anālayo's efforts have achieved.' – **Sharon Salzberg**

'I was taught by some Mahāyāna Buddhist teachers that non-Mahāyāna forms of Buddhism, including pre-Mahāyāna schools of Buddhism, lack deep teachings on compassion and emptiness, which made them inferior to Mahāyāna Buddhism's. After I began to study the Pali texts on my own, such claims no longer seemed cogent to me. They seem to be part of an unfortunate Buddhist sectarianism that is still prevalent. This scholarly book is more than timely with its demonstrations that teachings on emptiness and compassion that are helpful to practitioners of any form of Buddhism are abundant in early Buddhist texts.' – **Professor Rita M. Gross**

Also by Bhikkhu Anālayo

*Satipaṭṭhāna: The Direct Path to Realization*
*The Genesis of the Bodhisattva Ideal*
*A Comparative Study of the Majjhima-nikāya*
*Excursions into the Thought-world of the Pāli Discourses*
*Perspectives on Satipaṭṭhāna*
*The Dawn of Abhidharma*

# Compassion and Emptiness in Early Buddhist Meditation

Bhikkhu Anālayo

Windhorse Publications

Windhorse Publications
17e Sturton Street
Cambridge
CB1 2SN
UK

info@windhorsepublications.com
www.windhorsepublications.com

© Bhikkhu Anālayo, 2015
Reprinted 2019

The right of Anālayo to be identified as the author of this work has been asserted by him in accordance with the Copyright, Designs and Patents Act 1988.

As an act of Dhammadāna, Anālayo has waived royalty payments for this book.
The index was not compiled by the author.

Cover design by Dhammarati

Typesetting and layout by Ruth Rudd
Printed by Bell & Bain Ltd, Glasgow

**British Library Cataloguing in Publication Data:**
A catalogue record for this book is available from the British Library.

ISBN: 978 1 909314 55 9

# CONTENTS

# ABOUT THE AUTHOR

Born in 1962 in Germany, Bhikkhu Anālayo was ordained in 1995 in Sri Lanka, and completed a PhD on the *Satipaṭṭhāna-sutta* at the University of Peradeniya, Sri Lanka, in 2000 – published in 2003 by Windhorse Publications under the title *Satipaṭṭhāna: The Direct Path to Realization.*

Anālayo is a professor at the Numata Center for Buddhist Studies of the University of Hamburg and researches at the Dharma Drum Institute of Liberal Arts in Taiwan. His main research area is early Buddhism and in particular the topics of the Chinese *Āgama*s, meditation, and women in Buddhism. Besides his academic pursuits, he spends about half of his time in meditation under retreat conditions and regularly teaches meditation courses in Asia and the West.

# ACKNOWLEDGEMENTS AND DEDICATION

I am indebted to Shaila Catherine, Adam Clarke, Sāmaṇerī Dhammadinnā, Dawn P. Neal, Mike Running, Jill Shepherd, and Shi Syinchen for having helped me to improve my presentation. Any shortcomings in the following pages are entirely due to my own ignorance.

I would like to dedicate this book to the memory of Godwin Samararatne (1932–2000), a Sri Lankan meditation teacher believed by many to have reached an advanced level in his cultivation of the bodhisattva path, for having in a very practical way taught me compassion and emptiness in their inseparability.

# PUBLISHER'S ACKNOWLEDGEMENTS

Windhorse Publications wishes to gratefully acknowledge and thank the individual donors who gave to the book's production via our "Sponsor-a-book" campaign in 2014 and 2015.

# FOREWORD BY H.H. THE 17TH KARMAPA

I am pleased to have the opportunity to introduce this book by Professor Dr Bhikkhu Anālayo, not only as a contribution to our understanding of early Buddhist meditation, but as a work of bridge-building on many levels.

First of all, *Compassion and Emptiness in Early Buddhist Meditation* is the result of rigorous textual scholarship that can be valued not only by the academic community but also by Buddhist practitioners. This book serves as an important bridge between those who wish to learn *about* Buddhist thought and practice and those who wish to learn *from* it. I believe this bridge-building is valuable, as academic scholarship on Buddhist texts is greatly enriched by taking into consideration the uses to which such texts are put in the lives of practitioners. As a monk engaging himself in Buddhist meditation as well as a professor applying a historical-critical methodology, Bhikkhu Anālayo is well positioned to bridge these two communities who both seek to deepen their understanding of these texts.

Secondly, I also believe that those studying Buddhism within one tradition are well advised to consider the texts preserved in other traditions' canons. Too often, we allow language to become a barrier and overlook the versions of our own texts extant in other languages. The bridge built in this book between Pāli, Sanskrit, Chinese, and Tibetan texts reveals just how widely shared the concern with cultivating compassion and understanding emptiness is. It also allows us to reflect on the nuances of the differences in their presentation in varying contexts.

Finally, this book brings together the two topics of compassion and emptiness within a single work, and highlights the value of treating them as mutually complementary. In this way, as we might say in Mahāyāna Buddhism, Bhikkhu Anālayo has ensured that the two wings of the bird remain united, allowing meditative experience and philosophical understanding to truly take flight.

17th Karmapa Ogyen Trinley Dorje
Bodhgaya, India
18 November 2014

# INTRODUCTION

With the present book I explore the meditative practices of compassion and emptiness by examining and interpreting relevant material from the early discourses. Similar to my previous study entitled *Perspectives on Satipaṭṭhāna*,[1] in the present case I approach matters of practice from the perspective that emerges through a comparative study of the versions that parallel the Pāli discourses, which are extant mainly in Chinese as well as at times in Sanskrit and Tibetan. Although my presentation is based on academic methodology, as a whole this book is meant for practitioners and relevance to meditation practice informs my exploration.[2]

In Chapter 1 I explore the nature of compassion, before moving on in Chapter 2 to a contextualization of compassion within the standard set of the four divine abodes, *brahmavihāras*. In Chapter 3 I study the fruits to be expected from maturing compassion. The next three chapters are dedicated to emptiness, mainly based on the gradual meditative entry into emptiness described in the *Cūḷasuññata-sutta* and its parallels. In Chapter 7, I provide practical instructions on how meditation practice can proceed from compassion to emptiness.

1 Anālayo 2013c.

2 For the same reason I have placed a more detailed discussion of the following topics in separate papers: in Anālayo 2015b I take up the evolution of the commentarial instructions on cultivating the *brahmavihāras* with individual persons as the object; in Anālayo 2015a I survey the opinions voiced by other scholars regarding the relationship between the *brahmavihāras* and awakening; and in Anālayo 2014d I discuss the problematic usage of the term *hīnayāna*.

Chapter 8 offers translations of the *Madhyama-āgama* parallels to the *Karajakāya-sutta*, the *Cūḷasuññata-sutta*, and the *Mahāsuññata-sutta*, three discourses that are of central importance throughout my study.

In order to keep alive a sense of actual practice, I try as much as possible to consider passages in light of their relevance to meditation. When on a few occasions I quote academics or meditation teachers[3], my intention is not to present their statements as directly corresponding to or in some way authenticating what I am discussing. Such references only reflect the fact that in my own practice I have found what I quote helpful, even though, without having practised under these teachers, I am unable to verify the context and implications of their instructions fully. The form of practice I present in the following pages is meant to offer just one possible mode of approach, without any implicit claim that this is the only right understanding or description that fits the early discourses. I only intend to provide one of several possible avenues to encourage readers to develop their own approach.

When translating the parallel versions preserved in Chinese and other languages,[4] I do not intend to imply a judgement of any kind about their relative value vis-à-vis the Pāli canon. Instead, I offer these translations merely as an expedient means to enable the reader to gain a first-hand impression of the situation in these parallel versions. The wealth of discourses preserved in the Chinese *Āgama*s is largely unknown to the general public, mostly due to a lack of translations. Hence I attempt to provide translations of a selection of relevant passages. All translations are my own; at times my understanding of a particular passage differs from an already existing translation referred to in my footnotes, in which I refer to the standard English translations of the relevant Pāli passages in order to facilitate comparison beyond the selected observations that I am able to provide regarding variations between the parallels.

From an academic viewpoint it is not possible to reconstruct with absolute certainty what the historical Buddha said. Within the limits of the source material at our disposal, however, the comparative

3 Burbea 2014 came too late to my notice to be taken into account.

4 My translations throughout are based on the CBETA edition of the Chinese canon; at times I have followed variant readings or emendations suggested by the CBETA team. Since the present work is aimed at a general readership, I have not marked such instances in my translations and only explicitly note my own emendations of the text.

study of the early discourses takes us back as close as possible to the original delivery of a particular teaching. This offers a window onto the earliest stages of Buddhist thought on compassion and emptiness. Given that this early stage would have been the common starting point of the different Buddhist schools and traditions, I hope that my examination will be of interest to followers of any Buddhist tradition. In order to present such common ground, I have endeavoured to base my exploration predominantly on material that has been preserved in the canonical discourses of more than one school. On the rare occasions when I depart from this approach, I alert the reader to the fact that the passage taken up is only preserved in one tradition.

In the excerpt translations in the following chapters, I have tried to avoid gendered terminology, in order to ensure that my presentation does not give the impression of being meant for male monastic practitioners only.[5] The actual texts often have a monk as their protagonist and I have kept to the original formulation in the complete translations of the three main discourses given at the end of this book, so as to offer the reader a text that is as faithful to the original as possible within the confines of my translation abilities. In excerpts that come interspersed in my study, however, I have usually replaced "monk" with "... one", in order to ensure that the meditation instructions are of similar appeal to any reader, monastic or lay, male or female.

When translating from the Chinese, here and elsewhere I employ Pāli terms in my translation for the sake of ease of comparison, without thereby intending to take a position on the language of the original used for translation into Chinese. Exceptions are terms like "Dharma" and "Nirvāṇa", both of which are now commonly used in Western publications.

---

5 In its usage in the early discourses, the term *bhikkhu* does in fact appear to be gender-inclusive; cf. in more detail Collett and Anālayo 2014.

# I

# CULTIVATING COMPASSION

In the present chapter I examine aspects of the cultivation of compassion, proceeding from active expressions of compassion to its meditative practice.

## I.1 THE NATURE OF COMPASSION

The early discourses do not offer a succinct definition of the term "compassion". The giving of precise definitions is a concern mainly of later literature, so that determining the meaning of a particular term in its early Buddhist usage often requires some interpretation. Particularly helpful in this respect are similes.

A simile that provides help for understanding the nature of compassion occurs in a discourse in the *Aṅguttara-nikāya* and its *Madhyama-āgama* parallel, which take up ways of overcoming resentment. The simile in question describes a situation that arouses feelings of compassion to illustrate the attitude one should cultivate towards someone who is immersed in unwholesomeness. Here is my translation of the simile in the *Madhyama-āgama* version:

> It is just like a person who is on an extended journey along a long road. Becoming sick halfway he is exhausted and suffering extremely. He is alone and without a companion. The village behind is far away and he has not yet reached the village ahead.
>
> Suppose a person comes and, standing to one side, sees that this traveller on an extended journey along a long road has become sick

> halfway, is exhausted and suffering extremely. He is alone and without a companion. The village behind is far away and he has not yet reached the village ahead. [The second person thinks:][1] "If he were to get an attendant, emerge from being in the wilderness far away and reach a village or town, and were to be given excellent medicine and be fed with nourishing and delicious food, be well cared for, then in this way this person's sickness would certainly subside."
>
> So that person has extremely compassionate, sympathetic, and kind thoughts in the mind towards this sick person.[2]

This simile shows that an essential component of compassion is the concern for others to be relieved from suffering and affliction. Although this is hardly surprising, a subtle but important point to be noted here is that the simile does not qualify the act of seeing the actual suffering as compassion. Rather, compassion is concerned with the other being free from affliction. The way the simile proceeds makes this quite clear, where the vision of the sick person being cared for, or even actually caring for this person, is what corresponds to the "extremely compassionate, sympathetic, and kind thoughts" of the person who has come by.

Drawing a clear distinction between the realization that others are suffering and the wish for them to be free from suffering is important, since mentally dwelling on the actual suffering would be contemplation of *dukkha*. Such contemplation offers a basis for the meditative cultivation of compassion. The cultivation of compassion itself, however, finds its expression in the wish for the other to be free from *dukkha*. In this way, the mind takes the vision of freedom from affliction as its object. Such an object can generate a positive, at times even a joyful state of mind, instead of resulting in sadness.

This is vital in so far as the meditative cultivation of compassion can only lead to deeper concentration if it is undertaken with a positive or even joyful mind. From a practical perspective this means that one's cultivation of compassion needs to steer clear of sadness. This is not easy, since what causes the arising of compassion can naturally lead to being afflicted oneself by sadness. Therefore it is

1 The Chinese original could also be read as if the person actually helps the traveller, although it seems to me more probable that the passage describes a reflection, not an action.

2 MĀ 25 at T I 454b18 to b25 (translated Bingenheimer et al. 2013: 169) and AN 5.162 at AN III 189,8 (translated Bodhi 2012: 776).

important to monitor closely one's own response to the affliction of others. This should ideally proceed from the opening of the heart that is genuinely receptive to the pain and suffering of others, to the positive mental condition of being filled with the wish for others to be free from affliction and suffering.

Understood in this way, compassion does not mean to commiserate to the extent of suffering along with the other. This would be falling prey to what later tradition considers to be the "near enemy" of compassion. According to the *Visuddhimagga*, cruelty is the "far enemy" of compassion, in the sense of being directly opposed to it, whereas worldly forms of sadness are its "near enemy".[3] Needless to say, both enemies are best avoided.

The early discourses do not explicitly draw a distinction between near and far enemies of compassion. However, they do mention that compassion is directly opposed to the wish for others to be harmed (corresponding to the far enemy of compassion). An explicit statement contrasting cruelty to the meditative cultivation of compassion can be found in the *Mahārāhulovāda-sutta* and its *Ekottarika-āgama* parallel.[4] The same also emerges from one of a set of six elements of release (*nissaraṇa*), listed in the *Dasuttara-sutta* and its parallels. In what follows I translate the relevant part from the Sanskrit fragment version:

> [Suppose someone] should speak in this way: "I have practised, cultivated, and made much of the concentration of the mind by compassion, yet cruelty still remains having pervaded my mind."
>
> Such a one should be told: "Do not say this. Why is that? It is impossible, it cannot be that cruelty remains pervading the mind of one who has practised, cultivated, and made much of the concentration of the mind by compassion; that is an impossibility. This is the release from all cruelty, namely the concentration of the mind by compassion."[5]

---

3 Vism 319,13 (translated Ñāṇamoli 1956/1991: 311).

4 MN 62 at MN I 424,28 (translated Ñāṇamoli 1995: 530) and its parallel EĀ 17.1 at T II 581c19.

5 Mittal 1957: 78. In the parallels DN 34 at DN III 280,27 (the relevant part is abbreviated, the full text is found in DN 33 at DN III 248,16, translated Walshe 1987: 500) and DĀ 10 at T I 54b6 (this is also abbreviated; cf. T I 54b3), the initial statement is followed by the indication that in this way one actually misrepresents the Buddha. Such a statement is not found in another parallel, T 13 at T I 236a9. Among the Pāli discourses, the six elements of release recur in AN 6.13 at AN III 290,20 (translated Bodhi 2012: 867).

This passage makes it unmistakeably clear that one who has truly developed compassion will no longer be overwhelmed by cruelty, and that this holds not only for the time one is actually engaged in the practice. Although falling short of the complete removal of cruelty without remainder, the meditative cultivation of compassion clearly affects one's character trait, making it impossible for one to be completely overpowered by cruelty. Once this has happened, there will no longer be any scope for a broad range of unwholesome activities to take place. In this way the cultivation of compassion has important ethical ramifications and can offer a substantial contribution to progress towards liberation, a topic to which I will return later.[6]

### I.2 COMPASSION AND MORALITY

Moral conduct stands in direct relation to compassion. In fact moral conduct is an expression of compassion. This comes up explicitly in the more detailed description of the first of the unwholesome bodily deeds given in the parallels to the *Karajakāya-sutta*, a discourse to which I will return repeatedly in different parts of my study of compassion. The passage in question indicates that one who kills living beings lacks compassion. According to the *Madhyama-āgama* version, such a one "has the wish to injure and is without compassion for living beings".[7]

This in turn implies that one who abstains from killing living beings thereby acts with compassion. The presence of compassion is to some degree also implicit in abstaining from other forms of unwholesome behaviour. Refraining from theft, for example, can certainly be considered compassionate activity, just as refraining from the type of sexual conduct that inflicts harm on others. In this way, all physical activity that avoids the harm of others can be seen as an expression of the wish for others to be free from affliction and thus of compassion.

6 See Anālayo 2015a and below p.59.
7 MĀ 15 at T I 437c3 (translated below p.170, with a parallel in D 4094 *ju* 236b5 or Q 5595 *tu* 270a8. Whereas this detailed exposition seems to have been lost from AN 10.208 (see below note 45), a reference to compassion can be found in the description of abstaining from killing living beings in the preceding discourse AN 10.206 at AN V 295,6 (translated Bodhi 2012: 1535, given as number 217), repeated in abbreviated form in AN 10.207 at AN V 298,26.

The relation of compassion to verbal activities comes under more detailed scrutiny in the *Abhayarājakumāra-sutta*.[8] The discourse describes the types of speech the Buddha would use, distinguishing them according to three criteria:[9] is such speech truthful? Is it beneficial? Is it agreeable to others? The *Abhayarājakumāra-sutta* clarifies that the Buddha will not engage in speech that is not in accordance with the truth or that is not beneficial. However, in the case of speech that is truthful and beneficial, the Buddha will at times say what is not pleasing to others. The discourse explicitly indicates that the Buddha's speaking in these ways is an expression of his compassion.

From a practitioner's perspective, then, to express compassion verbally does not mean that one only says what others find pleasing and agreeable. Of course, an effort should always be made to avoid hurting others. But at times it may be necessary to say something displeasing, if it is true and beneficial. In other words, the compassionate vision that informs one's verbal activities does not consider only harmony in the present moment. Instead it evaluates a situation in the light of both short-term and long-term repercussions. Motivated by the wish to help others emerge from the conditions that cause their unhappiness, such compassion has the courage to do what is temporarily unpleasant, whenever this is required. In this way verbal activity can become the fitting expression of a mind that is filled with compassion.

### I.3 COMPASSION AND THE FOUR NOBLE TRUTHS

Already from these few passages a clear relationship emerges between compassionate concern and physical as well as verbal deeds. Nevertheless, it is worth noting that the early discourses do not show the Buddha or his arahant disciples engaging in charitable activities. Instead, his lay disciple Anāthapiṇḍika features as exemplary in

---

8 Unfortunately the relevant part of the discourse has not been preserved among what is extant from a parallel to the *Abhayarājakumāra-sutta* in Sanskrit fragments and a discourse quotation extant in Chinese translation. Hoernle fragment Or. 15009/100, Hirabayashi 2009: 167, has preserved only the beginning part of the discourse. A discourse quotation in the **Mahāprajñāpāramitopadeśa*, T 1509 at T XXV 321b15 to b25, records the first part of the discussion between the Buddha and his interlocutor, but stops short of the part with which I am concerned here.

9 MN 58 at MN I 395,8 (translated Ñāṇamoli 1995: 500).

this regard in the early discourses. His deeds of charity had already gained him repute when he first met the Buddha.[10] This implies that his philanthropic activities were not an outcome of his conversion to Buddhism, but rather something he had been engaging in before.

The Buddha himself is on record for undertaking charitable activities before his awakening, during one of his previous lives. According to a *jātaka* tale, which strictly speaking belongs to the commentarial strata of Pāli literature, the bodhisattva who was to become Gotama Buddha had a place constructed for the destitute and for pregnant women.[11] No such activities are on record for the time that followed his awakening. Instead, the form his compassion took from then onwards was teaching the Dharma.[12]

The *Ariyapariyesanā-sutta* and its *Madhyama-āgama* parallel report that the Buddha at first wished to share his discovery of the path to liberation with his two former teachers. On finding out that they had passed away, he decided instead to teach his five former companions.[13] In this way, the Buddha's compassionate teaching activities began by disclosing the four noble truths to them.

It deserves to be noted that the Buddha's compassionate impulse to teach others first manifests as a sense of gratitude. Even though the practice advocated by his first two teachers and the asceticism upheld by his five former companions had not led him to awakening, they did form part of the path he had traversed. Apparently in recognition of his debt of gratitude to those who supported him in his search,

---

10 MĀ 28 at T I 460c10 (translated Bingenheimer et al. 2013: 198) and its parallels SĀ 592 at T II 158b12 and SĀ[2] 186 at T II 441a18 report that he informed the Buddha during their first meeting that his actual name was Sudatta, but that he was referred to as the one who feeds the destitute, Anāthapiṇḍika, because of his charitable deeds. This of course implies that he had already become famous for his philanthropic activities before becoming a Buddhist lay follower. The version of their first encounter in SN 10.8 at SN I 212,10 (translated Bodhi 2000: 312) and Vin II 156,19 (translated Horner 1952/1975: 219) differs, as here the Buddha divines his name Sudatta. Nevertheless, the continuation of the story in the Pāli *Vinaya* makes it clear that at that time he was already being called Anāthapiṇḍika; cf. Vin II 157,20.

11 Jā 546 at Jā VI 333,5 (translated Cowell and Rouse 1907: 158).

12 Bodhi 2013: 24 notes that, from the viewpoint of tradition, "while social work is certainly praiseworthy, of all benefits that can be conferred on others the most precious benefit is the gift of the Dhamma." The superiority of the gift of Dharma over all other types of gifts is also recorded in Aśoka's ninth rock edict at Girnār, Dhaulī, and Jaugaḍ; cf. Woolner 1924/1993: 19.

13 MN 26 at MN I 170,25 (translated Ñāṇamoli 1995: 263) and MĀ 204 at T I 777b4 (translated Anālayo 2012c: 32).

the Buddha's compassionate impulse to teach the path to liberation first turned to them.

Since his aim was to convey to his five former companions what he considered a discovery previously unheard of,[14] he had to employ novel expressions and depart at least to some extent from what in the ancient Indian setting were well-known philosophical or religious notions. In this situation, his realization of awakening finds expression in a scheme that appears to take its inspiration from medical diagnosis. Although there is no firm evidence that such a scheme was in use in ancient Indian medicine at the time of the Buddha, several discourses do compare the four noble truths to medical diagnosis.[15] This makes it fairly probable that such a scheme was in existence. The scheme in its Buddhist application is as follows:

| | |
|---|---|
| disease: | *dukkha* |
| pathogen: | craving |
| health: | Nirvāṇa |
| cure: | eightfold path |

In this way the Buddha's compassion made him act as the supreme physician by offering the medicinal treatment of the noble eightfold path that can lead to a condition of complete mental health.

The centrality of this pragmatic scheme in early Buddhist thought emerges also from the *Mahāhatthipadopama-sutta* and its *Madhyama-āgama* parallel, according to which the relationship of the four noble truths to wholesome states is comparable to that of an elephant's footprint to the footprints of other animals.[16] Owing to the large size of its circumference, combined with its depth due to the elephant's weight, this footprint is able to comprise the footprint of any other animal. In the same way, the four noble truths comprise all

---

14 For a comparative study of the Chinese parallels to the *Dhammacakkappavattana-sutta* cf. Anālayo 2012a and Anālayo 2013a.

15 SĀ 389 at T II 105a24 (translated in Anālayo 2011c: 23f), SĀ² 254 at T II 462c9, T 219 at T IV 802a16, a quotation in the *Abhidharmakośopāyikā-ṭīkā*, D 4094 *nyu* 1b1 or Q 5595 *thu* 32b6, a quotation in the *Abhidharmakośavyākhya*, Wogihara 1936: 514,27, a partial quotation in the *Arthaviniścaya-sūtra*, Samtani 1971: 159,6, and a version preserved in Uighur fragments, Kudara and Zieme 1995: 47–52; for a more detailed discussion cf. Anālayo 2011c.

16 MN 28 at MN I 184,26 (translated Ñāṇamoli 1995: 278) and its parallel MĀ 30 at T I 464b23 (translated Bingenheimer et al. 2013: 219). According to Ñāṇaponika 1966/1981: 2, the simile conveys that "the Four Noble Truths comprise ... all that is beneficial, i.e. all that is truly worth knowing and following after."

wholesome states. This clearly invests the four noble truths with central importance in early Buddhist thought.

Besides being an expression of the Buddha's compassion, the four noble truths themselves also stand in a direct relationship to compassion. This relationship emerges from a discourse in the *Aṅguttara-nikāya* and its *Madhyama-āgama* parallel, which distinguish between "penetrative wisdom" and "vast wisdom". Here are the definitions of these two types of wisdom given in the *Madhyama-āgama* version:

> If ... one has heard that "this is *dukkha*" and through wisdom moreover rightly sees *dukkha* as it really is; [if] one has heard of "the arising of *dukkha*" ... "the cessation of *dukkha*" ... "the path to the cessation of *dukkha*", and with wisdom moreover rightly sees the path to the cessation of *dukkha* as it really is; then in this way ... one is learned with penetrative wisdom ...
>
> If ... one does not think of harming oneself, does not think of harming others, does not think of harming both; and instead ... one thinks of benefiting oneself and benefiting others, benefiting many people out of compassion for the affliction in the world, seeking what is meaningful and of benefit for *deva*s and humans, seeking their ease and happiness; then in this way ... one is bright, intelligent, and with vast wisdom.[17]

So penetrative wisdom comes through insight into the four noble truths; vast or great wisdom finds its expression in intending to benefit oneself and others, being motivated by compassion. This clearly points to a close relationship between the four noble truths and compassion as two complementary facets of wisdom, which should be penetrative as well as vast.

In this way, compassionate activity should ideally be based on the perspective afforded by the four noble truths. The resulting compassionate vision sees not only the actual pain and affliction of others (first truth), but also the conditions that have led to their predicament (second truth), and the conditions that can lead out of it (fourth truth). The motivating force of compassion is the wish for others to be free from pain and affliction (third truth). This is what makes compassion become thoroughly Buddhist, namely by way of being combined with the wisdom of the four noble truths.

---

17 MĀ 172 at T I 709b22 to b25 and 709c5 to c9, with a parallel in AN 4.186 at AN II 178,27 (translated Bodhi 2012: 555).

### I.4 COMPASSION AND TEACHING

Following the example set by the Buddha's teaching of the four noble truths out of compassion, active expressions of compassion in the early discourses predominantly take the form of teaching the Dharma. The connection between compassion and teaching was apparently felt to be so close and well established that a request for an instruction regularly comes accompanied by a reference to such a teaching being given "out of compassion". The term used in such contexts is *anukampā*, which in the early discourses often functions to express compassion in action, whereas *karuṇā* is the regular choice in contexts related to the meditative practice of compassion.[18] From a practical perspective, both stand for complementary facets of the early Buddhist notion of compassion.

Not only those who request a teaching but also those who deliver it consider such teaching activity to be an expression of compassion. A teaching given by the Buddha to his disciples at times ends with the emphatic indication that he has done for them out of compassion what a teacher should do.[19] In this way, once the Buddha has done his duty as a compassionate teacher, it is the disciples' turn to put into practice what he has taught.

In reply to a challenge by Māra, the Buddha emphasizes that his engaging in teaching activities is not related to any form of bondage, but simply an expression of his compassion.[20] How to teach out of pure compassion is taken up in another discourse. One should not teach with the wish to inspire listeners so that they make offerings to oneself.[21] Instead, the proper way to teach is when one is just motivated by the wish to benefit others.

---

18 The two cannot be completely set apart from each other, however, as at times *karuṇā* does stand for compassion in action, and *anukampā* can occur in what clearly is a meditative context. An example for the first would be Sn 426 (translated Norman 1992: 45), which refers to speaking with *karuṇā*. Contrary to the assumption by Aronson 1980/1986: 16 that *anukampā* never occurs in relation to meditation practice, an example of such an occurrence would be It 1.27 at It 21,10 (translated Ireland 1991: 20) and AN 8.1 at AN IV 151,1 (translated Bodhi 2012: 1112), where a reference to the boundless radiation of *mettā* leads on to a mental attitude of *anukampā* for all beings. Clearly here *anukampā* refers back to the radiation of *mettā* and functions as part of a description of what is a meditation practice.

19 An example is MN 19 at MN 118,20 (translated Ñāṇamoli 1995: 210) and its parallel MĀ 102 at T I 590a18.

20 SN 4.14 at SN I 111,19 (translated Bodhi 2000: 204) and its parallel SĀ 1097 at T II 288c8.

21 SN 16.3 at SN II 199,14 (translated Bodhi 2000: 665) and its parallels SĀ 1136 at T II 300a8, SĀ[2] 111 at T II 414b27, and T 121 at T II 544c28.

Besides teachings given by the Buddha himself, those by his disciples are also seen by others as being given out of compassion. So when a group of monks request that Sāriputta instruct another monk, they ask him to do so out of compassion.[22] The same formulation recurs when he is asked to visit and deliver a teaching to a sick layman.[23] In this way, a disciple is shown to engage in the same type of compassionate teaching activity as the Buddha himself.

The expectation in the early texts that the Buddha's disciples act with compassion finds reflection in another passage. This passage reports Sāriputta being rebuked for failing to take up his responsibility as a guide for other monks and thereby implicitly for failing to act with sufficient compassion. After the Buddha had dismissed a group of newly ordained and unruly monks for being too noisy, Sāriputta did not realize that it was now his duty to provide guidance to this group of monks. Instead he decided to remain uninvolved. As a consequence of his failure to take care of the monks, he had to face the Buddha's stern rebuke.[24] This throws into relief the importance accorded to teaching and providing guidance to others, to taking up responsibility for others. Such taking up of responsibility in situations where others are in need of guidance or assistance offers a very practical way of cultivating compassion, which can find its expression in the deliberate effort to help and advise others.

The same need to take up responsibility recurs in another discourse that describes Sāriputta being vexed by another monk who repeatedly contradicts him. Instead of intervening, Ānanda thinks it better to keep quiet. As a consequence of this, he incurs the Buddha's public censure for lacking compassion.[25] This passage confirms the importance accorded in the early discourses to taking responsibility and reacting with compassion. Such importance is somewhat dramatically highlighted by the fact that these two outstanding disciples of the Buddha, Sāriputta and Ānanda, are publicly criticized when they do not live up to the high standard

22 SN 22.85 at SN III 110,25 (translated Bodhi 2000: 932) and its parallel SĀ 104 at T II 31a4 (translated Anālayo 2014f: 12).

23 SN 55.26 at SN V 380,28 (translated Bodhi 2000: 1816) and its parallel MĀ 28 at T I 458c16 (translated Bingenheimer et al. 2013: 189).

24 MN 67 at MN I 459,18 (translated Ñāṇamoli 1995: 562) and EĀ 45.2 at T II 771b6.

25 AN 5.166 at AN III 194,22 (translated Bodhi 2012: 779) and MĀ 22 at T I 450a21 (translated Bingenheimer et al. 2013: 148).

of compassion and concern for others the Buddha was apparently expecting of them.

The importance of benefiting others through teaching comes up again in a discourse in the *Aṅguttara-nikāya* and its *Madhyama-āgama* parallel. The discourse features a Brahmin who upholds the view that by going forth one only benefits oneself. In reply, the Buddha points out that one who goes forth and reaches liberation will benefit many through being able to show them the path to freedom. The *Madhyama-āgama* version records the Buddha's statement as follows:

> One tells others: "I myself undertook such a path, such a track that, having undertaken this path, having undertaken this track, I eradicated all the influxes (*āsava*) and attained the influx-free liberation of the mind and liberation by wisdom, and I dwell having known by myself, having awakened by myself, having realized by myself: 'Birth has come to an end, the holy life has been established, what had to be done has been done, there will be no more experiencing of existence'; knowing it as it really is.
>
> "Come, all of you, and undertake yourselves such a path, such a track that, having undertaken this path, having undertaken this track, you will eradicate all the influxes and attain the influx-free liberation of the mind and liberation by wisdom, and will dwell knowing by yourselves, awakening by yourselves, realizing by yourselves: 'Birth has come to an end, the holy life has been established, what had to be done has been done, there will be no more experiencing of existence'; knowing it as it really is."[26]

Confronted with this description, the Brahmin had to admit that his previous assessment was wrong. By going forth to tame oneself, one can indeed benefit many. The view earlier upheld by the Brahmin is in fact understandable, since to go forth implies a withdrawal from social obligations and relations. This can easily give the impression that one is similarly withdrawing from compassionate concern for others. Yet this is not necessarily the case.

The same principle applies not only to going forth but also to temporarily withdrawing into seclusion for dedicated practice.

26 MĀ 143 at T I 650c17 to c25. Whereas in MĀ 143 the one who becomes liberated and then teaches others is introduced as a recluse or Brahmin, the parallel AN 3.60 at AN I 168,24 (translated Bodhi 2012: 262) refers more specifically to the Tathāgata as the one who has reached liberation and then shows others the path.

Here, too, what at first sight might appear to be a lack of compassion can instead become a powerful source for compassionate activity, as long as such practice is undertaken with the wish to benefit others.

### I.5 COMPASSION AND SECLUSION

Regarding withdrawal into seclusion, another aspect worth noting is that teaching out of compassion need not be confined to verbal instructions. It can also take place through teaching by example. In this way, even the Buddha's regular dwelling in seclusion stands in direct relation to compassion. According to the *Bhayabherava-sutta*, one of the two reasons for the Buddha's regular dwelling in seclusion was his "compassion for later generations".[27] A parallel preserved in the *Ekottarika-āgama* explains that his dwelling in secluded places served "to deliver incalculable [numbers of] living beings."[28] These statements highlight that with his secluded lifestyle the Buddha set an example to be emulated. In this way, his seclusion was not just undertaken for its own sake, but was motivated by compassion.

Besides the Buddha, his disciples can also function as examples to be emulated. The early discourses explicitly reckon the undertaking of various ascetic practices by Mahākassapa to have been similarly motivated by compassion for later generations,[29] by setting an inspiring example for them. In the *Mahāgosiṅga-sutta* and its parallels, Mahākassapa makes a point of combining the ascetic practices or other aspects of the path with commending such practices to others.[30] In this way one can encourage others to follow one's own example.

So when, according to a famous instruction recorded in a broad range of sources, the Buddha sent his first arahant disciples to tour the country and teach others,[31] he would have intended teaching

27 MN 4 at MN I 23,35 (translated Ñāṇamoli 1995: 107).

28 EĀ 31.1 at T II 666c25 (translated Anālayo 2011b: 219).

29 SN 16.5 at SN II 203,5 (translated Bodhi 2000: 667) and its parallels SĀ 1141 at T II 301c17 and SĀ² 116 at T II 416b19. Aronson 1980/1986: 11 comments that "Mahākassapa, like [the] Buddha, ... undertook beneficial activities with the hope that others would follow him and benefit similarly."

30 MN 32 at MN I 214,2 (translated Ñāṇamoli 1995: 309) and its parallels MĀ 184 at T I 727c2, EĀ 37.2 at T II 711a7, and T 154 (§16) at T III 81b16; for a survey of the different qualities listed in the parallel versions cf. Anālayo 2011a: 212.

31 SN 4.5 at SN I 105,24 (translated Bodhi 2000: 198) and its parallels SĀ 1096 at T II 288b3; the Dharmaguptaka *Vinaya*, T 1428 at T XXII 793a7; the

verbally as well as by way of example. Both can express one's compassionate concern for others.

In sum, then, from an early Buddhist viewpoint to cultivate compassion does not stand in conflict with withdrawing into meditative seclusion. As long as one's motivation comprises the aspiration to benefit others, regularly retreating for dedicated practice is certainly an integral part of the cultivation of compassion. In fact to some extent it could even be considered a requirement for proper compassionate activity to do so, in as much as dedicated training of the mind lays the proper foundation for being able to react with patience and compassion when interacting with others. The more the mind is purified from defilements, the better one will be able to react compassionately and thereby truly benefit others.

The basic underlying principle behind this finds its expression in a simile in the *Sallekha-sutta* and its parallels. The *Madhyama-āgama* version formulates it in this way:

> If one is not tamed oneself and wishes to tame someone else who is untamed, that is impossible. [If] one is drowning oneself and wishes to rescue someone else who is drowning, that is impossible. [If] one has not extinguished one's own [defilements] and wishes to make someone else with unextinguished [defilements] extinguish them, that is impossible...
>
> If one is tamed oneself and wishes to tame someone else who is untamed, that is certainly possible. [If] one is not drowning oneself and wishes to rescue someone else who is drowning, that is certainly possible. [If] one has extinguished one's own [defilements] and wishes to make someone else with unextinguished [defilements] extinguish them, that is certainly possible.[32]

The simile in the *Sallekha-sutta* and its parallels clearly puts a spotlight on the need to build a proper foundation for compassionate activity

---

*Mahāvastu*, Senart 1897: 415,8; the Mahīśāsaka *Vinaya*, T 1421 at T XXII 108a7; the Mūlasarvāstivāda *Vinaya*, T 1450 at T XXIV 130a20; the Sarvāstivāda *Vinaya*, T 1440 at T XXIII 511a12; and the Theravāda *Vinaya*, Vin I 21,1. Gombrich 1988: 19 comments that this injunction "shows that concern for the happiness of all beings is the foundation of the Saṅgha's very existence".

32 MĀ 91 at T I 574b2 to b8. A version of the simile in the parallel EĀ 47.9 at T II 784a20 also illustrates this principle with the example of drowning; in the simile in MN 8 at MN I 45,3 (translated Ñāṇamoli 1995: 130) the problem is more specifically that one is sinking in the mud.

through cultivation of one's own mind.[33] The need to build a basis in self-culture is also taken up in two stanzas in the different *Dharmapada* collections as well as in the *Udānavarga*. Here I translate the relevant lines from the Sanskrit *Udānavarga*:

> First one should establish oneself,
> in what is proper,
> then advise others.[34]

Whereas this indication is straightforward, the second stanza I have chosen for translation might at first sight seem somewhat controversial. It reads:

> One should not give up one's own welfare,
> even for the sake of much welfare of others.[35]

The principle expressed here in a poetic way recurs in a passage found in a discourse in the *Aṅguttara-nikāya* and its Chinese parallel. The passage distinguishes four types of persons according to whether they benefit themselves, others, neither, or both. Somewhat surprisingly, benefiting oneself is considered superior to benefiting others. This echoes the point made in the second stanza above. As a basis for further exploration of this issue, I translate the Chinese parallel to the *Aṅguttara-nikāya* discourse that lists these four types of persons:

> There are four types of persons: one person aids himself without aiding others, one person aids others without aiding himself, one person neither aids himself nor aids others, and one person aids himself and also aids others.
>
> The person who neither aids himself nor aids others is the most inferior person. [If] a person aids others without aiding himself, he is superior [to that]. If a person aids himself without aiding others,

33 Mahāsi 1981/2006: 34 comments on this simile that "only the man who has disciplined himself ... and extinguished the fires of defilements will be able to help another man in regard to discipline ... and extinction of defilements."

34 Stanza 23.7, Bernhard 1965: 292, with parallels in Dhp 158 (translated Norman 1997/2004: 24), the Patna *Dharmapada* 317, Cone 1989: 187, and the Gāndhārī *Dharmapada* 227, Brough 1962/2001: 155.

35 Stanza 23.10, Bernhard 1965: 294, with parallels in Dhp 166 (translated Norman 1997/2004: 25), the Patna *Dharmapada* 325, Cone 1989: 189, and the Gāndhārī *Dharmapada* 265, Brough 1962/2001: 160.

> he is superior [to that]. If a person aids himself and also aids others, he is the highest; a person like this is supreme.[36]

Right away the next discourse in the *Aṅguttara-nikāya* explains that to be practising only for one's own welfare means to be intent on purifying oneself, without encouraging others to do so.[37] Practising only for the welfare of others then stands for encouraging others to purify themselves, without doing so oneself. This explains the at first puzzling indication in the *Udānavarga* stanza that one should not give up one's own welfare for the sake of others. It also explains the similarly surprising indication that benefiting oneself is superior to benefiting others. These presentations are made from the perspective of cultivating the path to liberation. From this viewpoint, it is indeed important that one does not neglect first establishing oneself in what one recommends to others.[38] In this way, one's verbal teaching will be grounded in one's own practice and will be complemented by teaching undertaken by way of example.

Early Buddhist compassion thus requires a carefully maintained balance between concern for others and purifying oneself. This is conveniently illustrated in a simile of two acrobats who perform together.[39] To perform successfully, they need to establish their own balance as a basis for being able to take care of each other.

Similarly, by withdrawing into seclusion to practise intensively one becomes increasingly better able to maintain one's own inner balance and thereby also better able to take care of others. Practice done in a retreat setting turns into compassionate activity through

---

36 T 150A.9 at T II 877a26 to b2 (on this text cf. Harrison 1997). The parallel AN 4.95 at A II 95,15 (translated Bodhi 2012: 476) illustrates this with two similes. The first simile compares the one who benefits neither himself nor others to a cremation brand that is burning at both ends and in the middle smeared with dung, which cannot be put to any purpose. The other simile illustrates the one who benefits both himself and others with cream of ghee, which in ancient India was considered the supreme product to be obtained from a cow's milk.

37 AN 4.96 at AN II 96,11 (translated Bodhi 2012: 477).

38 Schmithausen 2004: 151 comments that "it is obvious that persons who do not exhort or encourage others but who at least themselves practise wholesome behaviour are regarded as being superior to those who merely give good advice, without practising themselves what they recommend to others."

39 SN 47.19 at SN V 168,18 (translated Bodhi 2000: 1648) and its parallel SĀ 619 at T II 173b7 (translated Anālayo 2013c: 244f); cf. also the *Bhaiṣajyavastu* of the Mūlasarvāstivāda *Vinaya*, T 1448 at T XXIV 32b10.

the transforming power of one's aspiration to pursue awakening for one's own benefit and for the benefit of others.

The meditative cultivation of compassion and compassionate activity through teaching and a secluded lifestyle reinforce each other. Both are integral parts of a dynamic circle of compassion which benefits both oneself and others.[40]

### I.6 COMPASSION IN MEDITATION

The foundation for actively responding to situations with a compassionate attitude is the meditative cultivation of compassion, and one's compassionate responses in actual life will in turn strengthen the compassionate disposition of one's own mind. The impact of meditative compassion on one's activities is taken up in a passage in the *Karajakāya-sutta* and its parallels. The *Madhyama-āgama* version of the passage in question reads as follows:

> [The Buddha said:] "Suppose there is a small boy or girl, who since birth is able to dwell in the liberation of the mind through compassion.[41] Later on, would [he or she] still perform unwholesome deeds by body, speech, or mind?" The monks answered: "Certainly not, Blessed One."[42]

This passage throws into relief the potential of cultivating compassion or the other divine abodes, *brahmavihāra*s, as a "liberation of the mind". Such cultivation transforms the way one acts, speaks, and thinks. In this way the cultivation of compassion can offer a substantial contribution to progress on the path to liberation.

---

40 Jenkins 1999: 27 aptly speaks of a "circle of compassion", "in which self-cultivation benefits others and benefitting others enhances self-cultivation".

41 A Tibetan parallel, D 4094 *ju* 238a6 or Q 5595 *tu* 272a5 (translated Dhammadinnā 2014a: 68), also mentions a boy and a girl, whereas AN 10.208 at AN V 300,2 (translated Bodhi 2012: 1542, given as number 219) refers only to a boy. Since all versions later on mention a man and a woman, the presentation in MĀ 15 and the Tibetan version seems to fit the context better.

42 MĀ 15 at T I 438a15 to a17 (translated below p.170) gives this passage in full only for the first and the last of the four *brahmavihāra*s. In order to keep with my main topic, I here give the passage for compassion, even though in the original this is only given in abbreviation after the passage that takes up the case of *mettā*.

In order to appreciate this contribution, however, it should be noted that the expression "liberation of the mind", *cetovimutti*, here refers to the experience of temporary liberation. Early Buddhist thought distinguishes between different types of liberation, some of which can be of a temporary type, whereas with the different levels of awakening one reaches liberation of the final and irreversible type.[43] In short, then, compassion contributes to, but is not in itself, final liberation.[44]

The *Madhyama-āgama* parallel to the *Karajakāya-sutta* describes the actual practice that leads to compassion as a temporary liberation of the mind in the following way:

> A learned noble disciple leaves behind unwholesome bodily deeds and develops wholesome bodily deeds, leaves behind unwholesome verbal and mental deeds and develops wholesome verbal and mental deeds.[45]
>
> Being endowed with diligence and virtue in this way, having accomplished purity of bodily deeds and purity of verbal and mental deeds, being free from ill will and contention, discarding sloth-and-torpor, being without restlessness or conceit, removing doubt and overcoming arrogance, with right mindfulness and right comprehension, being without bewilderment, the learned noble disciple dwells having pervaded one direction with a mind imbued with compassion, and in the same way the second, third, and fourth directions, the four intermediate directions, above and below, completely and everywhere.[46] Being without mental shackles, resentment, ill will, or contention, with a mind imbued with compassion that is supremely vast and great, boundless and well developed, [the learned noble disciple] dwells having pervaded the entire world.

43 For a more detailed discussion cf. Anālayo 2012b: 289–296.

44 See in more detail below p.63 and Anālayo 2015a.

45 This part appears to have been lost from AN 10.208; cf. in more detail Anālayo 2012c: 503 and Dhammadinnā 2014a: 64f.

46 The description of the meditative radiation in AN 10.208 at AN V 299,20 at this point reads *sabbatthatāya*, translated somewhat freely by Woodward 1936/1955: 193 as "for all sorts". The translation by Bodhi 2012: 1542, "to all as to himself", instead follows the commentarial gloss on the alternative reading *sabbattatāya* in the Asian editions of AN 10.208. A more detailed study of this phrase suggests that the preferable reading would be *sabbatthatāya*, conveying the sense "in every way"; cf. in more detail Anālayo 2015b.

> Then [the learned noble disciple] reflects like this: "Formerly my mind was narrow and not well developed; now my mind has become boundless and well developed."[47]

This passage makes several points worthy of note. Firstly, it clearly grounds the meditative practice of compassion and the other divine abodes in moral conduct. This reflects the close relationship between moral conduct and compassion mentioned above and at the same time also corresponds to a general feature of early Buddhist meditation theory, according to which a firm ethical basis is an indispensable foundation for successful meditative culture of the mind.

The above-quoted passage continues by showing that the foundation laid through moral conduct in this way has wholesome repercussions on the mind, enabling the overcoming of various mental hindrances that are impediments for successful mental culture.[48] The removal of these hindrances and the establishing of mindfulness and comprehension then lay the foundation for the meditative cultivation of compassion (or the other *brahmavihāras*).

This meditative cultivation takes the form of radiating the mental attitude of compassion in all directions. Such radiation is the standard mode of practice of the *brahmavihāras* described in the early discourses, with only minor differences between the parallel versions preserved by different reciter lineages and in various languages. This radiation has some similarity to *kasiṇa* practice, where a particular meditative object like earth, for example, comes to encompass the "totality" of one's experience.[49]

---

47 MĀ 15 at T I 438a3 to a12; as above, here, too, the original gives the passage in full only for the first and the last of the four *brahmavihāras*, and compassion is only mentioned in an abbreviated manner. I have again applied the description given for the first *brahmavihāra* to the case of compassion in order to keep with my main topic.

48 The fact that the actual listing of the hindrances in MĀ 15 does not mention sensual desire seems to me to be less significant, since the previous section that described the unwholesome mental deeds to be left behind does refer to overcoming covetousness and greed. The same is the case for the Tibetan version, which in fact does not list any of the hindrances explicitly. AN 10.208 at AN V 299,17 (translated Bodhi 2012: 1542, given as number 219), which appears to have lost the exposition of the unwholesome bodily, verbal, and mental deeds, starts here with a reference to freedom from desire, an expression that uses one of the two terms that in the Pāli discourses stand for the first of the five hindrances.

49 Such a basic similarity suggests itself from the description of the *kasiṇas* in MN 77 at MN II 14,31 (translated Ñāṇamoli 1995: 640; this whole part is not found in the parallel MĀ 207), which employs the same terms as

The passage translated above concludes by indicating that the mind, which formerly was narrow, has become boundless through meditative radiation. Such boundlessness is an intrinsic quality of the *brahmavihāras* as they are presented in the early discourses. This is the case to such an extent that an alternative term to qualify these mental states is "boundless" or "immeasurable", *appamāṇa*.

The same notion of a vast and spacious mental condition is to some extent also implicit in the term *brahmavihāra* in the Pāli discourses, given how according to ancient Indian cosmology the Brahmā gods dwell in their heavenly abode, *vihāra*. The *Saṅkhārupapatti-sutta* distinguishes different Brahmās by the extent to which they dwell pervading their respective worlds. Whereas one type of Brahmā may dwell pervading a thousand worlds, another type of Brahmā may dwell pervading a hundred thousand worlds.[50] This description gives the impression that a central notion underlying the term *brahmavihāra* is a form of mental pervasion that covers a vast amount of space. Fully cultivated, such mental pervasion then becomes "boundless", *appamāṇa*. In this way, one who radiates compassion in all directions at that very time dwells in a mental abode, *vihāra*, that mirrors the abode of Brahmā.[51]

The comprehensive and pervasive character of such radiation becomes particularly evident in a simile used in several discourses. The simile illustrates the meditation practice with the image of a conch-blower whose sound is heard in all four directions. Here is a version of this simile from the *Madhyama-āgama*:

> It is just as if there were a person skilled at blowing a conch. He goes to a place where nobody has ever heard it [i.e., the sound of a

---

used elsewhere for the radiation of the *brahmavihāras*, both descriptions pointing to a form of pervasion that is undertaken "above, below, around ... boundless".

50 MN 120 at MN III 101,4 (translated Ñāṇamoli 1995: 960), a discourse that does not seem to have a parallel properly speaking; cf. the discussion in Anālayo 2011a: 678f. King 1980/1992: 56 explains in relation to the *brahmavihāras* that "the sense of 'boundlessness' no doubt is derived from ... the near-infinity of the gods in terms of time and space, as well as indicating the possibility of achieving the goal of complete universalization by extension of these attitudes to all beings in all universes."

51 On the term itself, Norman 1991/1993: 274 comments that "it is noteworthy that what we might suppose to be the ways to gain *brahma-vihāra* ... are in fact given the name *brahma-vihāra* by the Buddha." In this way the meditative dwelling itself is the divine abode, not only the rebirth to be expected from successful practice.

> conch]. He climbs up a high mountain at midnight, and with all his might he blows the conch. A wonderful sound comes out of it that pervades the four directions.[52]

The discourse continues by indicating that in the same way a meditator pervades all four directions with the divine abodes.

### I.7 THE OBJECTS OF MEDITATIVE COMPASSION

A particularly noteworthy aspect of the above description of the boundless radiation of compassion is that it lacks any reference to an object. No person or living being is explicitly mentioned, a feature common to early discourses transmitted by different reciter lineages. Here is another description of such radiation practice, this time taken from the *Ekottarika-āgama* parallel to the *Vatthūpama-sutta*.

> With a mind of compassion one pervades one direction, being naturally delighted, and the second direction, the third direction, the fourth direction, as well as the four intermediate [directions], above and below, in every [place], completely and everywhere in the whole world, with a mind that is boundless and unlimited, that cannot be calculated, that is without aversion or anger and naturally at ease. Being pervaded within by this mind of compassion one has gained gladness and joy, and the mind has become straight.[53]

Compared to the passage translated earlier, this description shows some minor differences. Particularly noteworthy is the reference to being delighted and to gaining gladness and joy, as a result of which the mind becomes straight. The reference to gladness and joy confirms a point made above, in that the meditative cultivation of compassion requires avoiding that the mind succumb to sadness. Instead of mentally commiserating with instances of suffering and affliction, at the heart of compassion stand the wish and aspiration for others to be free from suffering and affliction. Such a wish can and should be free from sadness and grief.

---

52 MĀ 152 at T I 669c10 to c12. The parallel MN 99 at MN II 207,22 (translated Ñāṇamoli 1995: 816) is shorter and just describes a vigorous conch-blower who makes himself heard in all four directions.

53 EĀ 13.5 at T II 574a11 to a15. The parallel MN 7 at MN I 38,24 (translated Ñāṇamoli 1995: 120) does not mention delight, gladness, or joy, nor does it indicate that the mind becomes straight.

The above passage also confirms the nature of the practice as being free from a specific object. It describes a boundless radiation of compassion in all directions that encompasses the whole world, but without explicitly mentioning an object. As the **Mahāvibhāṣa* explains, the reference to the directions should be understood as intending the living beings in these directions.[54] Nevertheless, it is significant that the standard description in the early discourses does not concretize this in any way.

This stands in contrast to the mode of practice recommended in the *Visuddhimagga* for the meditative cultivation of the *brahmavihāra*s, which explicitly takes actual persons as its object.[55] The basic pattern in the *Visuddhimagga* involves taking up other persons, such as a friend, a neutral person, and an enemy. Meditation should then be developed up to absorption level with each of these persons as the object in turn, after which one is ready to cultivate the boundless radiation by gradually extending the object of one's practice until it becomes universal.

In the early discourses this type of approach, which takes up individual friends or enemies, is not found at all. The standard references to the meditative practice of the *brahmavihāra*s in the early discourses do not involve any distinctions such as "friend" or "enemy". Of course, once the mind has been trained in this way, one will become able to react with compassion even towards an enemy. But the meditative cultivation of compassion to be undertaken for this purpose takes the form of a boundless radiation that does not depend on a personified object.

An approach that takes various individual persons as the object of practice can also be found in the *Abhidharmakośabhāṣya*. This work recommends such a form of practice when the mind is in a defiled condition and one is unable to practise the boundless radiation.[56]

An objectless form of compassion meditation is recognized in the *Pañjikā* on Śāntideva's *Bodhicaryāvatāra* as well as in Asaṅga's *Bodhisattvabhūmi*.[57] In both works such a form of practice represents

54 T 1545 at T XXVII 423c7.

55 For the case of compassion cf. Vism 314,20 (translated Ñāṇamoli 1956/1991: 306); for a more detailed discussion of the development that appears to have led to this description cf. Anālayo 2015b.

56 Pradhan 1967: 454,6.

57 The *Pañjikā* on the *Bodhicaryāvatāra*, Tripathi 1988: 234,29 (§9.76), distinguishes between three modes of cultivating compassion, of which the first takes living beings as the object, the second dharmas, whereas the superior third

an advanced stage compared to the more basic approach of taking living beings as the object.

These sources help to contextualize the use of persons as the object of meditation practice. Such a use of individuals certainly can have its proper place in the initial stages of meditation practice. It can also be helpful when one's mind is in a defiled condition, offering a skilful tool to build up the practice. But eventually practice should take the form of a boundless radiation, unless for some particular reason one wishes to direct one's compassion to a particular person in need.[58]

### I.8 SUMMARY

Compassionate activity in early Buddhist thought finds its predominant expression in teaching the Dharma as a way of helping others to reach freedom from affliction. Such teaching is not confined to verbal instructions, but can also take the form of providing an example for others through one's own moral conduct and meditative lifestyle. Moral conduct and a meditative lifestyle set the foundation for being able to help others and at the same time can become expressions of compassion themselves.

When faced with manifestations of *dukkha*, the early Buddhist compassionate response expresses itself in the positive wish for others to be free from affliction. This response ideally approaches such a situation by relying on the framework of the four noble truths. In practical terms this means seeing the conditions that have led to *dukkha* and those that lead out of it, as well as combining the vision of freedom from *dukkha* with an understanding of the practical path whose undertaking will make this vision come true.

---

mode is without an object; cf. also the *Śikṣāsamuccaya*, Bendall 1902/1970: 212,12 (translated Bendall and Rouse 1922/1990: 204), for an application of this pattern to *maitrī*. The *Bodhisattvabhūmi*, Wogihara 1930/1936: 241,17, has a similar presentation for all four *brahmavihāras*. For a more detailed discussion cf. Jenkins 1999: 188–227 and Schmithausen 2000: 447f.

58 Another possible use of particular individuals as the object of meditation practice could be to test one's ability to face particularly difficult people with compassion. Regarding such testing, however, it seems to me that sufficient occasions for that will manifest naturally when encountering others in daily life, so that actual meditation need not incorporate special forms of practice aimed at ensuring one does not avoid facing difficult people. Moreover, whereas in one's meditative imagination one might feel able to face even an enemy, it is only when the situation actually arises that such ability is truly put to the test.

Compassion as a meditation practice takes the form of a boundless radiation in all directions that does not depend on a specific person as its object. Later instructions introduce individual persons as objects of the practice as skilful means for a gradual meditative development. This should eventually culminate in a boundless radiation and thereby in the experience of a temporary liberation of the mind.

# II

# COMPASSION CONTEXTUALIZED

In this chapter I contextualize compassion by examining its relation to and position among the other divine abodes (*brahmavihāra*s). Compassion, *karuṇā*, features in the early discourses as the second among the four *brahmavihāra*s. This placing is significant and a proper understanding of compassion can benefit greatly from a closer examination of the relationship between *karuṇā* and the other three *brahmavihāra*s. These three form the context in early Buddhist thought within which the cultivation of compassion takes place. In what follows, I will examine each of these three *brahmavihāra*s in turn.

## II.1 BENEVOLENCE

The first of the four *brahmavihāra*s is *mettā*, often translated as "loving-kindness", although I would prefer the translation "benevolence".[1] The term has its etymological root in *mitra*, "friend", and conveys a basic sense of friendliness and an attitude of friendship, as well as nuances of mutual benefit and assistance.[2]

---

1 Instead of imposing my preferred translation, in what follows I will mainly use the Pāli term *mettā*. This has by now become so well known that it will probably be easiest for the reader to follow my presentation in this way.

2 On *mitra* cf. the detailed discussion in Gonda 1973. Collins 1987: 52 explains that the basic idea of friendship inherent in the term can carry a sense of mutual assistance and exchange, in that "the relationship involved can be a straight-forwardly reciprocal, indeed, quasi-contractual, exchange of goods and services."

In the early discourses *mettā* does not seem to convey the feelings of love a mother has for her child, contrary to the position taken, for example, in the *Visuddhimagga*.[3] Such love or affection would find its expression in the Pāli discourses instead in terms like *ape(k)khā*, *pema*, or *piya*.[4] A stanza in the *Metta-sutta*, however, could easily give the impression that *mettā* stands for a mother's love.[5] Here is my translation of the stanza in question:

> Just as a mother who has an only son would protect her own son with her life, so one should cultivate a boundless mind towards all living beings.[6]

The stanza describes the protection a mother would be willing to give to her only son, to the extent of being willing to risk her own life. Her love of her son is not the main theme here – the main point is protection. The providing and receiving of protection is in fact a

3 Vism 321,10 (translated Ñāṇamoli 1956/1991: 314) illustrates *mettā* with the feelings a mother has for her small child. Vism 313,26 (translated Ñāṇamoli 1956/1991: 306) then relates a story where someone throws a spear at a cow who was giving milk to her calf. The tale goes that the spear bounced off due to the "*mettā*" the cow felt for the calf; cf. also the discussion in Maithrimurthi 1999: 53f.

4 Sn 38 and Sn 41 (translated Norman 1992: 4f) employ *apekhā* and *pema* to describe what one feels for one's sons. Th 33 (translated Norman 1969: 5) uses *piya* to describe a woman's feelings for her only son; the verse continues by referring to her being good (*kusala*) towards him to illustrate the attitude one should have towards all living beings. The finer distinction introduced in Th 33 between *piya* and *kusala* in this way reflects the difference between the affection the mother feels for her only son and the attitude one should cultivate towards others.

5 Although in general in my study of compassion and emptiness I try to base myself on material preserved in more than one tradition, in this case I need to make an exception and present a translation of this passage which, as far as I am able to tell, is only preserved in the Theravāda tradition.

6 Sn 149 (translated Norman 1992: 17). Although no parallel to this discourse appears to be known, the motif of a mother's love recurs in EĀ 38.11 at T II 725c9 and EĀ 49.9 at T II 805b8 to illustrate the Buddha's compassion. Both discourses are also without a parallel. Another occurrence can be found in MĀ 70 at T I 523b7 (translated Bingenheimer et al. 2013: 497), which in a description of mother and son reuniting after a long time speaks of their mutual affection and their kind and compassionate mental condition. The corresponding section in the parallel DN 26 at DN III 73,17 (translated Walshe 1987: 402) has no such reference. Another parallel in DĀ 6 at T I 41b4 has such a reference, but it speaks of the feelings of both parents for their only son and does not in any way relate this to kindness or compassion. Overall this gives the impression that the association of *mettā* and/or compassion with the love of a mother is a later development.

recurrent aspect in the conception of *mettā* in the early discourses. Examples are the belief that *mettā* can protect from snake bites,[7] or that it will protect against non-human beings.[8]

The simile in the *Metta-sutta* encourages the cultivation of an attitude of protection towards others, not the cultivation of a form of love towards others that models itself on a mother's feelings for her child. In contrast to the bounded love of a mother for her child, which easily comes with an admixture of attachment, *mettā* should be boundless and free from attachment.[9]

In the early discourses *mettā* is the most frequently mentioned *brahmavihāra*, described in various ways and contexts. Underlying this emphasis on the first of the four *brahmavihāras* is its foundational role for the cultivation of the other three.[10]

The *Mahāyānasūtrālaṅkāra* expresses the same foundational role of *mettā* with the help of a simile. This simile is part of a series of similes that illustrate the nature of compassion with the example of a tree. In relation to the tree of compassion, *mettā* is the water that nourishes the root of this tree.[11]

---

7 AN 4.67 at AN II 72,29 (translated Bodhi 2012: 456) presents *mettā* towards various types of snakes as a protection against snake bite. Similar stanzas have been preserved in Sanskrit (cf. Hoernle 1897: 224f, de La Vallée Poussin 1911: 776f, Waldschmidt 1957: 40 and 1958: 403f) as well as in the otherwise unrelated discourses SĀ 252 at T II 61a27 and T 505 at T XIV 773b22. For a detailed study of the protective functions associated with *mettā* cf. Schmithausen 1997.

8 SN 20.3 at SN II 264,4 (translated Bodhi 2000: 707) and its parallel SĀ 1254 at T II 344c13; and again SN 20.5 at SN II 265,17 (translated Bodhi 2000: 708) and its parallels SĀ 1255 at T II 344c25 and a Sanskrit fragment, Hoernle 1916: 45.

9 Ohnuma 2012: 15 explains in relation to the Buddha that "while mother-love is particular to one's own child alone and does not extend to anyone else, the Buddha's love is universal and extends, with equal intensity, to all living beings. There is thus a stark contrast between *one person* and *all beings*, or between *particular* and *universal* love."

10 This foundational role appears to be explicitly recognized in the *Vibhaṅga* of the Theravāda Abhidharma collection, which indicates that *mettā*, unlike the other three, functions as a condition or root (*hetu*); cf. Vibh 283,27 (translated Thiṭṭila 1969: 374).

11 Lévi 1907: 126,5; cf. also the *Bhāvanākrama*, Namdol 1997: 86,1 (translated Sharma 1997/2004: 53), where *maitrī* similarly functions as water for what here is the seed of compassion.

This simile beautifully illustrates how *mettā* contributes to the growth of compassion.[12] In this foundational role, *mettā* can find expression through bodily, verbal, and mental activities. In the context of a set of six principles that lead to cordiality, for example, three such principles are *mettā* expressed through bodily, verbal, and mental acts.[13] This passage confirms the central role of *mettā* in bringing about cordiality in one's relationship to others.

Notably, *mettā* is the only *brahmavihāra* whose broad range of application by way of bodily, verbal, and mental activities is explicitly highlighted in the early discourses. By covering the entire range of possible interactions with others, *mettā* expressed bodily, verbally, and mentally thus provides the testing ground for one's meditation practice. One who has truly cultivated *mettā* will be able to remain established in this mental attitude even when having to face difficult people and situations.

Being undertaken in these three modes, *mettā* comes to permeate all aspects of one's behaviour and activities, thereby providing fertile soil in which compassion and the remaining *brahmavihāra*s can grow and flourish. The cultivation of compassion will be greatly facilitated by such building of a foundation through kindness in one's activities, the way one communicates, and most importantly one's mental attitude.

Cultivating *mettā* in these three ways provides a broader practical scope for expressing one's compassionate intent than just teaching activities. As discussed in Chapter 1, the predominant practical expression of compassion in the early discourses is through teaching the Dharma. This clearly features as the compassionate action par excellence. Yet this does not mean that the early discourses neglect the importance of cultivating the appropriate attitude in relation to other and perhaps more ordinary daily activities. Such

---

12 Jenkins 1999: 35 explains that "part of the reason that *karuṇā* is not often mentioned in early texts is that, as a technical term, '*mettā*' ... subsumes *karuṇā* and other affective qualities within it. It is the prime term for expressing empathetic sensitivity and concern in these contexts." According to Nattier 2003: 146, "in the early period of development of ideas about the bodhisattva path it may have been primarily *maitrī* that was cultivated, only gradually being eclipsed by the focus on *karuṇā*."

13 MN 104 at MN II 250,24 (translated Ñāṇamoli 1995: 859) and its parallel MĀ 196 at T I 755b23. The other three principles are willingness to share one's gains, maintaining moral conduct, and upholding the type of view that leads to liberation.

daily activities are best undertaken in a mode of *mettā*, of kindness and benevolence. This will go a long way in strengthening one's cultivation of compassion.

### II.2 KINDNESS IN DAILY CONDUCT

A detailed description showing how such a foundation in *mettā* can be laid occurs in the *Cūḷagosiṅga-sutta* and its parallels, which report the harmonious living together of a group of three monks. In what follows I translate the relevant part of this description from the *Madhyama-āgama* version in full, as it helps to bring out practical aspects relevant to everyday life:

> There were three clansmen staying together: the venerable Anuruddha, the venerable Nandiya, and the venerable Kimbila. Those venerable ones were practising in the following way:
>
> Whichever one of them comes back first from begging for almsfood, he sets out the sitting [mats], draws water, puts out the utensils for washing the feet, places the foot mat and the cloth for wiping the feet, the water containers, and the jar for bathing. If he is able to finish the food he has begged for, he finishes the food. If there are leftovers, he places them in containers, covers them, and puts them aside. Having completed his meal, he stores away his [robe] and bowl, washes his hands and feet, and, with a sitting mat over his shoulder, enters a hut to sit in meditation.
>
> Whichever one of them comes back last from begging for almsfood, if he is able to finish the food, he finishes the food. If it is not enough, he takes what is sufficient from the previously leftover food and eats it. Whatever leftovers remain, he pours them out on to a clear piece of ground or into water that contains no living beings.
>
> He takes those containers for [leftover] food and, having washed them clean and wiped them, puts them away to one side. He gathers and rolls up the sitting mats, collects the foot mat, gathers the cloth for wiping feet, and puts away the utensils for washing feet, the water containers, and the jar for bathing. Having swept the dining hall with a broom and taken out the sweepings so that all is clean, he stores away his robe and bowl, washes his hands and feet, and with a sitting mat over his shoulder enters a hut to sit in meditation.
>
> In the afternoon, whichever one of those venerable ones first rises from sitting in meditation looks whether the water containers or the

> jar for bathing are empty of water. [If they are], he takes them and goes to fill them. If he is able to carry them [after filling them], he carries them back and sets them up to one side.
>
> If he is unable to carry one of them, then he beckons to another monk with his hand, and both of them lift it together, carry it back, and set it up to one side, without speaking to each other or asking each other anything. Once in every five days those venerable ones assemble and either discuss the Dharma together or maintain noble silence.[14]

This passage provides a vivid description of how daily activities can be permeated with a spirit of kindness. The description relates back to a theme already broached in Chapter 1, namely the need to take responsibility as an aspect of compassion. Here, the monks are shown taking care of their common needs in a responsible manner, which provides ideal conditions for their meditative practice. Although this description is specific to monastic life in ancient India, its main points can easily be applied to one's own living situation in the modern world.

The one who comes back first makes sure everything is ready for those who come later. The one who is last sees to it that everything is properly stored away and cleaned up, doing this in a manner that does not damage the natural environment. All this takes place under the overarching purpose of creating conducive conditions for their meditation practice. The practice of meditation is given such clear priority that, if something needs to be done, they just communicate by signs, without talking. Alongside such silent cooperation, they make sure to meet regularly to discuss the Dharma or else just meditate together.

The *Cūḷagosiṅga-sutta* and its parallels also offer indications regarding the mental attitude that underpins such harmonious cohabitation. Here is the relevant part from the *Madhyama-āgama* discourse, where Anuruddha informs the Buddha of how he manages to live at ease without lacking anything:

---

14 MĀ 185 at T I 729c3 to c21. In the parallel MN 31 at MN I 207,12 (translated Ñāṇamoli 1995: 302), a comparable description is instead given by Anuruddha to the Buddha (in the other parallel, EĀ 24.8 at T II 629a15, such a description is also provided by the narrator of the discourse). Another difference is that MN 31 does not explicitly mention that after cleaning up they would sit in meditation, and it also does not envisage that their regular meetings could be spent together in silence instead of Dharma discussion. Due to such differences, the description in MĀ 185 (and to some extent also in EĀ 24.8) is pervaded by a stronger meditative flavour.

> Blessed One, I think to myself: "It is well gained by me, it is a great blessing, that is, to have such companions with me practising the holy life together."
>
> Blessed One, I constantly practise towards these companions in the holy life bodily deeds of *mettā*, whether seen or unseen, equally and without difference. I practise [towards them] verbal deeds of *mettā* ... I practise [towards them] mental deeds of *mettā*, whether seen or unseen, equally and without difference.
>
> Blessed One, I think to myself: "Let me now set aside my own mental [attitude] (*citta*) and follow the mental [attitude] of those venerable friends." Then I set aside my own mental [attitude] and follow the mental [attitude] of those venerable friends. I never harbour a single disapproving mental [attitude]. Blessed One, in this way I am always at ease and lack nothing.[15]

The other two monks give the same description. The Buddha concludes that these three monks are living together blending like milk and water.

This description offers several helpful indications. One is that it highlights a basic attitude of appreciation towards others, a topic to which I will return below when discussing the *brahmavihāra* of sympathetic joy. Each of the three monks considers it a gain and a blessing to have such companions. The example set in this way suggests the possibility of making it a regular practice to recollect the benefit one derives from those with whom one is close, even consciously rejoicing in being able to associate with them. Only too easily one takes for granted what others do for oneself. Making an effort to counter such a tendency can become a helpful asset in one's cultivation of compassion and kindness.

Based on such sincere appreciation then comes *mettā* expressed by body, speech, and mind. Such threefold expressions of *mettā* are not confined to manifestations that are obvious to others and that will be noticed by others for what they are. Instead, they can also

---

15 MĀ 185 at T I 730a6 to a13. This passage well exemplifies a point made by Gombrich 1988: 114 that "Buddhist loving kindness was no mere abstraction, no mere topic for meditation, but to be practised by the Sangha in their daily lives." Engelmajer 2003: 42 identifies three main themes in the description given of the monks in MN 31: "loving kindness towards others, putting others' needs before one's own, and taking responsibility" (for things that need to be done). For a study of MN 31 cf. also Ariyaratne 2010.

take place "unseen", in a hidden manner. Here the inner strength of *mettā* is such that it need not clamour for public recognition. Rooted in a mind steeped in *mettā*, any outer expression of *mettā* is sufficient unto itself, even if nobody takes notice.

Another significant indication is that such conduct requires the willingness to let go of one's own preferences. One learns to be willing to go along with what others prefer. Here such willingness is practised by all three monks. So the point is not merely to submit to the leadership of a strong personality. Instead, what this passage implies is an attitude that does not pin one's personal happiness on being able to get everything the way one wants it. To be at ease and lack nothing comes about precisely through letting go of wanting to have things one's own way.

### II.3 FACING AGGRESSION

The mental attitude of *mettā* that the *Cūḷagosiṅga-sutta* and its parallels show to be such an efficient tool in daily life situations can also come to one's aid when having to face others who act aggressively. A particularly vivid illustration of this can be seen in the *Kakacūpama-sutta* and its *Madhyama-āgama* parallel. Here is the relevant passage from the *Madhyama-āgama* version:

> You should train so that, if others punch you, stone you, beat you with sticks, or cut you with knives, your mind does not change, you will not utter malevolent words, and, based on that, you arouse a mental [attitude] of *mettā* and compassion for those who beat you...
>
> You should train so that, if thieves were to come by and cut you apart piece by piece with a sharp saw, your mind does not change, you will not utter malevolent words to those who are cutting you up and, based on that, you arouse a mental [attitude] of *mettā* and compassion.
>
> With your mind imbued with *mettā*, dwell having pervaded one direction, and in the same way the second, the third, and the fourth direction, and also the four intermediate [directions], above and below, completely and everywhere. Being without mental shackles, resentment, ill will, or contention, with a mind imbued with *mettā* that is supremely vast and great, boundless and well cultivated, dwell pervading the entire world.

In the same way with a mind imbued with compassion ... with sympathetic joy ... with equanimity ...[16]

The rather drastic example of the saw given in the simile needs to be understood for what it is: an example. Its purpose is to illustrate the potential and scope of *mettā*. The simile of the saw does not mean that one should just let others cut oneself into pieces or inflict harm on oneself in other ways. If there is a way to avoid such a gruesome experience, for one's own sake and also for the sake of the bandits who will accrue dreadful karmic retribution by such a deed, one should certainly try to escape.

After the simile, the *Kakacūpama-sutta* and its *Madhyama-āgama* parallel in fact continue with the Buddha querying if, on keeping this simile in mind, the monks could imagine any kind of unpleasant speech that they would not be able to bear. This shows that the simile of the saw is dramatic for a specific purpose, namely in order to encourage patience and forbearance in other situations that are considerably less threatening.

### II.4 MENTAL BEAUTY

Not only when anger and aggression influence the actions of others, but also when they arise within oneself, *mettā* is the required antidote. The opposition between *mettā* and ill will comes up in the context of a listing of six elements of release (*nissaraṇa*) in the *Dasuttara-sutta* and its parallels, which I already took up in Chapter 1 in relation to compassion. There I translated the Sanskrit fragment version; here I translate for a change the relevant part from the Chinese *Dīrgha-āgama* version:

If a monk speaks like this: "I have cultivated *mettā*, yet ill will still arises in my mind", [then] another monk [should] tell him: "Do not say this. Do not misrepresent the Tathāgata. The Tathāgata does not speak like this, [saying] that ill will still arises in one who is

16 MĀ 193 at T I 746a8 to a10 and a15 to a21. The parallel MN 21 at MN I 129,15 (translated Ñāṇamoli 1995: 223) does not take up being punched or hit as a case on its own, but proceeds directly from the topic mentioned in both versions just before, where one is confronted with unpleasant ways of speech, to the simile of the saw. Another difference is that MN 21 does not continue from the boundless radiation of *mettā* to the other *brahmavihāras*.

intent on the cultivation of the liberation [of the mind] by *mettā*. This is not possible. The Buddha said: 'Having overcome ill will, one consequently achieves *mettā*.'"[17]

In this way, *mettā* is directly opposed to ill will, so much so that ill will in its various manifestations will be overcome once one truly achieves dwelling in *mettā*. This is because *mettā* de-nourishes the hindrance of ill will,[18] depriving ill will of its nourishment and sustenance. Therefore *mettā* is the way to face anger, ill will, and aggression when these have arisen within oneself or when one is confronted with others who act under their influence.

An attitude of *mettā* is also the best way to proceed when one has to reprimand another, which should not be done with an angry mind.[19] The same would apply to engaging in any kind of criticism. This will have a better effect on others (and also on one's relationship with them) if it is done with *mettā*. Conversely, when one is being criticized, whether the criticism is justified or not, an attitude of *mettā* will be equally beneficial.

The *Mahāsaccaka-sutta* and its Sanskrit parallel report an occasion when the Buddha was challenged by a debater. At the end of their exchange, the debater expressed his surprise at the way the Buddha reacted when being challenged and criticized. The debater relates that he was used to other eminent religious teachers displaying anger on being verbally attacked by him. In the case of the Buddha, however, he not only noticed the absence of anger, but found that on being attacked the Buddha's skin and face brightened up and became clear.[20] Although this is not explicitly stated in the discourse, it seems fair to conclude that this physical effect was a visible mark of the Buddha reacting with *mettā* and compassion in such a situation.

A discourse in the *Aṅguttara-nikāya* and its *Madhyama-āgama*

---

17 DĀ 10 at T I 54b2 to b6. The parallel DN 34 at DN III 280,27 (the relevant part is abbreviated, the full text is found in DN 33 at DN III 248,1, translated Walshe 1987: 500) also indicates that in this way one actually misrepresents the Buddha, a statement not found in the other parallels, Mittal 1957: 78 and T 13 at T I 236a5.

18 SN 46.51 at SN V 105,23 (translated Bodhi 2000: 1600) and its parallels SĀ 715 at T II 192c9 (translated Anālayo 2013c: 184) and D 4094 *ju* 285b7 or Q 5595 *thu* 31a2.

19 AN 5.167 at AN III 196,15 (translated Bodhi 2012: 781) and its parallel SĀ 497 at T II 129c2.

20 MN 36 at MN I 250,24 (translated Ñāṇamoli 1995: 343) and its parallel in Sanskrit fragment 339v2, Liu 2010: 243.

parallel point out that those who become angry thereby come to be of ugly appearance, however much they are well washed and anointed.[21] The relationship highlighted in this way between anger and ugliness can easily be verified in one's own experience. When someone flies into a rage, this definitely does not make him or her look particularly beautiful.

According to the *Cūḷakammavibhaṅga-sutta* and a range of parallels, the relationship between anger and ugliness holds not only for the moment anger actually manifests. A tendency to become angry also leads to being reborn ugly.[22] Needless to say, the point of this indication is not to blame those who have been born unattractive, which in view of the complexity of karma and its fruit need not be because they harboured anger in the past. The point is more specifically to highlight the long-time repercussions of allowing oneself to be carried away by irritation and anger.

Given that *mettā* is the antidote to anger, it comes as no surprise that a discourse in the *Saṃyutta-nikāya* and its *Saṃyukta-āgama* parallel should proclaim that the cultivation of *mettā* leads the mind to supreme beauty. The *Saṃyukta-āgama* version formulates this as follows:

> A mind well cultivated in *mettā* is supreme in beauty.[23]

Besides the physical repercussions of the cultivation of *mettā* on one's countenance, this statement also indicates that the cultivation of *mettā* can become the foundation for developing mental beauty. Such beauty can shine through any bodily appearance, however much this falls short of satisfying current fashion standards. The mental beauty of *mettā* permeates one's actions and words, communicating to others in various ways one's own firm rootedness in kindness and compassion.

The passages surveyed above show the contributions that the practice of *mettā* can make to the cultivation of compassion. A mental

---

21 AN 7.60 at AN IV 94,8 (translated Bodhi 2012: 1066, given as number 64) and MĀ 129 at T I 617b25.

22 MN 135 at MN III 204,18 (translated Ñāṇamoli 1995: 1054) and its parallels MĀ 170 at T I 705a29, T 78 at T I 887c27, T 79 at T I 889c25, T 80 at T I 892a28, T 81 at T I 897a8, T 755 at T XVII 589a27, Lévi 1932: 37,18 and 185,25, as well as D 339 *sa* 301a4 or Q 1006 *shu* 312b8.

23 SĀ 743 at T II 197c11. The parallel SN 46.54 at SN V 119,17 (translated Bodhi 2000: 1609) expresses the same correlation in terms of beauty being the culmination of the cultivation of the liberation of the mind by *mettā*.

attitude of kindness and benevolence recommends itself for any kind of situation, ranging from ordinary activities like cleaning up after a meal to the most excruciatingly threatening situation of being helplessly at the mercy of cruel bandits. Cultivated in this way, *mettā* becomes the forerunner on the path to true beauty, the beauty of the compassionate mind.

Besides being best cultivated based on a well-established foundation in *mettā*, compassion finds its complements in the remaining two *brahmavihāras*, sympathetic joy and equanimity. These, in a way, round off the cultivation of compassion.

### II.5 COMPASSION AND SYMPATHETIC JOY

Sympathetic joy, *muditā*, etymologically speaking stands in a close relationship to terms like *pāmojja*, "delight", and *anumodana*, "rejoicing". From a practical perspective there is considerable overlap between these different nuances or manifestations of wholesome joy. Sympathetic joy stands out among these for being the type of joy that, on being cultivated as a boundless radiation, can lead to a temporary liberation of the mind.

Such sympathetic joy can come into being in relation to the compassionate activity of teaching the Dharma. Those who are the recipients of such compassionate teaching activity can use this as an opportunity to cultivate sympathetic joy. Sympathetic joy comes up in such a context explicitly in a discourse in the *Saṃyutta-nikāya* and its *Saṃyukta-āgama* parallels. Here a teaching given by Sāriputta has inspired his monastic audience to such an extent that one of them extols the event in verse. In one of the stanzas delivered on this occasion, the monk poet reports that the monks listened to Sāriputta with sympathetic joy.[24]

Another aspect of sympathetic joy can be seen in a discourse in the *Aṅguttara-nikāya*, of which no parallel seems to have been preserved.[25] Here is the relevant part from the Pāli version:

> Monks, at a time when the monks dwell in harmony, in concord,

---

24 SN 8.6 at SN I 190,20 (translated Bodhi 2000: 286) and its parallels SĀ 1210 at T II 329c12 and SĀ² 226 at T II 457a9.

25 Although in general I try to base myself on material preserved in more than one tradition, in this case I would again like to make an exception and present a translation of the relevant passage, even though as far as I am able to tell this is only preserved in the Theravāda tradition.

> without quarrelling, blending like milk and water, looking at each other with kindly eyes, monks, at such a time the monks generate much merit. Monks, at such a time the monks dwell in a divine abode, namely the liberation of the mind by sympathetic joy. Being delighted [in this way] joy arises. For one whose mind is joyful, the body becomes tranquil. One whose body is tranquil feels happiness. The mind of one who is happy becomes concentrated.[26]

This passage relates to the *Cūḷagosiṅga-sutta* and its parallels, where mutual appreciation and living together in harmony and without quarrelling were central themes. Once *mettā* by way of the three doors of action – bodily, verbal, and mental – has led to the absence of quarrelling, the actual dwelling in harmony and mutual appreciation could then be seen as an instance of the *brahmavihāra* of sympathetic joy.

As in the *Cūḷagosiṅga-sutta* and its parallels, in the present passage from the *Aṅguttara-nikaya* harmonious cohabitation is immediately set in relation to meditation practice. This takes place by showing how joy leads via tranquillity and happiness to concentration. The mental qualities mentioned here point to the cultivation of the awakening factors, a topic to which I will turn in Chapter 3.

The *Upāli-sutta* and its parallels report a series of stanzas spoken by another early Buddhist poet, this time a lay disciple. In these stanzas, the lay disciple Upāli eulogizes various qualities of the Buddha, one of which is sympathetic joy. In the *Upāli-sutta* and a reconstructed Sanskrit fragment parallel this qualification is preceded by the indication that the Buddha had vomited out worldly gains,[27] in the sense that he was not greedy for offerings by the laity.

According to the narrative background to these stanzas, Upāli had been a staunch adherent of the Jains and had come to debate with the Buddha. During what appears to have been his first and only meeting with the Buddha before his poetic outpouring, Upāli was convinced by the Buddha's arguments and declared his wish to become a Buddhist lay disciple. In reply, the Buddha advised that Upāli should carefully consider his decision and suggested that Upāli should continue to support the Jains with offerings as he had done earlier. Judging from the narrative context, it appears to

26 AN 3.93 at AN I 243,20 to 243,26 (given as number 95 in Bodhi 2012: 328).

27 MN 56 at MN I 386,6 (translated Ñāṇamoli 1995: 490) and a parallel in a Sanskrit fragment, Waldschmidt 1979: 6; cf. also MĀ 133 at T I 632c2.

be this magnanimous suggestion by the Buddha, his lack of envy for the gains received by others, that inspired Upāli's reference to sympathetic joy as one of the praiseworthy qualities of the Buddha.

On this understanding, the passage implicitly shows sympathetic joy to be the opposite of envy and jealousy. Just having successfully converted an eminent lay follower of a rival religious group, the Buddha tries to avoid the loss of this lay follower resulting in a loss of material support for this rival group.

Besides this implicit pointer to the absence of envy as an aspect of sympathetic joy, the early discourses explicitly set sympathetic joy in contrast to discontent (*arati*). This contrast can be seen in the listing of the elements of release, according to which one who has cultivated the liberation of the mind by sympathetic joy will no longer be overwhelmed by discontent.[28] Elsewhere discontent often features as a problem for a monastic who does not find delight in a celibate lifestyle in seclusion.[29]

Whereas in the case of *mettā* and compassion the opposite qualities are related to other living beings in the form of ill will and cruelty, discontent as the opposite to sympathetic joy is a quality that does not have such a direct relationship to others. The removal of discontent in relation to a monastic lifestyle or dwelling in solitude would be concerned predominantly with oneself. Of course, discontent can also occur in relation to others. But the more general import of the term fits in with the fact that sympathetic joy also appears to have a more general range of meaning, when compared to *mettā* and compassion.

## II.6 COMPASSION AND EQUANIMITY

Equanimity or equipoise, *upek(k)hā*, from an etymological perspective suggests a mental attitude of "looking upon", not an indifferent "looking away". The term thus conveys an awareness of whatever is happening combined with mental balance and the absence of favouring or opposing.

Now for compassion to relate to sympathetic joy seems natural, especially once it is appreciated that compassion does not mean to

28 DN 34 at DN III 280,27 (the relevant part is abbreviated, the full text is found in DN 33 at DN III 249,3, translated Walshe 1987: 500) and its parallels Mittal 1957: 79 and DĀ 10 at T I 54b6; cf. also T 13 at T I 236a16.

29 Trenckner et al. 1924: 417 give *s.v. arati* the explanation "not feeling at ease with (forest) solitude ... or monk-discipline."

commiserate and become sad oneself. In contrast, it can at first sight seem considerably less straightforward that compassion also relates to equanimity or equipoise.

This can appear particularly problematic when compassion is cultivated in the form of a bodhisattva's wish to liberate others. It is not easy to see how such an aspiration could lead to an attitude of equanimity towards others. In later traditions this has led to a reinterpretation of the function and nature of equanimity, as well as to a change in the place accorded to equanimity within the set of the four *brahmavihāra*s.

An instance of reinterpretation can be found in the *Bodhisattvabhūmi*, where the *brahmavihāra* of equanimity is defined as the intention to liberate living beings from their defilements.[30] The presentation in the *Bodhisattvabhūmi* is based on a distinction relating to the objects of the other three *brahmavihāra*s, according to which compassion takes as its object living beings who are suffering, sympathetic joy is concerned with living beings who are happy, and *mettā* applies to living beings who are neither. Each of these situations relates to a particular defilement: those who suffer tend to aversion, those who are happy tend to passion, and those who are neither tend to ignorance. Equanimity then comes in as the wish for each of these three types of living beings to be free from the respective defilement. In this way equanimity manifests as the aspiration that those for whom one has compassion become free from aversion, those for whom one has sympathetic joy become free from passion, and those for whom one has *mettā* become free from ignorance.

From the viewpoint of the early discourses, however, wishing that those who suffer from aversion become free from it, for example, would be an expression of one's compassion. It would not be an expression of the fourth *brahmavihāra* of equanimity.

Another solution adopted in later times involves shifting equanimity to first place among the *brahmavihāra*s. In this way equanimity functions as a preliminary exercise, in the sense of establishing a minimal degree of mental equipoise through the absence of gross forms of hatred or desire. This then forms the basis for being able to cultivate the other *brahmavihāra*s. Such a relocation of equanimity to

30 Wogihara 1930/1936: 242,13.

first place among the four *brahmavihāra*s can be found, for example, in Kamalaśīla's *Bhāvanākrama*.[31]

From a practical perspective this shift in position of equanimity can function as a skilful means in a situation where one is struggling with a defiled condition of the mind. However, such skilful means need not be the sole mode of engaging in the practice of equanimity. In order to explore the full range and benefits of the *brahmavihāra*s, it would seem recommendable for equanimity, if it is to be used as a preliminary aid for cultivating the *brahmavihāra*s at all, to then lead on to a form of practice that embraces all four, including equanimity as the culmination point of *brahmavihāra* meditation.

The circumstance that equanimity forms the culmination point of the four *brahmavihāra*s does not mean that equanimity replaces the others; one who cultivates the *brahmavihāra*s continues to dwell in all four.[32] It does mean, however, that in some way compassion can result in, or mature as, equanimity. Understood in this way, equanimity is of course not a condition of indifference, but rather a mental equipoise that rounds off a systematic opening of the heart which has been brought about through cultivation of the other three divine abodes.

The *Sakkapañha-sutta* and its parallels explicitly distinguish between two types of equanimity, of which only one should be developed, whereas the other should be avoided.[33] The decisive difference is whether such equanimity has wholesome or unwholesome repercussions. Applying this basic distinction to the case of equanimity as the fourth *brahmavihāra*, equanimity needs to be cultivated in such a way that it enhances and complements the other divine abodes, instead of having the unwholesome effect of weakening or even opposing them.

---

31 Namdol 1997: 85,2 (translated Sharma 1997/2004: 52); cf. also Longchenpa 2007: 70f.

32 Aronson 1979a: 8 explains that the position of equanimity as the fourth and last among the *brahmavihāra*s "does not mean that equanimity is to supplant the first three sublime attitudes in one's future practice". Stoler Miller 1979: 210 notes that the practice of the four *brahmavihāra*s "is cumulative, not linear", and "cultivation of all four is essential to effecting the radical change of heart that is the goal of the exercise." As summed up by Gethin 1992: 157, equanimity "should not be regarded as supplanting or superseding the other three. The four always remain essentially complementary."

33 DN 21 at DN II 279,3 (translated Walshe 1987: 329) and its parallels DĀ 14 at T I 64c29, T 15 at T I 249a20, and MĀ 134 at T I 636c1.

The importance of avoiding mere indifference can be seen from the passages I took up in Chapter 1, where Sāriputta and Ānanda had to face the Buddha's stern rebuke for remaining unconcerned in situations where their compassionate response was called for.[34]

A complementary relationship between equanimity and compassion emerges in relation to teaching activity. Someone teaching the Dharma engages in the most prominent expression of compassion in the early discourses. The reaction of the audience to teachings can then take the form of sympathetic joy. However, this is not always the case. At times a teacher has to face disciples who not only lack sympathetic joy, but are even in part or wholly inattentive. The *Saḷāyatanavibhaṅga-sutta* and its parallels preserved in Chinese and Tibetan indicate that in such a situation the Buddha would dwell in equanimity.[35]

A practical illustration of the transition from compassion to equanimity can be found in the *Bhaddāli-sutta* and its parallels, even though they do not explicitly employ these two terms. The situation they describe revolves around a monk who openly refuses to follow an injunction given by the Buddha to take only a single meal per day.[36] In what appears to be a reaction first motivated by compassion, the Buddha offers him an alternative way of conduct that strikes a compromise between the rule and the monk's apprehensions about getting sufficient food. When the monk still refuses, the Buddha undertakes no further action. In other words, he remains equanimous. In the long run this has its effect, as the monk in question eventually comes to realize the inappropriateness of his behaviour and approaches the Buddha to apologize and mend his ways.

---

34 See above p.14. The same point is also made in AN 4.100 at AN II 101,1 (translated Bodhi 2012: 481), of which no parallel seems to be known. The discourse reports someone proposing that to refrain completely from praising and criticizing others is a superior attitude, as this is an expression of equanimity. The Buddha disagreed, explaining that one should praise and criticize others when this is appropriate.

35 MN 137 at MN III 221,3 (translated Ñāṇamoli 1995: 1071), MĀ 163 at T I 693c23, and D 4094 *nyu* 59a1 or Q 5595 *thu* 101a8; for a more detailed discussion cf. Anālayo 2013c: 240–243.

36 MN 65 at MN I 437,25 (translated Ñāṇamoli 1995: 542) and its parallels MĀ 194 at T I 746b27, EĀ 49.7 at T II 800c2 (translated Anālayo 2014b: 9), and the Mahāsāṅghika *Vinaya*, T 1425 at T XXII 359b14.

Another example can be seen in the *Upakkilesa-sutta*, where the term "compassion" features explicitly as part of a request that the Buddha should approach a group of monks involved in a serious quarrel.[37] When the Buddha finds that his compassionate intervention is not sufficient to stop the monks from quarrelling, he takes his robes and bowl and wanders off on his own. It seems safe to conclude that in this case, too, his attitude has shifted from compassion to equanimity.

These examples show that, even for the Buddha, equanimity could at times be the appropriate attitude. This helps us to understand the function of equanimity as a divine abode. When compassionate activity meets with a careless or cold response, then perhaps the time has come to move on to equanimity.[38] This requires giving up attempts to control the situation and change it for the better. Instead one allows others to take responsibility for their own actions and attitudes. In this way equanimity can indeed round off compassion, by liberating compassionate activity from the expectation of results. Compassion that can lead to equanimity, if needed, is no longer attached to its activities bearing fruit and being successful. In this way, if that is what the situation demands, compassion can turn into equanimity.

Another aspect of equanimity emerges from the listing of elements of release in the *Dasottara-sutta*, which indicate that someone who has cultivated the liberation of the mind by equanimity will no longer be overwhelmed by lust.[39] According to the parallel versions, the mind of one who has cultivated the liberation of the mind by equanimity will also no longer be overwhelmed by ill will or aversion.[40] From

37 MN 128 at MN III 153,6 (translated Ñāṇamoli 1995: 1008). The parallel MĀ 72 at T I 532c11 begins directly with the Buddha addressing the quarrelling monks and does not report his previously being invited to do so, hence it has no explicit reference to compassion (although the same would be implicit).

38 The need for equanimity when one is unable to establish another in wholesome conduct is mentioned explicitly in MN 103 at MN II 242,11 (translated Ñāṇamoli 1995: 851), a discourse of which no parallel seems to be known.

39 DN 34 at DN III 280,27 (the relevant part is abbreviated, the full text is found in DN 33 at DN III 249,15, translated Walshe 1987: 500).

40 Mittal 1957: 79, DĀ 10 at T I 54b7, and T 13 at T I 236a20. Elsewhere the Pāli discourses also recognize that equanimity counters aversion; cf., e.g., MN 62 at MN I 424,32 (translated Ñāṇamoli 1995: 531).

a practical perspective this is intuitive, namely that equanimity counters not only lust, but also ill will and aversion.

A helpful approach for remaining in equipoise when facing abuse can be found in a discourse in the *Saṃyutta-nikāya* and its parallels. The discourse features a Brahmin pouring insults on the Buddha. In reply, the Buddha calmly asks the Brahmin what would happen to food offered to visitors who do not accept it. The Brahmin replies that such food remains his own property. In the same way, the Buddha comments, he does not accept the Brahmin's abuse, so this abuse remains the Brahmin's own property.[41]

This delightful image can be of considerable aid in situations when one is facing actual abuse. When one's own equanimity is lost, one easily takes possession of anything insulting, making it one's own. Instead of making any insult one's own, it is better to remain with equanimity in the face of someone else's anger.

A stanza in the *Udānavarga*, with parallels in the different *Dharmapada* collections, offers a poetic image that can help to establish an attitude of equanimity. The stanza runs as follows:

> Just as a solid rock
> is not shaken by the wind,
> so the wise are not shaken
> by blame and praise.[42]

The *Mahāhatthipadopama-sutta* and its *Madhyama-āgama* parallel show how equanimity that is free from aversion can be encouraged by recollecting the simile of the saw, found in the *Kakacūpama-sutta* and its *Madhyama-āgama* parallel.[43] The two discourses depict a situation where one is subject to physical aggression in the form of being hit or having stones thrown at one. In such a situation one should bring to mind the simile of the saw to help oneself become established in equanimity, an equanimity that both versions explicitly qualify as wholesome.[44]

Another mode of reflection in such a situation is described in the

---

41 SN 7.2 at SN I 162,16 (translated Bodhi 2000: 256) and its parallels SĀ 1152 at T II 307a17 and SĀ² 75 at T II 400b18.

42 Stanza 29.49, Bernhard 1965: 387, with parallels in Dhp 81 (translated Norman 1997/2004: 12), the Patna *Dharmapada* 93, Cone 1989: 128, and the Gāndhārī *Dharmapada* 239, Brough 1962/2001: 157.

43 See above p.35.

44 MN 28 at MN I 186,21 (translated Ñāṇamoli 1995: 280) and its parallel MĀ 30 at T I 465a16 (translated Bingenheimer et al. 2013: 222).

*Puṇṇovāda-sutta* and its parallels. The different versions show a monk ready to bear any type of attack with the reflection that his aggressors are kind in that they are not attacking him in ways even worse than what they are already doing. His equanimity is such that he is able to face calmly even the prospect of being killed. He does so with the thought that, while some have to make an effort to commit suicide, he is now able to achieve the same result without needing to make any effort.[45] As in the case of the simile of the saw, the last and rather dramatic example is not a practical recommendation. Rather, it serves as an illustration of a patient and equanimous attitude in which one is able to face anything. The basic pattern that emerges from the *Puṇṇovāda-sutta* and its parallels is the reflection "it could be much worse", providing a support for maintaining equanimity.

### II.7 COMPASSION AND THE OTHER DIVINE ABODES

As mentioned at the outset of Chapter 1, the basic thrust of compassion is the wish for others to be free from affliction. By having as its object those who are afflicted, compassion will often be concerned with those who are less well off than oneself. The same orientation towards those in an inferior position can recur when compassionate activity finds its standard expression in teaching activities. The teacher is usually in a higher position than the students, especially in the ancient Indian setting.

From this it follows that a potential pitfall of compassion could arise from it being directed towards others perceived as being in a lower and inferior position. This requires counterbalancing in order to avoid becoming a habit. Such an attitude might even give rise to conceit and a personal feeling of superiority. One way to protect against this possible pitfall is to contextualize *karuṇā* by combining its cultivation with that of the other *brahmavihāras*.

Here the foundation building can be done by way of *mettā*. As a basic attitude of kindness or well-wishing, *mettā* can take as its object those who are better or worse; in fact its central thrust is one of

45 MN 145 at MN III 269,10 (translated Ñāṇamoli 1995: 1119), found again at SN 35.88 at SN IV 62,24 (translated Bodhi 2000: 1169), and the discourse parallels T 108 at T II 503a6 and SĀ 311 at T II 89c10; cf. also the *Divyāvadāna*, Cowell and Neil 1886: 39,8, and the Mūlasarvāstivāda *Vinaya*, T 1448 at T XXIV 12b7 and D 1 *ka* 306b2 or Q 1030 *khe* 286a2.

treating everyone equally as one's friend. The foundation building practice of *mettā* also has a wider scope than compassionate activity. As the passages discussed above show, *mettā* extends to various daily activities like cleaning up and setting things in order. It can also function as the appropriate attitude when one is faced with various forms of aggression. In this way, *mettā* can become a vehicle for laying the proper foundation for the cultivation of compassion.

The cultivation of compassion as a mental attitude that is predominantly concerned with those in a less favourable situation has its natural complement in sympathetic joy, which will make sure that those in a more favourable situation will be integrated in one's *brahmavihāra* practice. Sympathetic joy also ensures that, after what is negative has received due attention during the cultivation of compassion, what is positive will equally be taken into account.

With equanimity a further complement comes into play, this time a complement to the other three *brahmavihāra*s in their reaching out towards other living beings. The basic positive affective orientation continues, but there is no longer an active reaching out towards others. In many a situation such equanimity is not called for, as the episodes with Ānanda and Sāriputta show. In some situations, however, it clearly is the appropriate reaction. In this way, equanimity rounds off the cultivation of compassion by freeing it from any trace of compulsion and obsession. The presence of equanimity makes the set of the four divine abodes complete. The four *brahmavihāra*s as a whole offer someone who is devoted to the meditative opening of the heart a complete array of choices for the appropriate mental attitude in any kind of situation.

In the early discourses the *brahmavihāra*s are mentioned frequently and seem to have been considered a prominent option for the systematic cultivation of the mind. Their eminent position in this respect suggests itself, for example, from a description given in the *Ānāpānasati-sutta* and its *Saṃyukta-āgama* parallel of the attainments reached and variety of meditative practices undertaken by the members of a substantial monastic gathering. The two versions agree that a number of those present on that occasion were practising the four *brahmavihāra*s.[46] The description gives the impression that the *brahmavihāra*s were a regular form of practice among ancient Indian

46 MN 118 at MN III 81,28 (translated Ñāṇamoli 1995: 943) and its parallel SĀ 815 at T II 209c21.

Buddhist monastics. A reason for this apparent popularity would have been the fruits and benefits to be gained from their practice. This is the theme I will explore in Chapter 3, namely the fruits to be expected from maturing compassion and the other *brahmavihāra*s.

### II.8 SUMMARY

Early Buddhist thought contextualizes compassion by presenting *mettā* undertaken by way of body, speech, and mind as its foundation. Such a foundation in *mettā* has a broad range of possible applications, from kindness in daily-life situations to facing the most dramatic forms of aggression. Based on *mettā*, compassion in turn finds its complement in sympathetic joy and equanimity. Contextualizing compassion in this way enriches actual practice and avoids possible pitfalls that could result from compassion being undertaken without the support of the other *brahmavihāra*s.

# III

# MATURING COMPASSION

In the present chapter I turn to the benefits that come from maturing compassion and the other divine abodes. The early discourses showcase various possible fruits to be expected from the cultivation of the four *brahmavihāras*, which range from mundane advantages to the gaining of liberating insight.

## III.1 THE BENEFITS OF BENEVOLENCE

The benefits of *mettā* are highlighted in several passages. According to a discourse in the *Saṃyutta-nikāya* and its *Saṃyukta-āgama* parallel, to cultivate the mental attitude of *mettā* even for a short while is superior to making offerings to hundreds of recipients three times a day.[1] This brings up a theme of considerable relevance in traditional Buddhist circles, namely the acquisition of merit through generosity.

As a side note it may be worth pointing out that the two parallel versions conclude with the Buddha giving an emphatic injunction that *mettā* should be cultivated, an injunction given to monks. This goes to show that in early Buddhist thought the laity were not alone in being concerned with what efficiently generates merit. Here the prospect of acquiring merit acts as an incentive for monks to engage in the cultivation of *mettā*. The present passage also shows that

---

1 SN 20.4 at SN II 264,19 (translated Bodhi 2000: 707) compares giving a hundred pots full of food three times a day to *mettā* practised for a moment, whereas the parallel SĀ 1253 at T II 344b26 speaks of giving 300 pots three times a day.

the practice of *mettā* was clearly seen as recommendable for both monastics and laity.

A graphic illustration of the importance accorded to *mettā* in early Buddhist thought can be found in a discourse in the *Itivuttaka* and its Chinese parallel. Here is the relevant passage from the Chinese version:

> It is just as among all minor and major stars the full moon is foremost. Why is that? The powerfully flourishing radiance of the full moon eclipses all the minor and major stars. Therefore the radiance of all those stars, compared to that of the full moon, is not equal to a sixteenth part of it.
>
> With all meritorious activities it is just like that. [If one] wishes to compare them to the [merit] of the liberation of the mind by *mettā*, they do not equal a sixteenth part of it.[2]

The eminent position accorded in this way to *mettā* is further highlighted in the *Velāma-sutta* and its parallels. Here is a translation of the *Madhyama-āgama* version:

> Superior to offering food to a hundred stream-enterers, [to offering food to] a hundred once-returners, [to offering food to] a hundred non-returners, [to offering food to] a hundred arahants, [to offering food to] a hundred paccekabuddhas, to constructing a monastery and giving it to the monastic community of the four directions, to taking refuge with a joyful mind in the triple gem – the Buddha, the Dharma, and the Saṅgha – and accepting the precepts, would it be if one were to dwell with a mental [attitude] of *mettā* towards all living beings just for the brief time it takes to milk a cow.[3]

---

2 T 765 at T XVII 670b20 to b25, a comparison found similarly in It 1.27 at It 19,26 (translated Ireland 1991: 19).

3 MĀ 155 at T I 677c23 to c28. MĀ 155 at T I 678a4 and one of its parallels, T 73 at T I 879c16, continue by presenting contemplation of all things or all formations as impermanent, *dukkha*, empty, and not-self as what is superior to *mettā*. AN 9.20 at AN IV 396,1 (translated Bodhi 2012: 1277) mentions just perception of impermanence; cf. also D 4094 *ju* 172a1 or Q 5595 *tu* 198a3 (which here leads on to dispassion, cessation, etc.). T 72 at T I 878c26 and EĀ 27.3 at T II 645a2 present as superior to *mettā* not delighting in anything in the whole world, whereas T 74 at T I 882a10 mentions the signless (concentration) of the mind that is free from discriminations. In sum, the parallels differ on what form of insight should be reckoned as the supreme, but agree on according to *mettā* the position of being next in importance.

According to this passage, any material assistance one may give to others, even to highly developed practitioners of the path, as well as taking refuge and the precepts oneself, fades away in comparison to *mettā*.

The practice of *mettā* can yield other benefits, apart from the acquisition of merit. A listing of eleven such benefits can be found, with some variations, in a discourse in the *Aṅguttara-nikāya* and its parallels. In what follows I translate the listing found in a version of this discourse extant in Chinese translation, adding numbers in parentheses to facilitate a discussion of these benefits.

> If the liberation of the mind by *mettā* is engaged in widely, practised, and carried out, one gains and gives rise to wholesome endowments and there will be eleven results in turn, eleven fruits. What are the eleven? One sleeps peacefully (1), one wakes up peacefully (2), one does not encounter bad dreams (3), heavenly beings protect one (4), human beings love one (5), one is respected by non-human beings (6), one will not be harmed by poison (7), by weapons (8), by water or fire (9), nor be subjected to torturing (10), and with the breaking up of the body at death one will be reborn in a god realm, in a Brahmā heaven (11).
>
> One will quickly attain all wholesome states and with wisdom one will be able to proceed to the eradication of the influxes. Monks, engaging widely in the liberation of the mind by *mettā*, practising it and carrying it out, one thereby gains and gives rise to wholesome endowments and there will be these eleven states. Monks, you should therefore make an effort in the liberation of the mind by *mettā*. Monks, you should train in this way![4]

The *Aṅguttara-nikāya* discourse and parallels in the *Ekottarika-āgama* as well as a Tibetan version agree that the practice of *mettā* will have positive repercussions on one's sleep, waking up, and dreams (1 to 3). These benefits bring out the soothing effect of *mettā* on the mind, which makes it easy to sleep well and wake up refreshed. They also agree that *mettā* will improve one's relationships, be these with humans or non-humans (4 to 6). Here an attitude of kindness and well-wishing sets the foundation for being loved and respected by others.

---

4 T 138 at T II 861a27 to b6.

Next in all versions come different aspects of protection that *mettā* was believed to afford (7 to 10), a topic I took up briefly at the beginning of Chapter 2. The reference to not being tortured in the passage translated above has as its counterpart in the *Ekottarika-āgama* discourse the benefit of being protected against robbers.[5] The parallels agree again that one will be reborn in the Brahmā heaven.

The listing in the *Aṅguttara-nikāya* and the Tibetan version consider the different nuances of protection as a single item and as a result have several additional benefits that make up their listing of eleven. These are the ability to concentrate quickly, to have a serene facial complexion, and to pass away without being confused.[6] The *Aṅguttara-nikāya* discourse and the Tibetan version do not refer to the destruction of the influxes (*āsava*).

The *Ekottarika-āgama* version takes up the related topic of reaching the unconditioned, which in its presentation also comes in the form of a postscript after the list of eleven benefits, here given in verse.[7] The presentations in the passage translated above and in the *Ekottarika-āgama* version make it clear that *mettā* can make a substantial contribution to progress towards the destruction of the influxes or reaching the unconditioned. The fact that both versions do not simply include the final goal in their list of eleven benefits also indicates that more than just *mettā* is required for this purpose. The passage translated above explicitly indicates that the additional requirement is the cultivation of wisdom. This is a topic to which I will return later in this chapter, namely the relationship of the *brahmavihāra*s to the gaining of liberating insight.

In what follows I first explore various aspects of the relationship between compassion (as well as the other divine abodes) and absorption. I begin by discussing whether the boundless radiation invariably stands for absorption attainment. Then I examine the advantage the *brahmavihāra*s as a liberation of the mind offer compared to other absorption practices.

---

5 EĀ 49.10 at T II 806a21.

6 AN 11.16 at AN V 342,8 (translated Bodhi 2012: 1573, given as number 15) and D 36 *ka* 270a5 or Q 752 *tsi* 286b1. Judging from what has been preserved from a Sanskrit fragment version of the discourse in SHT I 620R4, Waldschmidt et al. 1965: 276 (identified by Schlingloff 1967: 422), it seems that this version also mentioned the effect of *mettā* on one's facial complexion, followed by the benefit of being liked by *deva*s and humans.

7 EĀ 49.10 at T II 806a27.

## III.2 RADIATING COMPASSION AND ABSORPTION

The description of the boundless radiation of the *brahmavihāra*s clearly points to a concentrated mind, but it requires further investigation to see if this should be understood to invariably entail absorption attainment. Closer inspection of the context of one such description of the radiation practice gives the impression that this is not the case.

The discourse in question is the *Dhānañjāni-sutta* and its *Madhyama-āgama* parallel. According to both versions, Sāriputta had come to know that his former friend, the Brahmin Dhānañjāni, was engaging in unwholesome activities, apparently involving embezzlement. He then visited Dhānañjāni and gave him a teaching. This had the desired impact on Dhānañjāni who decided to mend his ways.

The discourse continues with Dhānañjāni falling seriously ill. On being informed of this, Sāriputta visits him again. Dhānañjāni describes his physical condition with a set of stock passages that indicate he suffers from agonizing headache, severe stomach cramps, and high fever. Sāriputta realizes that Dhānañjāni is on his deathbed and leads him in a sort of guided meditation through various possible rebirth realms, proceeding from rebirth in hell or as an animal up to the prospect of being reborn in the Brahmā world. Dhānañjāni becomes very enthusiastic as soon as the Brahmā world is mentioned, whereon Sāriputta teaches him the practice of the four *brahmavihāra*s as a boundless radiation in all directions.

Soon after Sāriputta has left, Dhānañjāni passes away and is reborn in the Brahmā world. The *Madhyama-āgama* version explicitly states that Dhānañjāni's rebirth in the Brahmā world took place because he had put Sāriputta's instructions into practice and cultivated the four *brahmavihāra*s.[8] The *Majjhima-nikāya* parallel similarly indicates that with this teaching Sāriputta had established Dhānañjāni in the Brahmā world, and that once Dhānañjāni had passed away, he was indeed reborn in the Brahmā world.[9]

Now Dhānañjāni's severe physical condition would have made it highly difficult if not impossible for him to practise absorption.[10]

---

8 MĀ 27 at T I 458b12 (translated Bingenheimer et al. 2013: 187).

9 MN 97 at MN II 195,20 (translated Ñāṇamoli 1995: 796).

10 My discussion takes it that in the early discourses absorption stands for a deeply concentrated mental condition that requires considerable meditative proficiency. It seems to me that such an understanding of absorption clearly emerges from what the early discourses have to indicate in this respect; cf. Anālayo 2003: 75–79, 2014c, and 2015d.

The way he is depicted in the earlier part of the discourse as a busy Brahmin administrator who engages in embezzlement makes it improbable that he should be considered a proficient meditator, capable of attaining absorption at will. With his weak moral basis, this would hardly have been possible.

In fact absorption abilities are ruled out by the different rebirth perspectives that Sāriputta presents to him. Had he been proficient in absorption attainment, there would have been little need for Sāriputta to begin his tour of possible rebirths for Dhānañjāni with the hell and animal realms. Such prospects for his next rebirth only make sense if Dhānañjāni had no proficiency in absorption and due to his earlier bad conduct still stood the chance of a lower rebirth, however much he had reformed himself in the meantime.

Without previous meditative proficiency, however, in his severely critical health condition on his deathbed it would have been impossible for him to learn how to enter absorption attainment through instructions that apparently he had not received before. Given that according to both versions Dhānañjāni was subsequently reborn in the Brahmā world, he nevertheless must have put Sāriputta's instructions to good use.

From this it would follow that the radiation of the *brahmavihāra*s can be undertaken successfully even by someone who is not in a condition to enter absorption. In fact, both versions report that Sāriputta, who was well aware of the physical condition of Dhānañjāni, explicitly introduced his teaching on how to develop the radiation of the *brahmavihāra*s as a way to rebirth in the Brahmā world.[11] Given that Sāriputta delivered such a teaching to someone who was not in the proper condition for developing absorption, it seems fair to conclude that this mode of practice can be undertaken even without absorption attainment. Needless to say, the radiation will of course be more powerful and stable if absorption is attained. So my point is only that the radiation experience is not confined to absorption, but can already be undertaken at lower levels of concentration.

Now the description of the radiation of the *brahmavihāra*s indicates that the mind has "become great", *mahāggata*, and "boundless", *appamāṇa*. At times the early discourses distinguish between these two qualifications. A temporary liberation of the mind that has "become great" takes place when one is able to pervade mentally

11 MN 97 at MN II 195,2 and MĀ 27 at T I 458b1.

a certain area, such as the area of a few trees, or a village, or even a country, with the object of one's meditation. A temporary liberation of the mind that has become "boundless", however, comes about through the radiation of the *brahmavihāra*s in all directions.[12] Here the mind not only pervades a certain measured space, however big or small, but has become totally without confines or boundaries.[13] In fact the term I have translated as "boundless", *appamāṇa*, could also be translated as "without measure". So the mental pervasion with the *brahmavihāra*s is a boundless experience that is indeed without measure in any way.[14]

Such boundlessness clearly points to a well-concentrated mental condition. Nevertheless, the qualifications "become great" and "boundless" at times feature in contexts that are not restricted to absorption attainment. An example can be found in a set of similes used by Sāriputta to illustrate his patience when being wrongly accused. In these similes he indicates that he faces the dishonest allegations with a mind that has "become great" and "boundless".[15] It seems safe to assume that the terms here are not meant to refer to absorption attainment, as they illustrate a situation where he is speaking up in order to defend himself. Sāriputta's broad mental attitude when defending himself would rather be an indication of his dwelling in a *brahmavihāra* condition in a day-to-day life situation.

The *Mahāparinibbāna-sutta* and its parallels report the Buddha praising Ānanda for having had bodily, verbal, and mental acts of *mettā* towards his teacher. These acts are qualified as having been "boundless".[16] This qualification cannot mean that, when doing things for the Buddha or speaking to him, Ānanda was immersed in absorption.

---

12 MN 127 at MN III 146,13 (translated Ñāṇamoli 1995: 1003) and its parallel MĀ 79 at T I 550a22.

13 This is the interpretation provided in the commentary on MN 127, Ps IV 200,21, which explains that the *brahmavihāra*s are boundless because there is no increase in their meditative object (*nimitta*).

14 The commentary on another discussion of the term "boundless" (found in MN 43), Ps II 353,19, explains that in the case of the *brahmavihāras* this qualification refers to the boundlessness of the pervasion, *pharaṇa-appamāṇatāya appamāṇā nāma*.

15 AN 9.11 at AN IV 375,2 (translated Bodhi 2012: 1262) and its parallel MĀ 24 at T I 453a7 (translated Bingenheimer et al. 2013: 162); another parallel, EĀ 37.6 at T II 713a12, does not use these expressions.

16 DN 16 at DN II 144,17 (translated Walshe 1987: 265) and its parallels in a Sanskrit fragment, Waldschmidt 1951: 298 (§22), and DĀ 2 at T I 25c9.

Another instance confirms that the expressions "become great" and "boundless" are not necessarily marks of absorption attainment. According to the *Kakacūpama-sutta* and its *Madhyama-āgama* parallel, even on being cruelly cut into pieces by bandits one's mind should remain unaffected and dwell in having "become great" and "boundless".[17] This depicts a rather extreme situation which leaves little scope for formal meditation practice leading up to entry into absorption. Yet, even in such atrocious circumstances, a mind that has previously been sufficiently trained can "become great" and "boundless".

In sum, the radiation of the *brahmavihāra*s in such a way that they "become great" and "boundless" does not seem to be confined to absorption attainment, but can be undertaken at levels of concentration that fall short of full absorption.[18]

### III.3 COMPASSION AS A LIBERATION OF THE MIND

Another noteworthy feature of the *brahmavihāra*s is their positioning within accounts of the path of practice in the early discourses. Whereas at times the divine abodes stand in place of the four absorptions, on other occasions the two sets occur alongside each other. At first sight this is surprising. Once the four absorptions are mentioned, it would be redundant to mention the four *brahmavihāra*s again, if these are just specific approaches to absorption attainment.[19]

The *Aṭṭhakanāgara-sutta* and its parallels, for example, follow a listing of the four absorptions with the *brahmavihāra*s, and then come to the immaterial attainments.[20] This gives the impression that the

---

17 MN 21 at MN I 129,22 (translated Ñāṇamoli 1995: 223) and its parallel MĀ 193 at T I 746a19.

18 Vism 152,16 (translated Ñāṇamoli 1956/1991: 148) indicates that the meditative sign of the earth *kasiṇa* can be extended so as to become all-pervasive when one is in access concentration, not only when one is in absorption, and then makes the same indication for the *brahmavihāra*s, Vism 320,6 (translated Ñāṇamoli 1956/1991: 312). Nevertheless, Vism 308,7 (translated Ñāṇamoli 1956/1991: 300) suggests that full ability in the radiation would require absorption attainment.

19 This problem is taken up in the **Mahāvibhāṣa*, T 1545 at T XXVII 420b8, which as one of three alternative explanations argues that the boundless states are supreme among what can lead to absorption attainment.

20 MN 52 at MN I 350,10 (translated Ñāṇamoli 1995: 454), corresponding to AN 11.17 at AN V 343,19 (translated Bodhi 2012: 1574, given as number 16), and the parallels MĀ 217 at T I 802b7 and T 92 at T I 916b17.

*brahmavihāra*s are sufficiently distinct to merit explicit mention, even when the absorptions have already been covered. In fact the sequence of presentation in the *Aṭṭhakanāgara-sutta* gives the impression that the *brahmavihāra*s might in some way be superior to the four absorptions.

Perhaps the listing of the absorptions and the *brahmavihāra*s side by side in this way reflects a distinct quality of the *brahmavihāra*s when practised in the radiation mode. With forms of meditation that are based on other objects, the condition of a temporary liberation of the mind (*cetovimutti*) comes about once absorption is attained. With the *brahmavihāra*s, however, experiencing a temporary liberation of the mind is possible already with a lesser degree of concentration, simply due to their boundless nature. From this viewpoint, then, they would indeed merit separate mention in a listing of different types of temporary liberations of the mind, alongside the absorptions and the immaterial attainments.

Understood in this way, the *brahmavihāra*s offer a distinct advantage over other forms of tranquillity meditation. Due to their boundless nature, the condition of a temporary liberation of the mind can be experienced already with lesser degrees of concentration and does not depend exclusively on the successful attainment of absorption.

For actual meditation practice this is significant, as it may help to avoid much of the pressure that can at times come with the practice of mental tranquillity. The belief that one has to reach a certain level of concentration through successful attainment of absorption in order to be capable of progressing on the path can for some practitioners have detrimental repercussions. If such a belief is held strongly, it can result in excessive forms of striving and mental tension. Such excesses easily become counterproductive, in the sense of actually preventing the mind from becoming truly tranquil. Here the cultivation of the *brahmavihāra*s as a boundless radiation offers a skilful approach that avoids such problems. The mental experience of boundlessness is by its very nature free from any strain or tension and thereby offers a natural way into deepening mental tranquillity.

Moreover, the very fact that one is engaging in compassion etc. makes it almost inevitable that one will be soft with oneself instead of pushing too hard. Besides encouraging a soft and allowing attitude towards oneself, the mental attitude engendered by the *brahmavihāra*s will also be of considerable assistance when one has to face external disturbances. Instead of resulting in the frustrating experience of wavering between being concentrated on the chosen object of meditation and having lost this object due to external sounds and other disturbances, meditation can continue smoothly. This can be achieved by making the sound or disturbance part of the practice: compassion informs one's attitude towards the disturbance or those responsible for it. In this way, problems can become the path. Even though the degree of mental tranquillity will not be as profound as it would have been without the disturbance, the actual practice continues seamlessly.

In this way, the main concern of one's practice would not be the reaching of a particular mark in concentrative depth, but the maintenance of the boundless radiation of the *brahmavihāra*s when facing any disturbance. Any disturbance, including any form of mental distraction, thus simply becomes food for the practice.

Through such cultivation, eventually the meditative practice of compassion and the other *brahmavihāra*s will lead to absorption attainment. Their ability to lead into absorption is why, as mentioned above, the divine abodes at times stand in place of the four absorptions, after the successful removal of the hindrances or other mental defilements.[21] The cultivation of the *brahmavihāra*s up to absorption level can then fulfil the training in mental tranquillity that in early Buddhist thought forms an integral part of the path to liberation.

## III.4 COMPASSION AND KARMA

Besides the benefits that the cultivation of tranquillity through the boundless radiation of compassion and the other *brahmavihāra*s offers in the present moment, the discourses also point to a relation between the divine abodes and the future fruition of karma. This is spelled out, for example, in the *Karajakāya-sutta* and its parallels. The passage in question comes in between the two passages that I took up in Chapter 1, which describe the boundless radiation practice and the effect of the cultivation of compassion and the other *brahmavihāra*s on a boy or girl, who by dint of such practice becomes incapable of performing an unwholesome deed. The piece that leads from

21 Cf. e.g. DN 25 at DN III 49,24 (translated Walshe 1987: 390) and its parallels DĀ 8 at T I 48c5 and MĀ 104 at T I 594b17; or MN 40 at MN I 283,25 (translated Ñāṇamoli 1995: 374) and its parallel MĀ 183 at T I 726b22.

the radiation practice to the other statement reads as follows in the *Madhyama-āgama* version:

> Then [the learned noble disciple] reflects like this: "Formerly my mind was narrow and not well developed; now my mind has become boundless and well developed."
>
> When the mind of the learned noble disciple has in this way become boundless and well developed, if because of [associating with] bad friends one formerly dwelled in negligence and performed unwholesome deeds, those [deeds] cannot lead one along, cannot defile one, and will not come back to meet one.[22]

The *Karajakāya-sutta* makes a similar indication in a more succinct manner, simply indicating that no limiting karma will remain or persist there.[23] In order to provide some background for appreciating the significance of this presentation, in what follows I briefly survey some key passages regarding the early Buddhist conception of karma.

Karma in early Buddhist thought is closely related to intention, since intention is what is responsible for deeds by body, speech, and mind.[24] Based on this focus on intention as the decisive factor that shapes karma, the early Buddhist conception of karma and its fruit acquires a dynamic aspect. What has been done in the past will in some way come to fruition, but the way this happens depends on what one does now.

This dynamism finds illustration in a simile of a piece of salt, found in a discourse in the *Aṅguttara-nikāya* and its *Madhyama-āgama* parallel.[25] According to this simile, the same piece of salt can have quite a different effect depending upon the quantity of water it is thrown into. If the piece is thrown into a small amount of water, such as the water contained in a little bowl, all the water will become salty. In contrast, thrown into the river Ganges the same piece of salt will hardly have a noticeable effect. In the same way, the present

22 MĀ 15 at T I 438a11 to a15; an explicit reference to karma is not found at this juncture in the Tibetan parallel D 4094 *ju* 238a5 or Q 5595 *tu* 272a5 (translated Dhammadinnā 2014a: 67).

23 AN 10.208 at AN V 299,25 (translated Bodhi 2012: 1542, given as number 219).

24 AN 6.63 at AN III 415,7 (translated Bodhi 2012: 963) and its parallel MĀ 111 at T I 600a24; cf. also the *Abhidharmakośavyākhyā*, Wogihara 1936: 400,20.

25 AN 3.99 at AN I 250,1 (translated Bodhi 2012: 332, given as number 100) and MĀ 11 at T I 433a21 (translated Bingenheimer et al. 2013: 63).

repercussions of a particular deed from the past depend to a great extent on the overall current condition of the one who performed this deed previously.

A rather stark example of the possibility of emerging from the constraints of previously performed unwholesome deeds is the tale of Aṅgulimāla. The *Aṅgulimāla-sutta* and its parallels report that the serial killer Aṅgulimāla was converted by the Buddha, gave up his bloody deeds, and went forth as a monk. In due course, he became an arahant.[26] This remarkable turn of events shows that in early Buddhist thought even a mass murderer was held to stand a chance at total transformation, so much so that he could reach the acme of spiritual perfection.

The *Aṅgulimāla-sutta* and several of its parallels report that Aṅgulimāla was attacked by people when as a monk he went begging.[27] Here karmic retribution takes an immediately evident form, since his earlier bloody deeds had obviously earned him the people's hatred that expressed itself in these attacks. Compared to the karmic results to be expected for mass murder, however, such karmic retribution seems indeed like a piece of salt thrown into the river Ganges.

It is against this dynamic conception of karma that the above-translated passage from the *Karajakāya-sutta* and its *Madhyama-āgama* parallel is best appreciated. A mind imbued with compassion and the other *brahmavihāra*s is a potent intentional state that will have its effect on how the results of other deeds done in the past will now be experienced.[28] In particular the boundless nature of the radiation is responsible for the fact that no limiting action can remain.[29] The limiting action becomes like a piece of salt thrown into

26 MN 86 at MN II 104,1 (translated Ñāṇamoli 1995: 715) and its parallels SĀ 1077 at T II 281a26 (translated Anālayo 2008: 137f), SĀ² 16 at T II 378c29, EĀ 38.6 at T II 721a7, T 118 at T II 509b23, and T 119 at T II 511a19.

27 MN 86 at MN II 104,3 and its parallels EĀ 38.6 at T II 721a22, T 118 at T II 510a6, T 119 at T II 511c23, and T 212 at T IV 704a26.

28 For a more detailed discussion of the relationship drawn in the *Karajakāya-sutta* between the *brahmavihāra*s and karma cf. Dhammadinnā 2014a: 71–89.

29 In the case of MN 99 at MN II 207,22 (translated Ñāṇamoli 1995: 816), the statement on no limiting karma remaining is followed by the conch-blower simile (the parallel MĀ 152 at T I 669c10 only has the conch-blower simile). Aronson 1979b: 31 relates the notion of no limiting actions remaining to this type of simile, in that the blowing of the conch "is not a measured performance. Similarly, when one cultivates love and the other attitudes according to the method given in the discourses, no measured intentions remain."

the boundlessness of the mind whose scope is incomparably vaster than even the waters of the Ganges.

Such considerations are relevant not only to rebirth prospects. Another aspect of the same dynamic is that present-moment intentions of the type that would lead to unwholesome deeds have no scope to remain in a mind established in the boundless radiation of compassion. In practical terms, when unwholesome thoughts arise and distract the mind, these can be made to vanish by just returning to the boundless condition of the mind. Regular mental inspection can confirm that unwholesome intentions require some degree of mental narrowness to thrive. Deprived of this mental narrowness, their power dissipates. The very boundlessness of the mind simply does not afford a basis for negativity to remain, which due to its limited nature dissolves and disappears just like a piece of salt thrown into a vast expanse of water.

A simile in the *Kakacūpama-sutta* and its parallel illustrates the absence of aversion that comes about through the radiation of *mettā* with the example of painting on space. The simile occurs as part of a series of illustrations on how disagreeable words will not affect one who remains patient and free from aversion, able to remain established in *mettā*. In what follows I translate this simile from the *Madhyama-āgama* parallel.

> [The Buddha said:] "It is just like a painter or a painter's apprentice who comes along carrying various colours and says: 'I will trace forms and images in empty space and adorn them with these coloured paints.' What do you think? Will that painter or that painter's apprentice be able, by these means, to trace forms and images in empty space and adorn them with coloured paints?"
>
> The monks replied: "No, Blessed One. Why is that? Blessed One, this empty space is immaterial, it is invisible and without resistance. Therefore that painter or that painter's apprentice is unable, by these means, to trace forms and images in empty space and adorn them with coloured paints. Blessed One, that painter or that painter's apprentice will just tire himself in vain."[30]

Just as space does not afford a material basis for painting, so too aversion has simply no basis to remain in a mind that is well

30 MĀ 193 at T I 745c11 to c19. In the simile in MN 21 at MN I 127,30 (translated Ñāṇamoli 1995: 221) the protagonist is not introduced as a painter or his apprentice.

established in cultivating the *brahmavihāras* as a boundless radiation. Unwholesome thoughts simply vanish against the spaciousness of the mind as soon as this has regained its former boundless condition.

### III.5 COMPASSION AND INSIGHT

Another significant indication in the *Karajakāya-sutta* and its parallels reflects the potential of compassion and the other *brahmavihāras* for the cultivation of liberating insight. The passage in question in the *Madhyama-āgama* version reads as follows:

> If the liberation of the mind by compassion has become boundless and well developed in this way, certainly non-returning will be attained, or else that which is still higher.[31]

The *Karajakāya-sutta* similarly indicates that cultivation of each *brahmavihāra* in this way leads to non-return for those who have not penetrated the highest liberation.[32] Significantly, the *Karajakāya-sutta* explicitly indicates that this is the case for one who has wisdom.[33]

As in the case of the above passage on karma, here, too, a proper appreciation of this statement requires a short excursion into the relationship between tranquillity and insight in the early Buddhist texts. A helpful passage to convey the main principles underlying this relationship occurs in the *Yuganaddha-sutta* and its *Saṃyukta-āgama* parallel. The speaker of the discourse is Ānanda, who describes four different approaches taken by those who have informed him that they reached the final goal. The two versions agree that three of these approaches involve tranquillity and insight. The fourth approach in the *Yuganaddha-sutta* involves neither, although the *Saṃyukta-āgama* parallel brings in both qualities even in this fourth instance.[34] The other three modes, presented similarly in the parallel versions, are as follows:

---

31 MĀ 15 at T I 438a22 to a24, which has this passage in full only for the first and the last of the four *brahmavihāras*. In order to keep with my main topic, I here supply the passage for compassion, even though in the original this is only given in abbreviation.

32 AN 10.208 AN V 300,12 (translated Bodhi 2012: 1542, given as number 219).

33 The Tibetan parallel agrees in this respect with MĀ 15, in that it does not explicitly mention wisdom; cf. D 4094 *ju* 238b2 or Q 5595 *tu* 272b2 (translated Dhammadinnā 2014a: 70f).

34 AN 4.170 at AN II 157,20 (translated Bodhi 2012: 535f) just speaks of overcoming restlessness in regard to the Dharma, an approach which in SĀ 560 at T II 147a5 still involves tranquillity and insight.

- insight preceded by tranquillity,
- tranquillity preceded by insight,
- tranquillity and insight conjoined.

This shows that there is no hard and fast rule that either tranquillity or else insight must be practised first. For some it will be better to start by placing emphasis on insight, and based on the initial degree of insight gained then give more room to tranquillity in their practice. Others will prefer to begin instead with calming down the mind and then turn to insight. Or else some develop a mode of practice that combines both.

This presentation allows various approaches, according to personal inclination and predisposition. At the same time, neither version envisages any monoculture, in the sense of proposing that either tranquillity or insight could lead on its own to liberation. Instead, tranquillity and insight need to be combined, in one way or another, in order to mature the mind sufficiently so that progress to full awakening can take place.

The contribution made by tranquillity and insight respectively to progress on the path receives another highlight in a discourse in the *Aṅguttara-nikāya* and its *Ekottarika-āgama* parallel. Although their actual formulation differs, the main point made remains the same. Here is the relevant part from the *Ekottarika-āgama* version:

> A forest monk should cultivate two dharmas. What are the two dharmas? They are: tranquillity and insight. If a forest monk gains the calmness of tranquillity, he will then be successful in his moral restraint without blemish of conduct and without violation of the precepts, generating all virtues.
>
> If a forest monk has gained insight, he will in turn contemplate that this is *dukkha*, knowing it as it really is, he will contemplate the arising of *dukkha*, contemplate the cessation of *dukkha*, and contemplate the way out of *dukkha*, knowing it as it really is.
>
> Having contemplated in this way, his mind attains liberation from the influx of sensuality, [his mind attains liberation from] the influx of becoming, and his mind attains liberation from the influx of ignorance. Having in turn attained liberation, he knows: "Birth and death have come to an end, the holy life has been established, what had to be done has been done, there will be no further experiencing of existence", knowing this as it really is.[35]

35 EĀ 20.7 at T II 600b1 to b9.

The corresponding discourse in the *Aṅguttara-nikāya* proceeds in a more succinct manner and without mentioning a forest monk.[36] It just indicates that through tranquillity the mind is developed and lust is abandoned; through insight wisdom is developed and ignorance is abandoned.

According to the passage translated above from the *Ekottarika-āgama*, a forest monk who cultivates tranquillity becomes able to maintain his moral conduct well. The reason behind this relationship can be filled out with the help of the *Aṅguttara-nikāya* discourse: because the cultivation of tranquillity has helped him to let go of lust. Letting go of lust the monk would indeed have abandoned one of the main causes for breaches of the monastic rules.

The succinct indication in the *Aṅguttara-nikāya* discourse that insight leads to wisdom and the abandoning of ignorance in turn receives a fitting illustration in the *Ekottarika-āgama* discourse, in that insight takes as its vehicle contemplation of the four noble truths, and this then leads to final liberation.

The important contribution made by tranquillity here is that it brings about a change in the attitudes of the mind, by providing it with a higher form of pleasure and inner satisfaction. This higher internal joy and happiness divests outer sensual objects of their attraction and in this way leads to a gradual diminishing of lust.

The contribution offered by tranquillity in this way does not stand on its own, however; in fact both passages make it clear that the factor that eradicates ignorance and leads to final liberation is insight. In this way, tranquillity and insight function in harmonious cooperation as the two essential qualities to be brought into being for progress on the path to awakening.

Returning to the *Karajakāya-sutta* and its parallels, the indication that the boundless radiation of compassion and the other *brahmavihāra*s can lead to non-return acquires its significance against the background of the *Yuganaddha-sutta* and the above passage. The *Yuganaddha-sutta* makes it clear that such a statement should not be interpreted as advocating monoculture. The point is not that compassion practised entirely on its own without any relation to insight can lead to non-return. Instead, compassion can make a significant contribution to progress to non-return due to its ability to transform the affective attitudes of the mind.

36 AN 2.3.10 at AN I 61,4 (translated Bodhi 2012: 152, given as number 31).

As stated explicitly in the *Karajakāya-sutta* and its parallels, one who cultivates the temporary liberation of the mind by compassion will become unable to engage in unwholesome deeds.[37] In other words, besides leading to concentration, the meditative radiation of compassion makes its own intrinsic contribution to the path by transforming one's mind, in particular by countering its tendency to cruelty. Through repeated radiation of compassion the mind becomes habituated to respond to whatever happens with a compassionate attitude. The same holds for the other *brahmavihāras*. The basic principle behind this transformative potential can be illustrated with a statement made in the *Dvedhāvitakka-sutta*. Here is my translation of the corresponding passage in the *Madhyama-āgama* parallel:

> In accordance with what one intends, in accordance with what one thinks, the mind takes delight in that. If ... one often thinks thoughts without sensual desire and abandons thoughts of sensual desire, then because of often thinking thoughts without sensual desire, the mind will take delight in that.
>
> If ... one often thinks thoughts without ill will ... thoughts without cruelty, and abandons thoughts of ill will ... thoughts of cruelty, then because of often thinking thoughts without ill will ... thoughts without cruelty, the mind takes delight in that.[38]

This in a way helps to bring to light another distinct advantage of the *brahmavihāra*s when compared to other forms of tranquillity meditation. The advantage that compassion or the other *brahmavihāra*s have to offer is that the mental attitude they engender is opposed to mental defilements whose removal and eradication is integral to the path to awakening.

Not only do the joy and happiness experienced with the boundless radiation of compassion divest lust and sensual desire of their former attraction, but the very nature of compassion undermines the tendency of the mind to react with aversion. These are the two main defilements that need to be overcome in the progression from the initial insight gained with stream-entry to the level of mental

---

37 See above p.20.

38 MĀ 102 at T I 589c5 to c9; the parallel MN 19 at MN I 116,27 (translated Ñāṇamoli 1995: 209) expresses the same principle with the slightly different formulation that the mind "inclines" towards such thoughts, which in a way complements the indication in MĀ 102 that the mind "delights" in such thoughts.

freedom that comes with non-return: desire and aversion. Both are being directly addressed through the meditative cultivation of compassion.

A discourse in the *Dīgha-nikāya* and its *Dīrgha-āgama* parallel reckon the four absorptions as instances of a practitioner's "happiness", and the *brahmavihāra*s as instances of a practitioner's "wealth".[39] The subtle distinction drawn in these two discourses shows that cultivation of compassion and the other *brahmavihāra*s is not only a cause of happiness, but also results in an acquisition of a mental condition that is comparable to wealth.

The point underlying this distinction could be that cultivation of the *brahmavihāra*s offers a distinct advantage over other forms of mental tranquillity. Meditating with the help of an object like a *kasiṇa*, for example, or else the breath, of course has the eminent potential to lead to concentration. Apart from the gain of concentration, however, the particular object chosen for meditation, be it a *kasiṇa* or the breath, does not in itself offer substantial additional benefits in support of progress on the path. The case of compassion and the other *brahmavihāra*s differs. In addition to their ability to lead to deep concentration, the fact that a particular *brahmavihāra* has been chosen for meditation cultivation will result in a change of one's attitudes and mental conditioning.

This could be compared to drinking two different types of tea. One type is tasty and supplies the body with liquid, whereas the other in addition has medicinal properties that help counter some bodily illness. The cultivation of the *brahmavihāra*s would be like drinking tea that is not only tasty and nourishing, but also curative.

In addition to transforming one's own mind, the practice of compassion also has positive effects on others. All those who come into contact with someone who engages in the meditative cultivation of compassion will sense the harmony and well-wishing that accompany the words and deeds of one whose mind is steeped in compassion. Understood in this way, the *brahmavihāra*s can indeed be reckoned a practitioner's "wealth", enriching both oneself and others.

When seen from the viewpoint of the eightfold path, the meditative cultivation of compassion can become a direct expression of harmlessness as one of the three modes of right intention, the second

39 DN 26 at DN III 78,4 (translated Walshe 1987: 405) and its parallel DĀ 6 at T I 42b4 (however, another parallel, MĀ 70 at T I 524c24, does not mention either wealth or the *brahmavihāra*s).

factor of the noble eightfold path. This builds a firm foundation for right speech and right action free from intention of harm. Engaging in the cultivation of compassion thereby also becomes an implementation of right effort, and its successful practice can come to fulfil the path factor of right concentration. Undertaken in this way, the cultivation of compassion can fulfil several aspects of the noble eightfold path.

The cultivation of compassion could even be used as one's main vehicle of practice. The *Aṭṭhakanāgara-sutta* and its parallel describe the way this can be done, showing how the absorptions and each of the four *brahmavihāra*s can be used as alternative routes to the final goal. In the case of compassion, according to the *Aṭṭhakanāgara-sutta* the experience of the boundless radiation should be contemplated as conditioned and therefore as subject to cessation.[40] Two Chinese parallels present the cultivation of insight in a more succinct manner, indicating simply that one should contemplate dharmas as dharmas.[41] This appears to be a reference to the fourth *satipaṭṭhāna*. A central aspect of the fourth *satipaṭṭhāna* found alike in the *Satipaṭṭhāna-sutta* and its parallels is the awakening factors, those qualities that need to be brought into being for awakening to take place. The relationship between these and compassion is my next topic.

### III.6 COMPASSION AND THE AWAKENING FACTORS

A discourse in the *Saṃyutta-nikāya* and its *Saṃyukta-āgama* parallel show how *mettā* as a *brahmavihāra* can be combined with the awakening factors. Below is a translation of the *Saṃyukta-āgama* version:

> How does ... one by cultivating the mental [attitude] of *mettā* attain great fruit and great benefit? Here ... imbuing the mind with *mettā* one cultivates the mindfulness awakening factor supported by seclusion, supported by dispassion, and supported by cessation, leading to letting go ... *up to* ... [imbuing the mind with *mettā*] one cultivates the equanimity awakening factor supported by seclusion, supported by dispassion, and supported by cessation, leading to letting go.[42]

40 MN 52 at MN I 351,28 (translated Ñāṇamoli 1995: 456), corresponding to AN 11.17 at AN V 345,6 (translated Bodhi 2012: 1575f, given as number 16).

41 MĀ 217 at T I 802b19 and T 92 at T I 916b29.

42 SĀ 744 at T II 197c17 to c21; cf. also D 4094 *ju* 164b7 or Q 5595 *tu* 190b1 (translated Martini 2011: 150).

The *Saṃyutta-nikāya* collection continues after the parallel to the present passage with another three discourses that apply the same pattern to compassion, sympathetic joy, and equanimity.[43] In order to appreciate the implications of this indication on how the *brahmavihāra*s can be employed as one's main meditation practice in such a way that this results in cultivating the awakening factors and thereby in progress to awakening, in what follows I briefly summarize key aspects of the cultivation of the awakening factors.[44]

The set of seven awakening factors singles out those mental qualities that are required in order to progress to awakening. These are:

- mindfulness,
- investigation-of-dharmas,
- energy,
- joy,
- tranquillity,
- concentration,
- equanimity.

For an actual bringing into being of these seven qualities, two main dynamics need to be taken into account. One of these two dynamics is a sequential build-up, where each factor leads to the next in the list.[45] Besides this gradual build-up, the other significant dynamic is that some awakening factors are commendable when the mind is sluggish, others when the mind is agitated. In the first case, when the mind is sluggish, one should strengthen in particular investigation, energy, and joy. When the mind is agitated, however, one should rather make tranquillity, concentration, and equanimity stronger. In both situations, mindfulness is equally helpful.[46]

Once the awakening factors are cultivated in this way and brought into harmonious balance, actual practice can lead to awakening on being combined with four insight-related themes. These are

---

43 SN 46.63 to 46.65 at SN V 131,16 (translated Bodhi 2000: 1619).

44 For a more detailed discussion cf. Anālayo 2013c: 195–226.

45 A description of the sequential building up of the seven awakening factors can be found in MN 118 at MN III 85,8 (translated Ñāṇamoli 1995: 946f) and its parallel SĀ 810 at T II 208b15 (translated Anālayo 2013c: 215f).

46 SN 46.53 at SN V 112,21 (translated Bodhi 2000: 1605ff) and its parallels SĀ 714 at T II 191c25 (translated Anālayo 2013c: 202ff) and D 4094 *nyu* 52a5 or Q 5595 *thu* 92b7.

mentioned in the extract translated above, namely seclusion, dispassion, cessation, and letting go.[47]

Practice undertaken in this way offers a possibility to progress on the path to awakening based on having made compassion the main vehicle of one's meditative cultivation. Needless to say, this needs to be counterbalanced by dedicating some time to cultivating the other *brahmavihāra*s and would probably benefit considerably from being combined with insight contemplation undertaken at times also in its own right.

### III.7 COMPASSION AND INFINITE SPACE

A discourse in the *Saṃyutta-nikāya* that also combines the *brahmavihāra*s with the awakening factors brings in an additional perspective that relates to the immaterial spheres. Whereas the *Saṃyukta-āgama* parallel does not mention the awakening factors, it does have a similar presentation on the immaterial spheres. The context for this presentation is to show in what way the Buddhist approach to the *brahmavihāra*s differs from the way the practice of the divine abodes was undertaken by contemporaries in ancient India. One such difference is that a Buddhist practitioner skilled in the *brahmavihāra*s knows what constitutes the culmination point of each.

In Chapter 2 I already took up briefly the culmination point of *mettā*, which is found in mental beauty.[48] In the case of the other three *brahmavihāra*s, however, their respective culmination points are the first three of the four immaterial spheres. Here is the relevant part from the *Saṃyukta-āgama* parallel:

> Cultivating the mental [attitude] of compassion, much cultivating it, has the sphere of [infinite] space as its culmination. Cultivating the mental [attitude] of sympathetic joy, much cultivating it, has the sphere of [infinite] consciousness as its culmination. Cultivating the

47 Here I would understand seclusion as referring in particular to seclusion from anything that is unwholesome. Dispassion I take to point to the gradual eroding and fading away of craving and attachment. Cessation I consider to reflect a focus on the disappearing aspect of phenomena, thereby bringing to the mental forefront the most challenging implication of impermanence. These three together culminate in a profound letting go, which I see as standing for a relinquishment of any identification or holding on, any clinging or craving, whatever it may be.

48 See above p.38.

mental [attitude] of equanimity, much cultivating it, has the sphere of nothingness as its culmination.[49]

The *Saṃyutta-nikāya* parallel adds that in each case to speak of these immaterial spheres as the culmination holds for one who has not penetrated to a superior liberation.[50] That is, these three immaterial spheres are the culmination point of the three *brahmavihāra*s within the realm of mental tranquillity. The presentation does not intend to posit these culmination points as superior to the gaining of awakening.

The experiences of infinite space, infinite consciousness, and nothingness share the boundless nature of the radiation of the divine abodes.[51] The parallelism goes further in as much as there appears to be a shared tendency towards diminishing at least to some degree one's holding on to a sense of self. Needless to say, fully going beyond a sense of self requires the cultivation of liberating insight, a topic to which I will return in the next chapters. Nevertheless, the *brahmavihāra*s and the experience of the immaterial spheres can make a considerable contribution to progress towards realization of not-self.

In the case of the immaterial spheres, the *Brahmajāla-sutta* and its parallels report that these experiences were seen by other practitioners in ancient India as forms of going beyond the self.[52] Whereas from an early Buddhist perspective the attainment of an immaterial sphere does not suffice to settle the issue of the sense of self, such attainment does have some potential to undermine at

---

49 SĀ 743 at T II 197c11 to c13.

50 For the case of compassion this indication is found in SN 46.54 at SN V 120,2 (translated Bodhi 2000: 1610). Besides not mentioning the awakening factors, SĀ 743 also does not refer to a training in viewing things as repulsive and not repulsive. In SN 46.54 such training leads to the correlation of the *brahmavihāra*s with the immaterial spheres. Aronson 1984: 24 comments on SN 46.54 that "the special contribution of the Buddha is his coupling of these attitudes to a cultivation of liberating insight. This *union* is the uniquely Buddhist way of cultivating love, compassion, sympathetic joy, or equanimity."

51 Bronkhorst 1993/2000: 94 comments on the correlation established in SN 46.54 and SĀ 743 that "in both the Brahmic States and the four Stages [i.e., the four immaterial spheres] we find a heavy emphasis on infinity."

52 DN 1 at DN I 34,32 (translated Walshe 1987: 84) and its parallels DĀ 21 at T I 93b4, a Tibetan discourse parallel in Weller 1934: 56 (§186), a discourse quotation in the **Śāriputrābhidharma*, T 1548 at T XXVIII 660b1, and a discourse quotation in D 4094 *ju* 151b5 or Q 5595 *tu* 174b8; for Sanskrit fragments cf. Hartmann 1989: 54 and SHT X 4189, Wille 2008: 307.

least the grosser manifestations of this sense of self in the form of clinging to one's body, physical possessions, etc. The same holds for the *brahmavihāras*, which are similarly able to diminish major forms of self-centredness through the experience of the boundless radiation of a mental attitude that wishes others to be well.

The immaterial attainments are a regular occurrence in the early Buddhist discourses. The last two of the set of four are the attainment of nothingness and the attainment of neither-perception-nor-non-perception, which according to the *Ariyapariyesanā-sutta* and its parallel had been learned by the Buddha-to-be from his two teachers Āḷāra Kālāma and Uddaka Rāmaputta.[53] Just like the *brahmavihāras*, the immaterial spheres are in this way presented as modes of meditation known in ancient India in general. Their correlation as presented above, however, is highlighted as a specifically Buddhist contribution.

The standard description of the meditative progression from the attainment of the four absorptions to gaining the immaterial spheres stipulates leaving behind any perception related to material form and to the experience of resistance, and not giving attention to any form of diversity.[54] Such transcendence of the material realm in order to be able to experience infinite space apparently underlies the relationship of infinite space to compassion. The *Visuddhimagga* and the *Yogācārabhūmi* agree in explaining that with infinite space one leaves behind all the physical afflictions that take place in the material realm, such as, for example, being beaten.[55] So the compassionate wish for others to be free from affliction would relate to the notion of being free from all forms of material resistance, since in this way a major portion of the types of affliction normally experienced will not happen in the first place.

With sympathetic joy, in the sense of the wish for others to be mentally joyful and at ease, a concern with the minds of others

53 MN 26 at MN I 164,14 (translated Ñāṇamoli 1995: 257) and its parallel MĀ 204 at T I 776b12 (translated Anālayo 2012c: 27); for a more detailed discussion of the Buddha's pre-awakening attainment of the immaterial spheres cf. Anālayo 2014a.

54 Cf., e.g., MN 137 at MN III 222,15 (translated Ñāṇamoli 1995: 1072) and its parallel MĀ 163 at T I 694b1 (translated below, p.92, notably a context where this also comes after a reference to being resolved on beauty (MN 137) or experiencing liberation by beauty (MĀ 163). This mirrors the present context, which after beauty as the culmination of *mettā* continues with infinite space as the culmination of compassion.

55 Vism 324,22 (translated Ñāṇamoli 1956/1991: 317) and Delhey 2009: 191,15 or T 1579 at T XXX 338b19.

emerges that could be seen to mirror a focus on consciousness experienced with the second immaterial sphere. With equanimity one takes a step back from being actively involved with others. Similarly, with the sphere of nothingness one takes a step back from involvement with any other notion and idea.

When evaluating these correlations, it is noteworthy that the four *brahmavihāra*s are correlated not just with the four immaterial attainments. This would have been a simple step to take, given that both describe an ascending series of four meditative experiences. Clearly the presentation chosen is not simply the result of matching categories, which suggests that there was some underlying rationale for this correlation.

Independent of whether one finds the above explanations for these correlations convincing, what invests this presentation with particular significance for my present study is that the perceptions corresponding to these three immaterial spheres feature in the *Cūḷasuññata-sutta* and its parallels as steps in the gradual cultivation of emptiness. By relating the above *Saṃyutta-nikāya* and *Saṃyukta-āgama* discourses to the presentation in the *Cūḷasuññata-sutta* and its parallels, the possibility of a meditative progression emerges that proceeds from the boundless experience of compassion to the boundless experience of space used as a step in a gradual entry into emptiness. In the following chapters I will explore this gradual entry into emptiness in more detail, before presenting a practical implementation of this meditative trajectory in Chapter 7.

### III.8 SUMMARY

The maturing of compassion and of the other *brahmavihāra*s through sustained cultivation of their boundless radiation as a temporary liberation of the mind can yield manifold benefits. Besides mundane benefits like good sleep and harmonious relationships through engaging in *mettā*, the divine abodes offer substantial support for progress on the path to awakening. By dint of their boundless nature, cultivation of compassion and the other *brahmavihāra*s enables the experience of a temporary liberation of the mind already when concentration has not yet matured up to absorption level.

Besides fulfilling the training in tranquillity, the *brahmavihāra* of compassion by its nature counters intentions of harm, and through the experience of inner joy divests sensual pleasures of their attraction. Neither has scope to remain in a mind that is immersed in the boundless radiation of compassion: they dissolve like a piece of salt thrown into the Ganges or vanish like images painted on space.

The culmination point of the development of tranquillity through compassion is the attainment of infinite space. Progression to the attainment of non-return or full awakening as the true culmination point of all early Buddhist meditation practice requires one to combine the practice of compassion with the cultivation of the awakening factors.

# IV

# EMPTY MATTER

With this chapter my examination shifts from compassion to emptiness. I begin by examining the significance of the qualification "empty" in the early discourses and then turn to the first part of the exposition of a gradual meditative entry into emptiness delineated in the *Cūḷasuññata-sutta* and its parallels. At the end of this chapter I return to the topic of compassion.

## IV.1 THE NATURE OF BEING EMPTY

The noun "emptiness" occurs only rarely in the early discourses, which more often use the adjective "empty" instead. This usage in a way discourages hypostasizing emptiness as a sort of entity and instead directs attention to the quality of being empty.

A straightforward sense of this quality of being empty can be found in the expression "empty place". Because such a place is empty of people and other potential disturbances and distractions, it features among locations that are conducive to meditative seclusion.[1]

The sense of being empty of people recurs also in a simile which describes a man who, while attempting to escape from six enemies set on killing him, comes across an empty village. Here is the *Ekottarika-āgama* explanation of the significance of this simile.

1 SN 54.1 at SN V 311,8 (translated Bodhi 2000: 1765) and its parallel SĀ 803 at T II 206a23 commend such an empty place for mindfulness of breathing.

> The six enemies stand for lustful cravings [through the six sense-spheres]. The empty village stands for the six internal sense-spheres. What are the six? The six sense-spheres are: the eye sense-sphere, the ear sense-sphere, the nose sense-sphere, the mouth sense-sphere, the body sense-sphere, and the mind sense-sphere.
>
> If a wise one contemplates the eye, then at that time it appears completely empty, with nothing [essential] in it and without stability. Again, if such a one contemplates the ear ... the nose ... the mouth ... the body ... the mind, then at that time it appears completely empty, with nothing [essential] in it, all void, all quiescent, and without stability.[2]

If one is haunted by lustful cravings and turns to the six senses for a solution, one will find to one's dismay that these are empty and insubstantial, that they are unable to offer real and lasting relief. This is similar to the lack of any real assistance one would find in a deserted village against six enemies set on killing one. Even if one tries to hide somewhere in the empty village, chances are that sooner or later one will be caught by them. In the same way, trying to assuage one's lustful cravings through the senses can only offer momentary relief, but does not result in a real and lasting solution. A real solution can be found only by once and for all getting rid of the six enemies, that is, getting rid of lustful craving. This can be achieved by fully realizing the empty nature of sense experience.

The empty nature of the six senses comes up again in an explanation of the dictum that the entire world is empty. In what follows I translate the relevant passage from the *Saṃyukta-āgama*:

> The eye is empty; it is empty of being permanent, of being perpetual, and of having an unchanging nature, and it is empty of what belongs to a self. Why is that? That is its intrinsic nature.
>
> Forms ... eye-consciousness ... eye-contact ... feeling arisen in dependence on eye-contact that is painful, pleasant, or neutral, is

---

2 EĀ 31.6 at T II 670a7 to a12. The parallel SN 35.197 at SN IV 174,30 (translated Bodhi 2000: 1238, given as number 238) differs in so far as it speaks of a single sixth murderer (in addition to the five aggregates as five murderers), which stands for delight and lust. Another parallel, SĀ 1172 at T II 313c14, agrees with EĀ 31.6 in as much as it speaks of six robbers that represent the six types of craving and delight (i.e., in relation to the six sense-spheres). Parts of this presentation have also been preserved in a Sanskrit fragment; cf. Hoernle fragment Or. 15009/252, Nagashima 2009: 259–261.

also empty; it is empty of being permanent, of being perpetual, and of having an unchanging nature, and it is empty of what belongs to a self. Why is that? That is its intrinsic nature.

The ear ... the nose ... the tongue ... the body ... the mind are also like that. This is [the implication] of the saying: "The world is empty."[3]

So the world is empty in the sense that each of the six senses is empty of a self and of anything that could belong to a self. This shows that in early Buddhist thought the qualification of being empty of a self applies to everything. Once the six senses and their objects etc. are mentioned, there is no scope left for anything to be excluded from emptiness. As far as the early Buddhist teachings are concerned, there cannot be any doubt about the comprehensive scope of the qualification of emptiness: all things, all phenomena, all aspects of experience, without any exception, are empty of a self and of anything that could belong to a self.

The same comprehensive scope holds for what in early Buddhist thought is the doctrinal equivalent to emptiness, namely the teaching on not-self. As a stanza in the *Udānavarga*, with parallels in the different *Dharmapada* collections, succinctly proclaims:

All phenomena are not-self.[4]

In agreement with its parallels, the *Udānavarga* makes a point of using the term "all phenomena" instead of "all formations", which is found in an otherwise similar statement made about impermanence. This makes it clear that the choice of the expression "phenomena" here is intentional: it serves to signal the comprehensive scope of the not-self teaching, which does not admit of any exception.

The empty and not-self nature of the whole world of experience is the topic of a series of similes, which approach this theme from the perspective of the five aggregates. Since these similes can be of considerable help for appreciating the implications of emptiness in early Buddhist thought, in what follows I translate the whole relevant section from the *Saṃyukta-āgama* version:

---

3 SĀ 232 at T II 56b24 to b29 (also translated in Choong 2004/2010: 73). The formulation in the parallel SN 35.85 at SN IV 54,7 (translated Bodhi 2000: 1163) simply indicates that the eye etc. are "empty of a self and empty of what belongs to a self".

4 Stanza 12.8, Bernhard 1965: 194, with parallels in Dhp 279 (translated Norman 1997/2004: 41), the Patna *Dharmapada* 374, Cone 1989: 203, and the Gāndhārī *Dharmapada* 108, Brough 1962/2001: 134.

It is just as a drifting collection of foam, following a great wave on the river Gaṅges, which a clear-sighted person carefully examines, [attends to], and analyses. When carefully examining, [attending to], and analysing it, [the clear-sighted person finds that] there is nothing in it, nothing stable, nothing substantial, it has no solidity. Why is that? It is because there is nothing solid or substantial in a collection of foam.

In the same way one carefully examines, attends to, and analyes whatever bodily form, past, future, or present, internal or external, gross or subtle, sublime or repugnant, far or near. [When] carefully examining, attending to, and analysing it ... [one finds that] there is nothing in it, nothing stable, nothing substantial, it has no solidity; it is like a disease, like a carbuncle, like a thorn, like a killer, it is impermanent, *dukkha*, empty, and not-self.[5] Why is that? It is because there is nothing solid or substantial in bodily form...

It is just as when during a great rain there are bubbles on the [surface] of water,[6] arising and ceasing one after another, which a clear-sighted person carefully examines, attends to, and analyses. When carefully examining, attending to, and analysing them, [the clear-sighted person finds that] there is nothing in them, nothing stable, nothing substantial, they have no solidity. Why is that? It is because there is nothing solid or substantial in water bubbles.

In the same way ... one carefully examines, attends to, and analyses whatever feeling, past, future, or present, internal or external, gross or subtle, sublime or repugnant, far or near. When carefully examining, attending to, and analysing it ... [one finds that] there is nothing in it, nothing stable, nothing substantial, it has no solidity; it is like a disease, like a carbuncle, like a thorn, like a killer, it is impermanent, *dukkha*, empty, and not-self. Why is that? It is because there is nothing solid or substantial in feeling...

It is just as when towards the end of spring or the beginning of summer, in the middle of the day when the sun is strong and there are no clouds and no rain, a shimmering mirage appears, which a clear-sighted person carefully examines, attends to, and analyses.

---

5 Among the parallel versions only T 105 at T II 501a13 and the Tibetan version D 4094 *ju* 239a5 or Q 5595 *tu* 273a7 (translated Dhammadinnā 2013: 74) bring in the comparison with a disease etc.

6 SN 22.95 at SN III 141,5 (translated Bodhi 2000: 951) adds that this happens during autumn.

When carefully examining, attending to, and analysing it, [the clear-sighted person finds that] there is nothing in it, nothing stable, nothing substantial, it has no solidity. Why is that? It is because there is nothing solid or substantial in a mirage.

In the same way ... one carefully examines, attends to, and analyses whatever perception, past, future, or present, internal or external, gross or subtle, sublime or repugnant, far or near. When carefully examining, attending to, and analysing it ... [one finds that] there is nothing in it, nothing stable, nothing substantial, it has no solidity; it is like a disease, like a carbuncle, like a thorn, like a killer, it is impermanent, *dukkha*, empty, and not-self. Why is that? It is because there is nothing solid or substantial in perception...

It is just as if a clear-sighted person in need of heartwood takes hold of a sharp axe and enters a mountain forest. Seeing a large plantain tree that is thick, straight, and tall,[7] [the clear-sighted person] cuts it down at the root, chops off the treetop and gradually takes off sheath after sheath, all of which are without solid core, which [the clear-sighted person] carefully examines, attends to, and analyses. When carefully examining, attending to, and analysing them, [the clear-sighted person finds that] there is nothing in them, nothing stable, nothing substantial, they have no solidity. Why is that? It is because there is nothing solid or substantial in a plantain tree.

In the same way ... one carefully examines, attends to, and analyses whatever formations, past, future, or present, internal or external, gross or subtle, sublime or repugnant, far or near. When carefully examining, attending to, and analysing them ... [one finds that] there is nothing in them, nothing stable, nothing substantial, they have no solidity; they are like a disease, like a carbuncle, like a thorn, like a killer, they are impermanent, *dukkha*, empty, and not-self. Why is that? It is because there is nothing solid or substantial in formations...

It is just as if a master magician or a master magician's disciple at a crossroads creates the magical illusion of an elephant troop, a horse troop, a chariot troop, or an infantry troop,[8] which a wise and clear-sighted person carefully examines, attends to, and analyses.

---

7 T 106 at T II 502a9 adds that on seeing the plantain tree the person is very happy.

8 SN 22.95 and T 106 do not specify what types of magical illusion are being created; T 105 at T II 501b10 and the Tibetan parallel D 4094 *ju* 240a5 or Q 5595 *tu* 274b1 proceed similarly to SĀ 265.

> When carefully examining, attending to, and analysing it, [the clear-sighted person finds that] there is nothing in it, nothing stable, nothing substantial, it has no solidity. Why is that? It is because there is nothing solid or substantial in a magical illusion.
>
> In the same way ... one carefully examines, attends to, and analyses whatever consciousness, past, future, or present, internal or external, gross or subtle, sublime or repugnant, far or near. When carefully examining, attending to, and analysing it ... [one finds that] there is nothing in it, nothing stable, nothing substantial, it has no solidity; it is like a disease, like a carbuncle, like a thorn, like a killer, it is impermanent, *dukkha*, empty, and not-self. Why is that? It is because there is nothing solid or substantial in consciousness.[9]

A practical implementation of these descriptions requires first of all recognizing the five aggregates within one's own personal experience. Here bodily form stands for the material body. Feelings represent the affective and perception the cognitive dimensions of one's experience, its *how* and *what*, in the sense of how one feels and what one cognizes. One's reactions and will power fall under the aggregate of formations, and the fact of experiencing, that which knows, corresponds to the aggregate of consciousness.

According to early Buddhist thought these aggregates are problematic in so far as they provide a basis for clinging and identification. This is what needs to be recognized in actual practice. Whenever there is clinging, which aggregate(s) is one clinging to? Once this is recognized, the above similes can be used as aids to deconstruct the basis on which clinging, attachment, and identification thrive. Their main thrust is to reveal that each of these aggregates, in whatever form it manifests (past, present, future, etc.), is invariably unstable, insubstantial, unsatisfactory – in short, it is empty.

In the case of the apparently so solid physical body, which can easily give the impression of providing a firm basis for the reassuring sense of who I am, according to the above simile this body is just like foam. The comparison of the material body to foam points to a deconstruction of the notion of solidity to which I will turn in more detail in a later part of the present chapter.

Besides conveying the sense of a lack of solidity, foam is also rather fragile and therefore easily affected by outside circumstances. The

9 SĀ 265 at T II 68c1 to 69a16 (translated Anālayo 2013b: 35ff).

same holds true for the body, which is quite vulnerable to outside circumstances. Besides its already fragile nature, the foam is moreover carried away by the river. Similarly, the apparently so durable body, providing the illusion of a stable basis for one's sense of identity, is actually being carried away by the quickly moving current of change, every moment coming closer to its final destiny in death.

Feelings of various types stand at the heart of many pursuits in the world. Closer inspection reveals that such pursuits are an obsession with ephemeral feelings that only too quickly pass away. Such impermanent feelings are just like bubbles on the water's surface, which arise in quick succession due to the impact of raindrops during a heavy rain.

Already being by nature so ephemeral, the arising of these bubbles will come to an end as soon as the rain is over. Just as the bubbles are merely the conditioned result of the contact of raindrops, so feelings are merely the conditioned result of various types of stimulation through contact. In other words, one's fleeting experience of pleasure or pain is about as serious a matter as a few bubbles on water.

The ability to recognize things is based on one's accumulated knowledge and experiences, which inform perceptions. "My" perceptions as the result of "my" accumulated knowledge are easily taken to be invariably accurate reflections of the way things are. In this way perceptions can become an apparently objective basis for strongly held subjective opinions and value judgements. Yet, according to the above simile, any perception is merely a mental projection comparable to a mirage.

Perception turns out to be as empty as the optical illusion created by the sun on a hot day. The creative ability of the sunshine of mental attention forms the basis for perceptions of seemingly real and independent solid objects out there. In reality what is perceived is just empty and conditioned processes, without any independent existence and without any solidity, coated with an overlay of subjective evaluations that the mind projects on what is perceived.

Intention and will power, the ability to make decisions and its concomitant feeling of being in control, can be central to one's notion of who one is and what one does. On closer inspection this turns out to lack any essence or core, comparable to a plantain tree, which has no core.

Sheaths over sheaths of conditioning make up one's apparently so well-informed decisions. When unrolled one after the other, no solid core is found. No real person or self stands behind intentions and the decision-making process. Just sheaths over sheaths of conditioning accumulated from the past.

Consciousness as what in a way provides the ground of mental experience easily tends to be appropriated as a subtle basis for the notion of a self. On examination it turns out to be just like a magical illusion. The creations of such a magical illusion have no basis whatsoever in reality.

Whereas perception is comparable to a mirage and thereby to what is at least a real optical phenomenon, based on a displacement of images of distant objects, consciousness is so thoroughly delusive that it is like a hallucination, totally void of anything real at all. I will return to the topic of the empty nature of consciousness in more detail in Chapter 5.

In sum, all the five aggregates as the central aspects of what is usually taken as "I" and "mine" are thoroughly empty. Just a bit of foam, a few bubbles, a mirage, some plantain sheaths, and a magical trick, that is all.

The powerful images that emerge from the above passage offer themselves as aids for contemplation of emptiness. Based on recognizing the five aggregates as components of one's personal experience that one tends to cling to and identify with, one proceeds to see them as thoroughly empty with the help of the images provided in these similes. Any instance of craving or attachment will in some form or another involve an obsession with the body, or a yearning for pleasure, or a holding on to one's preconceived notions, or the expectation that things will always go the way one wants them to, or a clinging to a particular experience, or else a combination of these. The above passage clarifies that one is actually obsessed with a bit of foam, yearns for a few bubbles, holds on to a mirage, expects what is impossible (such as heartwood in a plantain tree), and clings to a magical illusion.

Developing detachment through such reflective contemplation based on these images can function as a preparatory stage in the cultivation of emptiness leading on to a more meditative approach to emptiness. This could be the gradual entry into emptiness depicted in the *Cūḷasuññata-sutta* and its parallels, to which I now turn.

### IV.2 A GRADUAL MEDITATIVE ENTRY INTO EMPTINESS

A gradual meditative entry into emptiness is the topic of the *Cūḷasuññata-sutta* of the *Majjhima-nikāya* and its two parallels.[10] These are a discourse in the *Madhyama-āgama*, preserved in Chinese translation, and a discourse translated into Tibetan, representing the Sarvāstivāda and the Mūlasarvāstivāda traditions respectively.

The meditative trajectory in the three parallel versions proceeds through a series of perceptions that take up the forest and the earth as objects, followed by the immaterial attainments, and then the experience of signlessness. Each of these perceptions becomes a stage in the gradual meditative entry into emptiness through awareness of its empty nature. The increasing refinement and eventual deconstruction of perception undertaken in this way culminates in the realization of supreme emptiness with full awakening. This meditative progression forms the backbone of my presentation in this and the next two chapters.

The *Cūḷasuññata-sutta* and its parallels begin their exposition of the gradual entry into emptiness with Ānanda enquiring about a statement the Buddha had made on an earlier occasion. According to this statement, the Buddha dwelled much in emptiness. The Buddha confirms that he indeed made such a statement and then teaches Ānanda a gradual entry into emptiness that starts off by directing attention to the monastic dwelling place where they are staying.

This signals that the starting point for engaging in contemplation of emptiness can be just here and now, in whatever situation one may find oneself at present and as part of whatever community of practitioners. Such turning to one's situation right here and now lends a nuance of immediacy to contemplation of emptiness as something to be done wherever one currently is. It encourages pragmatically utilizing any external circumstance for the purpose of progress towards the realization of emptiness.

The monastic dwelling place in the forest where the Buddha and Ānanda were staying had an empty quality to it, in as much as it was empty of the hustle and bustle of city life. The *Cūḷasuññata-sutta* and its parallels express this by mentioning the absence of various kinds of domesticated animals and people. Instead of these, there was just the community of monks.

10 Dhammajothi 2008: 91 comments on the *Cūḷasuññata-sutta* that "the purpose of this Sutta is to give practical advice to lead the mind to ... experience the voidness of everything."

This in itself simple indication sets the pattern for what is to follow and thereby reveals a central principle in the gradual entry into emptiness. This principle requires seeing what a particular experience is empty of, and at the same time also directing awareness to what this experience is not empty of. In the present case, the monastic dwelling place was not empty of monks.

These monks would all have had a shaven head and would have been wearing similar monastic robes. So turning attention to the monks is to direct attention to a unified component in that situation, in contrast to the variegation one would experience when in town and seeing differently dressed people or various animals. Directing attention to the perception of monks in this way forms a starting point for a thrust towards unification that will become more prominent with subsequent steps.

Another aspect of drawing attention to the monks results from the fact that Ānanda, as well as the Buddha himself, were of course part of this monastic community. So for Ānanda or any other monk present to be attending to the perception of the monks present in the monastic dwelling appears to require some degree of integration of the external and the internal. What one attends to is not just something out there, but at the same time also something right here. This, too, is a pattern underlying the steps that follow, which embrace both what is external and what is internal, until eventually the subject–object distinction dissolves.

In early Buddhist thought in general, monastics are representative of the principle of renunciation. In this function the monastic community forms the object in which one takes refuge, together with the Buddha and his teaching, the Dharma.[11] This differs from the meditative practice of recollecting the Saṅgha, where the object is rather those who have reached different levels of awakening, be they lay or monastic.[12] In this case the notion of other practitioners

11 The standard formula for taking refuge in the early discourses speaks of the "community of *bhikkhus*"; cf., e.g., MN 27 at MN I 184,17 (translated Ñāṇamoli 1995: 277) and its parallel MĀ 146 at T I 658a24. Here the expression *bhikkhu* is probably best understood as an umbrella term for any monastic, male or female; cf. in more detail Collett and Anālayo 2014.

12 The typical expression for recollection of the Saṅgha refers to "the four persons, the eight types of beings", which covers those on the path to the four levels of awakening and those who have reached these four; cf., e.g., AN 6.10 at AN III 286,7 (translated Bodhi 2012: 863) and its parallels SĀ 931 at T II 238a6 (which lists the eight individually, followed by a summary

at various levels of awakening forms the basis for one's practice of recollection. Since the level of awakening someone has reached is not visible on the outside, however, for the formal act of taking refuge the object is instead the monastic community. Its outer appearance symbolizes renunciation and the adoption of the code of rules that, according to the *Vinaya,* was promulgated by the Buddha. Therefore monastics serve as an easily recognizable object in which one can take refuge and thereby express that one has become a follower of the Buddha, the founder and foremost member of the Buddhist monastic community.

The next step in the gradual entry into emptiness described in the *Cūḷasuññata-sutta* and its parallels requires cultivating the perception of the forest. In the setting of the discourse this obviously refers to the forest in which the monastic dwelling was situated. Here is the instruction from the *Mādhyama-āgama* version.

> If ... one wishes to dwell much in emptiness ... one should not give attention to the perception of village and not give attention to the perception of people, but should frequently give attention to the unitary perception of forest.
>
> In this way one knows that this is empty of the perception of village and empty of the perception of people. Yet there is this non-emptiness: just the unitary perception of forest. [One knows]: "Whatever weariness because of the perception of village there might be – that is not present for me. Whatever weariness because of the perception of people there might be – that is also not present for me. There is only the weariness because of the unitary perception of forest."
>
> Whatever is not present, one therefore sees as empty; whatever else is present, one sees as truly present. Ānanda, this is called truly dwelling in emptiness, without distortion.[13]

The shift from the monastic community (or people) to the forest reflects a perceptual shift towards something that is more stable. Whereas some of the monks might be moving around here and there, the vegetation that makes up the forest remains in place. The perception of the forest is also larger in scope and more encompassing, in contrast to the perception of the monastic community, which

---

reference to the four persons and eight types that is similar to AN 6.10) and SĀ[2] 156 at T II 432c27 (which just lists the eight individually).

13 MĀ 190 at T I 737a12 to a19.

is more limited in comparison. This reflects an undercurrent that becomes more prominent with the meditative steps that follow after the forest, which become ever more encompassing and stable.

In early Buddhist thought, the forest represents seclusion from worldly affairs. Such seclusion can manifest in a physical and a mental sense. Cultivating bodily and mental seclusion stands in close relation to the development of mental tranquillity and concentration, which serve as an important foundation for the meditative trajectory that in the *Cūḷasuññata-sutta* and its parallels sets in after the forest.

Physical seclusion requires withdrawal, at least temporarily, from involvement in worldly affairs, ideally undertaken in a secluded location that affords protection against outside disturbances. Mental seclusion similarly requires temporary withdrawal from involvement in worldly affairs, in this case achieved by emptying the mind of plans, worries, and memories, by letting go of past and future, and instead simply being aware of the empty nature of the present moment.

A poetic description of such mental seclusion from past and future concerns can be found in the *Ānandabhaddekaratta-sutta* and its *Madhyama-āgama* parallel. In what follows I translate the relevant section from the *Madhyama-āgama* version, which is part of a longer poem on how one should best spend one's time:

> Do not think of the past
> and do not long for the future,
> matters of the past have already ceased
> and the future has not yet come.
> In the present moment one should attend
> with mindfulness to the lack of stability
> of whatever phenomena there are;
> the wise awaken in this way.[14]

This short poem succinctly shows how the unstable nature of all phenomena as an aspect of emptiness can be brought to bear on day-to-day experience. This takes place by letting the mind remain anchored in the present moment and in full awareness of the lack of stability of whatever manifests itself. I will explore the topic of integrating emptiness into daily life in more detail in Chapter 5.

---

14 MĀ 167 at T I 700a15 to a18, parallel to MN 132 at MN III 190,20 (translated Ñāṇamoli 1995: 1042; cf. in full id. 1039).

### IV.3 EARTH

The ensuing step in the gradual entry into emptiness depicted in the *Cūḷasuññata-sutta* and its parallels takes up perception of earth. Here is the relevant section from the *Madhyama-āgama* version.

> If ... one wishes to dwell much in emptiness ... one should not give attention to the perception of people and not give attention to the perception of forest, but should frequently give attention to the unitary perception of earth.
>
> If ... one sees this earth as having hills and hollows, with clusters of snakes, with clumps of thorn-bushes, with sand and rocks, steep mountains and deep rivers, one should not attend to it so. If [instead] one sees this earth as level and flat like the palm of a hand, then one's manner of looking at it is beneficial and should be frequently attended to.[15]
>
> Ānanda, it is just as a cow hide which, when stretched and fastened with a hundred pegs, being fully stretched, has no wrinkles and no creases. [Similarly], if one sees this earth as having hills and hollows, with clusters of snakes, with clumps of thorn-bushes, with sand and rocks, steep mountains and deep rivers, one should not attend to it so. If [instead] one sees this earth as level and flat like the palm of a hand, then one's manner of looking at it is beneficial and should be frequently attended to.
>
> In this way one knows that this is empty of the perception of people and empty of the perception of forest. Yet there is this non-emptiness: just the unitary perception of earth.
>
> [One knows]: "Whatever weariness because of the perception of people there might be – that is not present for me; whatever weariness because of the perception of forest there might be – that is also not present for me. There is only the weariness because of the unitary perception of earth."
>
> Whatever is not present, one therefore sees as empty; whatever else is present, one sees as truly present. Ānanda, this is called truly dwelling in emptiness, without distortion.[16]

---

15 MN 121 at MN III 105,7 (translated Ñāṇamoli 1995: 966) does not have this illustration of the proper mode of attending to earth comparable to the palm of a hand. A similar presentation is found in the Tibetan version, however; cf. Skilling 1994: 156,9.

16 MĀ 190 at T I 737a19 to b4.

Progress in the gradual entry into emptiness requires leaving behind the earlier perceptions, in the present case the perception of people (which in the setting of the discourse are the monks who were present) and the perception of forest. Having emptied one's perception of these objects, one instead gives attention to the next step in the gradual entry into emptiness, which in the present case is perception of the earth element.

The description given of earth makes it clear that the point at stake is to arrive at a unitary perception. For this purpose one should disregard all variety, such as irregularities on the surface of the earth or different types of vegetation found on the earth. Instead, perception is concerned solely with the basic notion of earth, comparable to a hide that is without wrinkles or creases.

The detailed description given here on how to view earth properly differs from the treatment of the previous perception of forest, where no further details have been supplied. This difference reflects the fact that from this point onwards the modes of perceiving cultivated in the gradual entry into emptiness involve some degree of abstraction. The previous step concerned with the forest simply required directing attention to what would have been readily visible to anyone in the monastic dwelling where the Buddha and Ānanda were staying. It only involved attending to the forest as a unitary object. With the present step, however, the target of attention is no longer just the visible impact of the earth. This can be seen in the part of the instructions that recommends viewing the earth like a stretched hide. The comparison with a stretched hide suggests some degree of perceptual abstraction, whose target appears to be to point to the principle of solidity that underlies and is common to the various manifestations of earth.

In early Buddhist meditation theory, earth as the first of the four elements (the other three are water, fire, and wind) stands representative of the principle of solidity. This can be seen, for example, in the *Mahāhatthipadopama-sutta* and its *Madhyama-āgama* parallel, which conclude a description of various internal manifestations of the earth element by summing up that the internal earth element stands for whatever is solid within one's own body.[17] In addition to this internal earth element found within one's own

17 MN 28 at MN I 185,16 (translated Ñāṇamoli 1995: 279) and its parallel MĀ 30 at T I 464c7.

physical body, there is of course the external earth element, which covers whatever is solid outside.

The use of the earth element in early Buddhist meditation practice offers benefits for the cultivation of both tranquillity and insight. In relation to insight, the earth element functions as part of an analytical dissection of the human body into its material elements, described, for example, in the *Satipaṭṭhāna-sutta* and its parallels.[18] The purpose of such analysis is closely related to emptiness, since contemplating one's own body as made up of the material elements has the purpose of revealing the body's ultimately empty nature.

The *Satipaṭṭhāna-sutta* and its parallels illustrate the change in perception that can result from such practice with the example of a butcher who has slaughtered a cow. When cutting up the meat for sale, the butcher thinks no longer in terms of a cow, but rather in terms of various pieces of meat. In the same way a practitioner who mentally dissects the body into its material elements transcends the notion of the body as a compact solid unit to be identified with and to be clung to as "mine". Instead, the body is seen as just a product of these elements and thereby as something that is not at all different from manifestations of the same elements outside in nature.

The resultant insight finds its expression in the *Madhyama-āgama* parallel to the *Dhātuvibhaṅga-sutta*, a discourse on the topic of analysing the elements, in the following manner:

> Whatever is the internal earth element and whatever is the external earth element, all of it is summarily called the earth element. It is all not mine, I am not part of it, and it is not the self. By wisely contemplating it in this way, knowing it as it truly is, the mind does not become defiled with attachment in regard to the earth element.[19]

Moving the discussion from insight to tranquillity, the earth element also functions as a basis for a perceptual totality, called *kasiṇa*. The idea behind such a meditative cultivation is to develop a perception of the element of earth that is so all-embracing that it results in a unified experience and thereby leads to deep concentration.

The use of the element of earth in the present context in the

18 For a translation of the relevant passages and a discussion of their practical implications cf. Anālayo 2013c: 81–96.

19 MĀ 162 at T I 690c16 to c19, with parallels in MN 140 at MN III 240,27 (translated Ñāṇamoli 1995: 1089), T 511 at T XIV 780a15, and D 4094 *ju* 37a3 or Q 5595 *tu* 40b1.

*Cūḷasuññata-sutta* and its parallels in a way combines aspects of both of these trajectories of the earth element in early Buddhist meditation theory, as it has an insight component as well as a relation to tranquillity. In the present context the meditative use of the earth element does not carry the full analytical force of the *satipaṭṭhāna* exercise, for which purpose all four elements are required. Nevertheless, it does serve as a first pointer in the direction of emptiness, as is clear from the context within which the instructions occur.

Cultivating the emptiness aspect in the present context comes about through reducing one's perceptual experience of any manifestation of matter to the bare notion of solidity, the primary quality of the earth element, and viewing this as empty of that which still characterized the previous perceptions of people and the forest.

The tranquillity aspect comes into play, and perhaps more prominently than the insight aspect, in as much as the main thrust of the present stage in the gradual entry into emptiness is towards developing a unitary perception. The issue at stake is to build up unification of the mind and therewith a sufficiently strong degree of concentration to enable the mind to proceed with the ensuing steps.

The *Cūḷasuññata-sutta* and its parallels do not seem to be intending the practice of the earth *kasiṇa* in the way this is described in the commentarial tradition, however, where one fashions a disk of earth and then starts gazing at this device in order to develop an internal perception of earth as a basis for deepening concentration.[20] The instructions in the *Cūḷasuññata-sutta* and its parallels are clearly about looking at earth in the way it naturally appears outside in nature, with crevices and vegetation, and based on that one then develops a unitary perception of earth.

The development of a unitary perception is in fact already a feature of the preceding perception of the forest, which does not feature among the standard objects for *kasiṇa* meditation. The developing of a unitary perception of the forest does seem to intend simply a giving of attention to the forest as a whole, instead of attending to individual trees. The same holds for the perception of earth, with the additional requirement to view it like a stretched hide.

Ideally mental unification built up in this way should reach the concentrative depth of the fourth absorption, which is the usual basis

20 Vism 123,28 (translated Ñāṇamoli 1956/1991: 123).

for cultivating the immaterial spheres that in the gradual entry to emptiness come after the perception of earth. The instructions in the *Cūḷasuññata-sutta* and its parallels, however, speak of giving attention to the *perception* of the sphere of infinite space. They do not speak of *attaining* the sphere of infinite space itself. The same pattern holds for the subsequent instructions on the other immaterial spheres.

The formulation used in the *Cūḷasuññata-sutta* and its parallels makes it clear that the instructions are not meant to apply only to the fully fledged attainment of the sphere of infinite space etc., for which indeed attainment of the fourth absorption would be a requirement. Instead, the gradual entry into emptiness depicted in the *Cūḷasuññata-sutta* and its parallels presents a perceptual training that can be practised with lower degrees of concentration, as long as the hindrances are kept at bay. The actual instructions for the perception of infinite space read as follows.

### IV.4 INFINITE SPACE

> Again, Ānanda, if ... one wishes to dwell much in emptiness ... one should not give attention to the perception of forest and not give attention to the perception of earth, but should frequently give attention to the unitary perception of the sphere of infinite space.
>
> In this way one knows that this is empty of the perception of forest and empty of the perception of earth. Yet there is this non-emptiness: just the unitary perception of the sphere of infinite space.
>
> [One knows]: "Whatever weariness because of the perception of forest there might be – that is not present for me; whatever weariness because of the perception of earth there might be – that is also not present for me. There is only the weariness because of the unitary perception of the sphere of infinite space."
>
> Whatever is not present, one therefore sees as empty; whatever else is present, one sees as truly present. Ānanda, this is called truly dwelling in emptiness, without distortion.[21]

The meditative progression at this juncture requires replacing the unitary perception of earth with the unitary perception of the space that had been occupied by the earth. In this way, the object used for the previous step concerned with earth is allowed to disappear. This

21 MĀ 190 at T I 737b4 to b12.

involves a further level of abstraction, compared to the previous perception of earth. Such a further level of perceptual abstraction leaves behind and transcends the notion of solidity characteristic of any manifestation of matter.

The leaving behind of all that is characteristic of matter is one of the chief implications of the experience of infinite space as the first of the four immaterial attainments in early Buddhist thought. The standard descriptions of how to reach this experience make a point of explicitly marking this transcendence of all that is material. Here is the *Madhyama-āgama* version of such a description.

> Completely transcending perceptions of form, with the cessation of perceptions of resistance, not attending to perceptions of diversity, [being instead aware] of infinite space, one dwells having attained the sphere of infinite space.[22]

In this way, with the attainment of the sphere of infinite space all perceptions of form are left behind. In short, at this level of experience, matter no longer matters.

Needless to say, this is not an ontological statement, but only a step in a training of perception. The whole gradual entry into emptiness in the *Cūḷasuññata-sutta* and its parallels has the purpose of refining and to some extent also deconstructing ordinary perception up to the point where the meditative progression can culminate in the experience of Nirvāṇa, with which supreme emptiness is attained. So the issue at stake in the present step in the gradual entry into such supreme emptiness is only to reveal the empty nature of matter, not to proclaim its non-existence.

The need to steer clear of affirming non-existence as well as existence is the theme of a discourse in the *Saṃyutta-nikāya* and its parallels. Here is the relevant statement from the *Saṃyukta-āgama*:

> For one who rightly knows and sees as it really is the arising of the world, there will not be [the notion] that the world does not exist; for one who rightly knows and sees as it really is the cessation of the world, there will not be [the notion] that the world exists.[23]

---

22 MĀ 163 at T I 694b1 to b2, a description found similarly in its parallel MN 137 at MN III 222,15 (translated Ñāṇamoli 1995: 1072).

23 SĀ 301 at T II 85c26 to c28, a statement found similarly in its parallel SN 12.15 at SN II 17,10 (translated Bodhi 2000: 544) and in a Sanskrit fragment parallel, Tripāṭhī 1962: 169.

Instead of falling prey to these two extremes, the middle way of correct vision is to recognize the dependently arisen nature of things. Emptiness is in fact precisely about the conditioned nature of all phenomena, not about their non-existence.

The distinction to be drawn here can perhaps best be exemplified by briefly leaving the discussion of emptiness in early Buddhism and turning to quantum physics. From the viewpoint of quantum physics, matter turns out to be indeed for the most part just space. The size of the atomic nucleus compared to that of the whole atom is similar to the size of a grain of rice that is placed in a football stadium.[24] Applied to one's own body, if all nuclei in this body could be placed side by side, the area they would occupy would be merely a speck of dust. The rest is empty space.

These nuclei are themselves made up of quarks that are in a constant process of change. These constantly changing quarks are so difficult to pinpoint that their exact position and speed cannot be known both at the same time. We can only know either their speed or their position with precision, not both.

Reflecting on the material nature of one's own body and of manifestations of matter outside oneself along these lines, it seems that the perception of space does better justice to the way things really are than the common way of viewing matter as something solid that exists on its own out there.

Nevertheless, the point of all this is not that matter does not exist at all. In spite of all the fascinating discoveries of quantum physics, it is still not possible for us to walk through a wall. Because of the electromagnetic force between constantly changing energetic units, matter will by all means remain something solid that resists contact. Even though matter is clearly empty of any type of solid self-existence, its appearance is clearly solid. This comes into being as a product of constantly changing conditions that are not in any way solid themselves.

By training the mind in the perception of infinite space, this aspect of matter can be integrated into one's perceptual appraisal of the world and thereby lead to a more balanced and detached way of viewing manifestations of matter. The main issue at stake is to realize that solidity is not inherent in matter, which is for the most part just space.

---

24 Ricard and Thuan 2001: 95.

Once one realizes that matter is for the most part just space pervaded by the conditioning forces of electromagnetic attraction, the differences that matter manifests in daily life come to lose much of their importance. Distinctions between beautiful and ugly bodies, for example, become considerably less important if they just come down to the difference between two specks of dust in a lot of space. Being in this way deprived of their solid material foundation, evaluations of someone as being beautiful or ugly can more easily be seen for what they really are, namely projections of the mind. To be more precise, they are projections of one's mirage-like perceptions. In this way, cultivating the perception of infinite space as part of the gradual entry into emptiness has a remarkable potential to lead to dispassion and detachment in one's perceptual appraisal of the world.

In terms of a simile I already took up in Chapter 3,[25] just as a painter is unable to draw images on space, so attachment and aversion towards the outer appearance of the bodies of others lose much of their foundation once it is realized that they are concerned with what is mainly just space. The differences between the young fashion model on stage and the leprous beggar by the side of the road, between a diamond and dog excrement, dwindle to the differences between specks of dust.

Needless to say, such perceptual training should not go so far as to deny the existence of the bodies of others, which would remove the foundation not only of attachment and aversion, but also of genuine compassion for the physical afflictions of others. The cultivation of the perception of space as part of the gradual entry into emptiness is only meant to provide a counterbalance to the way the bodies of others (or matter in general) are usually perceived.

Practised as a boundless experience of space in all directions, the perception of infinite space not only goes beyond the colouring tendencies of gross defilements, but also leaves behind all experience of resistance. Just as the brush of the painter finds nothing to touch when trying to draw images on space, so all resistance and reference points dissolve in the limitlessness of the boundless meditative experience of space.[26]

---

25 See above, p.62.

26 Catherine 2008: 195 explains that the experience of the sphere of infinite space "is literally a perception without reference, formations, structures, distinctions, or particulars. It is without bounds. Infinite space cannot be described by its proportions, measurements, or dimensions."

Such experience stands in marked contrast to the average experience of bodily form as the first of the five aggregates. A discourse in the *Saṃyutta-nikāya* and its *Saṃyukta-āgama* parallel make a point of highlighting the nature of bodily form as something that is afflicted by all kinds of contact. The *Saṃyukta-āgama* version of this description reads as follows:

> Since it can resist and can break, it is called the bodily form aggregate of clinging. This refers to being resistant. If it is [contacted] by a hand, if it is [contacted] by a stone, if it is [contacted] by a stick, if it is [contacted] by a knife, if it is [contacted] by cold, if it is [contacted] by warmth, if it is [contacted] by thirst, if it is [contacted] by hunger, if it is [contacted] by mosquitoes, gadflies, or any poisonous insect, or by contact with wind and rain, this is called resisting contact. Because of [such] resistance, it is [called] the bodily form aggregate of clinging.[27]

Another discourse in the *Saṃyutta-nikāya* and its parallels also give a description of the body as something that is afflicted in various ways. Here is the relevant passage from the *Madhyama-āgama* version:

> This body, with its coarse form made of the four elements, born of father and mother, nourished by food and drink, covered by clothing, being massaged and bathed, and having to endure [external] force, is of an impermanent nature, of a nature to deteriorate, and of a nature to fall apart.[28]

The overcoming of all forms of physical affliction and experience of resistance with the immaterial spheres is also taken up in the *Apaṇṇaka-sutta*. Although several parts of this discourse have been preserved in Sanskrit fragments,[29] the section relevant to the present discussion is available to me only in the Pāli version, hence in what follows I translate this section from the *Apaṇṇaka-sutta* itself:

---

27 SĀ 46 at T II 11b26 to b29 (translated Anālayo 2014e: 37). The parallel SN 22.79 at SN III 86,23 (translated Bodhi 2000: 915) does not list various forms of being attacked. Being attacked is mentioned in the Tibetan parallel, D 4094 *ju* 16a4 or Q 5595 *tu* 17b7 (translated Dhammadinnā 2014b: 95).

28 MĀ 114 at T I 603a24 to a26. The description of the various activities to be undertaken in relation to the body in the parallels SN 35.103 at SN IV 83,24 (translated Bodhi 2000: 1183) and D 4094 *nyu* 72b1 or Q 5595 *thu* 117a3 is shorter.

29 For a survey of which parts of the discourse have been preserved in the published fragments cf. Anālayo 2011a: 339 n.147.

> "In relation to bodily form the taking up of stick and sword can be seen, and [the occurrence of] quarrels, disputes, contention, strife, slander, and false speech. This does not exist at all in the immaterial." Reflecting in this way one is practising for the disenchantment, dispassion, and cessation of bodily form.[30]

Bodily form can be affected by stones and sticks, changes of temperature, hunger and thirst, and various insects. It constantly requires nourishment, clothing, and bathing. Even being provided with all these, it will eventually fall apart. Yet, because of the body, there is quarrelling and fighting of all sorts. All this is left behind when materiality is allowed to dissolve into space.

A poetic description of those who have fully realized emptiness employs the motif of birds in the sky, which in a way complements the indications that can be gained from the above passages regarding the contrast between the limitations of matter and the unobstructed nature of space. Here is a version of this poem from the *Udānavarga*.

> Those who have extinguished becoming,
> who do not depend on the future,
> whose range is empty,
> signless and secluded,
> their path is hard to track,
> like that of birds in the sky.[31]

One who has realized supreme emptiness will no longer leave any tracks behind, just like a bird in the sky. This poetic image conveys not only the transcendence of rebirth by fully awakened ones, but also their transcendence of all types of defilements. These have completely disappeared from the vastness of their realization of emptiness, without leaving any vestige behind.

---

30 MN 60 at MN I 410,28 (also translated Ñāṇamoli 1995: 516). Another relevant passage is MN 62 at MN I 424,22 (translated Ñāṇamoli 1995: 530), which encourages the cultivation of a mind like space, as space is not established anywhere. In the case of MN 62, the whole exposition of the elements is not found in the parallel EĀ 17.1 at T II 581c15, but it does occur in EĀ 43.5 at T II 760a5.

31 Stanza 29.29, Bernhard 1965: 380. The parallels Dhp 93 (translated Norman 1997/2004: 14) and the Patna *Dharmapada* 270, Cone 1989: 173, speak of not being dependent on food instead of not being dependent on the future, and of liberation instead of seclusion.

### IV.5 INFINITE SPACE AND COMPASSION

The above passages on the empty nature of space in contrast to the material body are in line with indications given in the *Visuddhimagga* and the *Yogācārabhūmi* regarding the correlation between compassion and space, which I mentioned towards the end of Chapter 3.[32] According to this correlation, infinite space is the culmination point of the meditative cultivation of compassion.

The point underlying this correlation, according to the *Visuddhimagga* and the *Yogācārabhūmi*, is that with the experience of infinite space one mentally leaves behind the material realm that is the cause of a broad range of physical afflictions. This form of transcendence naturally reverberates with the compassionate wish for others to be free from such afflictions.

Another perspective on the relationship between compassion and emptiness that requires discussion is that later tradition sees the two as standing in some degree of tension in relation to each other. The perceived conflict is between the taking of living beings as the object of one's compassion (and of the other *brahmavihāra*s) and the notion that according to emptiness such living beings do not really exist.

The taking of living beings as the object of practice becomes a problem, for example, in the Pāli commentarial tradition. The Theravāda commentators set the practice of the *brahmavihāra*s apart from what is supramundane, because the divine abodes take living beings as their object.[33] So they consider *mettā*, for example, as coming close to holding the view of a self, since it takes living beings as its object.[34] The *Abhidharmakośabhāṣya* similarly holds that one of the reasons why the *brahmavihāra*s are incapable of removing defilements is that they take living beings as their object.[35]

Comparable problems are discussed in Mahāyāna texts. The *Bodhicaryāvatāra*, for example, queries to whom compassion could be directed, given that there are no living beings.[36] The *Buddhāvataṃsaka*, just to give another example, expresses the same conflict by stating that bodhisattvas, even though they understand that living beings do not exist, nevertheless do not give up all living beings.[37]

32 See above, p.72.
33 Mp II 41,27.
34 Pj I 251,5.
35 Pradhan 1967: 454,1.
36 Tripathi 1988: 234,4 §9.76 (translated Matics 1971: 218).
37 T 279 at T X 106c11 (translated Cleary 1984/1993: 466).

A phrasing of this problem in the *Aṣṭasāhasrikā Prajñāpāramitā* emphasizes the difficult task accomplished by bodhisattvas who have the wish to lead innumerable living beings to final Nirvāṇa, even though those living beings ultimately do not exist and are not to be found. The *Aṣṭasāhasrikā Prajñāpāramitā* summarizes the problem by stating that one might think space could be led (to liberation), if one thinks living beings could be led (to liberation).[38] The comparison with space here links directly to my present topic.

When examined from the perspective of the early discourses, the point raised in these different texts, ranging from the Theravāda commentarial tradition to various Mahāyāna texts, appears as less of a problem. For one, the practice of compassion takes the form of a boundless radiation, so that, as far as the meditation practice is concerned, the problem of arousing perceptions of individual living beings and then mistaking these perceptions to imply their existence as substantial entities does not arise in the first place.[39] Moreover, according to early Buddhism emptiness or not-self does not mean that there are no living beings. Instead, it only means that living beings do not have substantial and permanent selves; that is, they are empty of such a self. Thus the fact that compassion by nature is concerned with the affliction of living beings is not a problem, as long as these living beings are seen with insight as the impermanent products of conditions, and thus as not-self.

Living beings as changing and conditioned phenomena exist, just as walls and other manifestations of matter exist as changing and conditioned phenomena. Both exist precisely because of the conditioning force of the changing processes involved. I will return to this topic in more detail in Chapter 6, when examining the step in the gradual entry into emptiness that involves the perception of nothingness.

## IV.6 SUMMARY

Emptiness in the early discourses often takes the form of qualifying things as being "empty of" something. The qualification of being empty of a self then covers all aspects of experience, internally and externally, without any exception.

38 Mitra 1888: 445,5 (translated Conze 1973/1994: 259).

39 For a more detailed discussion of the taking of individual living beings as the object of *brahmavihāra* practice cf. Anālayo 2015b.

A gradual entry into emptiness in the *Cūḷasuññata-sutta* and its parallels begins with the immediate environment and then proceeds via earth qua solidity to the perception of infinite space, thereby deconstructing the notion of the solidity of material phenomena.

# V

# EMPTY MIND

In this chapter my examination continues with the gradual entry into emptiness described in the *Cūḷasuññata-sutta* and its parallels. By way of providing a background to the next step that involves the perception of infinite consciousness, I study the implications of consciousness in early Buddhist thought, in particular in relation to dependent arising (*paṭicca samuppāda*). I also examine the instructions given in the *Mahāsuññata-sutta* and its parallels regarding how to relate emptiness to daily activities.

## V.1 INFINITE CONSCIOUSNESS

The instructions given in the *Madhyama-āgama* parallel to the *Cūḷasuññata-sutta* for proceeding from the perception of infinite space to the perception of infinite consciousness in the gradual entry into emptiness are as follows.

> Again, Ānanda, if ... one wishes to dwell much in emptiness ... one should not give attention to the perception of earth and not give attention to the perception of the sphere of infinite space, but should frequently give attention to the unitary perception of the sphere of infinite consciousness.
>
> In this way one knows that this is empty of the perception of earth and empty of the perception of the sphere of infinite space. Yet there is this non-emptiness: just the unitary perception of the sphere of infinite consciousness.

> [One knows]: "Whatever weariness because of the perception of earth there might be – that is not present for me; whatever weariness because of the perception of the sphere of infinite space there might be – that is also not present for me. There is only the weariness because of the unitary perception of the sphere of infinite consciousness."
>
> Whatever is not present, one therefore sees as empty; whatever else is present, one sees as truly present. Ānanda, this is called truly dwelling in emptiness, without distortion.[1]

The instruction for the transition from one step to the next in the gradual entry into emptiness regularly begins with the need to avoid perceptions related to the two previous steps. In the present case, one should not give attention to the perceptions of earth and of infinite space. Instead one gives attention to the perception of infinite consciousness.

It is noteworthy that for progress from infinite space to infinite consciousness, earth is mentioned again. With infinite space this had already been left behind. The fact that earth is mentioned again gives the impression that, when proceeding from one perception in the series to the next, one needs to ensure that what had been accomplished previously is not lost. In the present case, this is the transcendence of the principle of solidity through the perception of infinite space.

The transition from infinite space to infinite consciousness follows the same pattern that underlies a meditative progression through the immaterial attainments. At the present juncture this requires turning attention to the mind itself. By earlier having become absorbed in the notion of infinite space, consciousness itself has come to be at one with the experience of infinity. Turning attention back to the mind itself then enables the development of the perception of infinite consciousness. Here consciousness, that which previously experienced infinite space as its object, becomes itself the object and content of one's experience.

Undertaking this step of practice as part of the gradual entry into emptiness reveals the foundational role that consciousness plays in subjective experience. The perception of infinite space includes the whole world, without any limit. The perception of infinite

---

1 MĀ 190 at T I 737b12 to b21.

consciousness turns attention to that which has been aware of infinite space, whereby the whole world is now seen to be, in a way, in one's own mind.

In order to properly appreciate the implications of the present step, it needs to be kept in mind that early Buddhist thought does not consider consciousness to be the source of the external world. The external world exists (as conditioned and impermanent processes) independently of my act of cognizing it. But as far as my subjective experience of the world is concerned, consciousness is its very foundation. My experience of the world is impossible without consciousness. In other words, for phenomena in the world to exist *for* me, to be experienced *by* me, consciousness is indispensable. So consciousness is indeed the source of *my* world, it provides the ground within which *my* world of experience can unfold.

Once space as the last vestige of the notion of an outer reality is left behind, the subjective experience of infinite consciousness becomes the pervasive theme of the meditative practice at this juncture. This step in the gradual entry into emptiness reveals the substantial contribution made by one's own mind to one's experience of the world, an experience which at the present juncture has been reduced to attending to the mind only. To avoid misunderstanding, the present step in the gradual entry into emptiness does not imply postulating some form of solipsism. The point is only that actual meditative experience at this point has the flavour of "mind only", since that is its predominant theme. But this is just a step in a series of perceptions, to be left behind with the next step.[2] For further clarification, in what follows I turn to the nature and conditionality of consciousness in early Buddhist thought.

## V.2 THE NATURE OF CONSCIOUSNESS

A frequent reference to consciousness in the early discourses forms part of an analysis of experience into the five aggregates, whose main thrust is to reveal the empty nature of all the aspects of experience that one might identify with and cling to as "I" and "mine". In

2 In relation to the perceptions of the immaterial spheres, Catherine 2008: 210 explains that "it is not helpful to try to ... replace conventional perceptions with these 'spiritually advanced' perceptions. Their value is simpler. They provide an opportunity to cease to cling to conventional perception. They are not intended to encourage attachment to an altered perspective."

terms of the canonical simile I took up in Chapter 4, consciousness as one of the aggregates is comparable to the performance of a magician.[3] In other words, consciousness has an effect comparable to a hallucination.

In the context of the five aggregates, consciousness represents only one aspect of the mind. Here it refers to being conscious of something as distinct from the aggregates of feeling, perception, and formations, which stand respectively for the affective, the recognizing, and the conative dimensions of the mind.

In other passages, however, consciousness can stand for the mind in its totality. One example is a recurring reference to "the body with its consciousness" as a way of conveying the sense of "body and mind".[4] Another example can be found in listings of elements that proceed from the four material elements (earth, water, fire, and wind) to space and consciousness.[5] Here, too, consciousness covers all that is mental.

This usage acquires a deeper meaning for one who has some meditative familiarity with the perception of infinite consciousness. With this perception all experience converges on consciousness, which has become all-embracing. The other aspects of the mind corresponding to the remaining mental aggregates have become subdued to such an extent that they are barely noticeable. In this way, in actual meditation practice consciousness can come to represent mind in its totality. Whereas the other aggregates have very much faded into the background, consciousness as that which knows and is aware stands squarely in the foreground of such meditative experience.

The quality of knowing and being aware is a constant given in mental experiences. This constancy, however, can easily result in the notion that consciousness is permanent. The *Mahātaṇhāsaṅkhaya-sutta* and its *Madhyama-āgama* parallel report a monk disciple of the Buddha coming to such a conclusion, namely assuming that the same consciousness will be reborn. Being informed about this, the Buddha asked him to explain his understanding. Here is their exchange as reported in the *Madhyama-āgama* version.

---

3 See above p.80.

4 An example is MN 112 at MN III 32,33 (translated Ñāṇamoli 1995: 906) and its parallel MĀ 187 at T I 733a13 (translated Anālayo 2012c: 234).

5 This type of usage can be found in a different passage in the same discourse mentioned in the previous note, MN 112 at MN III 31,16 (translated Ñāṇamoli 1995: 905) and its parallel MĀ 187 at T I 732c29 (translated Anālayo 2012c: 233).

> The Blessed One asked him: "Is it true that you speak in this way: 'I understand the Dharma taught by the Blessed One in this way: it is this consciousness now which is going to be reborn, not another?'"
>
> The monk Sāti replied: "Blessed One, I truly understand the Dharma taught by the Blessed One in this way: 'it is this consciousness now which is going to be reborn, not another.'"
>
> The Blessed One asked him: "What is this consciousness?"
>
> The monk Sāti replied: "Blessed One, this consciousness is that which speaks, feels, acts, instructs, gives rise to, appears, it is that which does good or bad deeds and experiences their results."
>
> The Blessed One reprimanded him: "Sāti, how come you understand the Dharma taught by me in this way? From whose mouth have you heard that I give such a teaching? You are a fool."[6]

The *Mahātaṇhāsaṅkhaya-sutta* similarly reports that the Buddha rebuked him in strong terms, calling him a fool; part of the expression "fool" has also been preserved in a Sanskrit fragment parallel.[7] Clearly, the idea that consciousness is a permanent entity that transmigrates from one life to the next did not find favour with the Buddha.

Another teaching on the impermanent nature of consciousness employs the simile of a monkey moving through a forest. Just as the monkey keeps grabbing one branch after another while moving through the forest, so consciousness continuously changes, taking up one object after another.[8] However stable it may appear, consciousness is just a flux of conditionally arisen moments of being conscious. Instead of speaking of "consciousness" one might better speak of "consciousness-ing", to avoid the nuance of stability and substantiality that can come with the use of a noun. Such "consciousness-ing" is just change itself. In fact if the cognizing part of the mind were beyond change, it would be forever frozen in the condition of knowing one single thing. The very ability to cognize different things inevitably implies change.

This flux of being conscious continues beyond a single life. The continuity of this flux provides the scope for the dependent

---

6 MĀ 201 at T I 767a6 to a14.

7 MN 38 at MN I 258,18 (translated Ñāṇamoli 1995: 350) and SHT V 1114b2, Sander and Waldschmidt 1985: 109.

8 SN 12.61 at SN II 95,5 (translated Bodhi 2000: 595) with its parallels SĀ 290 at T II 82a13 (translated Anālayo 2013c: 108) and a Sanskrit fragment parallel in Tripāṭhī 1962: 117.

arising of the fruits of previously done deeds. But it is not the same consciousness which is reborn – in fact it is not even the same consciousness that experiences the moment that follows after the present one. Instead, "consciousness-ing" is a stream of conditionally arisen moments of knowing.

## V.3 DEPENDENT ARISING

The conditionality of experience is a theme that to some degree underlies the instructions in the *Cūḷasuññata-sutta* and its parallels. Here conditionality underpins the reflection regarding what weariness has been overcome and what weariness is still there. The experience of infinite consciousness, for example, is a conditionally arisen mental state reached by leaving behind the conditions that led to earlier steps in the series, in the present case the perceptions of earth and infinite space. Their absence and attending to the perception of infinite consciousness are necessary conditions for the present step. By drawing attention to these, the instructions point to the conditions for the present moment's experience.

It is noteworthy that the discourse uses the expression "weariness" for the conditions that are to be left behind. This brings out an aspect shared by all that is conditioned, namely that one should eventually become weary of it. However sublime the actual experience may seem, it is just a conditioned product of the mind and as such something wearisome. The use of the qualification of each perception as a form of weariness combines insight into conditionality with a direct appreciation of *dukkha* as the ultimately unsatisfactory nature of all experience. This step-by-step approach prepares for the final aim of the gradual entry into emptiness, the stepping out of depending on any experience at all.

A description of a form of practice that no longer depends on any type of experience can be found in a discourse in the *Aṅguttara-nikāya* and its parallels in the two *Saṃyukta-āgama* collections. Here is a translation of one of the *Saṃyukta-āgama* versions:

> One meditates in such a way that one does not cultivate meditation in dependence on the earth, one does not cultivate meditation in dependence on water, fire, wind, [the sphere of boundless] space, [the sphere of boundless] consciousness, [the sphere of] nothingness, [the sphere of] neither-perception-nor-non-perception, not in

dependence on this world, not in dependence on that world, not [in dependence on] the sun or the moon, not [in dependence on] what is seen, heard, experienced, and cognized, not [in dependence on] what one has attained, not [in dependence on] what one searches for, not [in dependence on] what conforms with one's experience, not [in dependence on] what conforms with one's contemplation; yet one cultivates meditation.[9]

Such an independent form of meditation can be accomplished once one is able and willing to let go of each of these perceptions. Needless to say, this requires becoming disenchanted with them. It is precisely for this purpose that in the gradual entry into emptiness not only what one has just left behind, but even the present experience of infinite consciousness is explicitly qualified as a form of weariness. In fact progress takes place by leaving behind this weariness.

This aspect of the instructions appears to be aimed at ensuring that each stage in the gradual entry into emptiness is seen as merely a stepping stone on the meditative path. Even the exalted and sublime experience of infinite consciousness is just a type of weariness. It is indeed more refined than the forms of weariness experienced previously. Yet, however profound it may appear, it still is something to become weary of, since it still pertains to the realm of what is conditioned. It is merely part of a meditative progression towards the supreme form of emptiness through full liberation.

The conditionality of consciousness is a topic taken up in the *Mahānidāna-sutta* and its parallels. The relevant section of the discourse provides additional background to the present step in the gradual entry into emptiness.

Of particular interest for my present topic is that the *Mahānidāna-sutta* and its parallels show consciousness to stand in a reciprocally conditioning relationship to name-and-form. Here "form" corresponds to the first aggregate of bodily form and "name" stands for the functions of the mind apart from consciousness. These are elsewhere explained to be feeling, perception, intention, contact,

9 SĀ 926 at T II 236a11 to a15. The parallel AN 11.10 at AN V 325,1 (translated Bodhi 2012: 1561, given as number 9) does not mention the sun and moon. These are part of the corresponding description in another parallel, SĀ[2] 151 at T II 431a1, together with the stars.

and attention.[10] In the early discourses "name" does not include consciousness, contrary to its usage in later tradition.[11]

The *Mahānidāna-sutta* and its parallels begin with the Buddha highlighting the profundity of dependent arising. Here is the *Madhyama-āgama* version of this initial statement, which sets the context for the ensuing exposition:

> The Blessed One said: "Ānanda, do not think like that: 'This dependent arising is very simple, very simple!' Why is that? This dependent arising is very profound."[12]

The Buddha then follows up this initial statement by giving a detailed exposition of dependent arising (*paṭicca samuppāda*) in the reverse order, that is, by tracing each item to what forms its condition. In what follows I translate the part that proceeds from name-and-form to consciousness.

> "Ānanda, if someone asks: 'Is there a condition for name-and-form?', then one should answer in this way: 'There is a condition for name-and-form.' If someone asks: 'What is the condition for name-and-form?', then one should answer in this way: 'Consciousness is the condition.'
>
> "It should be understood what is meant by saying 'conditioned by consciousness there is name-and-form.' Ānanda, if consciousness were not to enter the mother's womb, would name-and-form manifest as this body?"
>
> [Ānanda] answered: "It would not."
>
> [The Buddha said]: "Ānanda, if consciousness, having entered the mother's womb, were to depart, would name-and-form combine with the semen?"
>
> [Ānanda] answered: "They would not combine."
>
> [The Buddha said]: "Ānanda, if the consciousness of a young boy or girl were to be cut off at the outset, destroyed and made non-existent, would name-and-form come to growth?"
>
> [Ānanda] answered: "It would not."

---

10 For a definition of name-and-form cf., e.g., SN 12.2 at SN II 3,34 (translated Bodhi 2000: 535) and its parallel EĀ 49.5 at T II 797b28, which similarly lists feeling, perception, attention, contact, and intention.

11 For a more detailed discussion cf. Anālayo 2015c.

12 MĀ 97 at T I 578b15 to b17.

> [The Buddha said]: "Ānanda, for this reason it should be understood that this is the cause of name-and-form, the source of name-and-form, the origin of name-and-form, the condition for name-and-form, namely consciousness. Why is that? Because conditioned by consciousness there is name-and-form.
>
> "Ānanda, if someone asks: 'Is there a condition for consciousness?', then one should answer in this way: 'There is also a condition for consciousness.' If someone asks: 'What is the condition for consciousness?', then one should answer in this way: 'Name-and-form is the condition.'"[13]

The translated excerpts show that the conditional relationship between consciousness and name-and-form in early Buddhist thought does cover rebirth. The reference to consciousness as that which enters a mother's womb is found similarly in the parallels to the above passage.[14] This leaves little scope for denying the rebirth aspect of dependent arising, as far as early Buddhism is concerned. At the same time, the above extract continues with a significant departure from the standard exposition of dependent arising, which from consciousness usually goes further backwards to formations and then ignorance. Instead, the present passage returns to name-and-form. This reveals a reciprocal conditioning between consciousness and name-and-form, each conditioning the other. The *Madhyama-āgama* discourse summarizes this reciprocal conditioning as follows:

> In this way, Ānanda, conditioned by name-and-form there is consciousness, and conditioned by consciousness there is name-and-form.[15]

This clearly refers not only to rebirth, but also shows consciousness in its everyday conditionality as a being conscious of name-and-form. This should make it clear that dependent arising cannot be confined merely to an explanation of rebirth either. The main point this particular teaching makes is rather to throw into relief the basic principle of conditionality, not just a particular manifestation of

13 MĀ 97 at T I 579c14 to c25.
14 DN 15 at DN II 63,2 (translated Walshe 1987: 226) and DĀ 13 at T I 61b9, T 14 at T I 243b18, and T 52 at T I 845b7.
15 MĀ 97 at T I 580a1f.

this principle in the form of twelve links. This is what makes the teaching on dependent arising indeed profound. At the same time, this profundity is accessible to direct meditative experience. The basic principle behind this profound teaching can be experienced in one's own practice here and now, without any need to develop the supernormal ability to know one's own past lives.

So the world of experience comes into being through a reciprocally conditioning relationship between the experiencing consciousness and the impact of outer phenomena, "form", together with the processing of such phenomena by the mind, "name". Out of this reciprocally conditioning relationship the dependent arising of *dukkha* evolves.

The reciprocal conditioning between consciousness and name-and-form finds an illustration in a simile in a discourse in the *Saṃyutta-nikāya* and its parallels. In what follows I translate the Sanskrit fragment version of this simile:

> It is just like two bundles of reeds which stand upright in an open space, leaning on each other.[16]

It is not possible to take out one of these two bundles without the other collapsing to the ground. Similarly, consciousness and name-and-form in a way lean on each other in reciprocal conditioning and the one cannot stand up without the other. Leaning on each other, both are dependent on the other and neither can in any way claim independent existence. Instead they are mere bundles, an image that points to the anyway composite nature of each, and these bundles moreover lean on each other.

In their reciprocally conditioning interrelation, consciousness and name-and-form function as the matrix of experience. It is out of this conditional matrix that experience arises in its various manifestations, and with that the possibility of attachment, defilements, craving, and

---

16 Tripāṭhī 1962: 110. SN 12.67 at SN II 114,17 (translated Bodhi 2000: 608) and a Tibetan parallel D 4094 *nyu* 70a5 or Q 5595 *thu* 114b2 also mention two bundles, whereas another parallel, SĀ 288 at T II 81b5, speaks of three bundles that will collapse once one or two of them are taken out. The presentation in SĀ 288 does not seem to fit the context so well, since the form bundle can be taken out without affecting the other two bundles, consciousness and name (e.g., in the case of an immaterial experience/realm). The imagery of the bundles of reeds works best if a single bundle corresponds to name-and-form together, in which case it is indeed not possible to take out one bundle without the other collapsing.

clinging. Seen for what it truly is, the foundation on which these defilements depend can be made to collapse to the ground, just as the two bundles of reeds collapse to the ground once they no longer lean on each other.

In this way, although consciousness is certainly not unconditioned, it can become unconditioning. How to go about unconditioning the mind is the theme of a succinct instruction given by the Buddha to the ascetic Bāhiya.

### V.4 THE BĀHIYA INSTRUCTION

The instruction to the ascetic Bāhiya is recorded in a discourse in the *Udāna* collection.[17] I first present the Bāhiya tale based on a summary of the *Udāna* account and then translate the *Saṃyukta-āgama* version of the same instruction given to the monk Māluṅkyaputta.

The *Udāna* tale begins with the Buddha dwelling at Jeta's Grove by Sāvatthī, whereas the ascetic Bāhiya is in a rather distant part of India, in the vicinity of modern Mumbai (Bombay). Bāhiya is a well-respected practitioner in that part of India who wonders if he might be an arahant. Becoming aware of this, a *deva* informs him that he is overestimating his level of accomplishment, as he is not even on the path to arahantship. Bāhiya enquires who then in this world are arahants or on the path to arahantship. The *deva* informs him of the Buddha and his whereabouts.

Profoundly stirred by this revelation, Bāhiya loses no time and walks straight across half the Indian subcontinent to Sāvatthī. Finding on arrival at Jeta's Grove that the Buddha has gone to beg for alms in town, Bāhiya decides to follow the Buddha immediately. Meeting the Buddha on the roads of the town, Bāhiya falls on his knees and requests to be given an instruction there and then. The Buddha replies that this is not the proper occasion for him to give teachings, since he is begging for alms. Yet, Bāhiya is not to be deterred and keeps pressing for an instruction.

---

17 Due to its importance for my present discussion, I depart from my usual policy of relying on material that is extant from more than one textual tradition and take up this tale, even though there does not seem to be any known parallel to this particular *Udāna* discourse. However, the instruction given to Bāhiya recurs in relation to a monk by the name of Māluṅkyaputta in the *Saṃyutta-nikāya*, and of this discourse we do have a parallel in the *Saṃyukta-āgama* and another parallel in Tibetan translation.

Thereupon the Buddha gives him a succinct instruction, according to which he should remain conscious of just bare sense experience, as a way to transcend *dukkha*. Bāhiya becomes an arahant on the spot.[18]

This story in the Pāli canon has an almost Zen-like quality to it. A non-Buddhist ascetic receives a short instruction on his first meeting with the Buddha, as a result of which he immediately becomes an arahant. Clearly the instruction was just what he needed to fulfil his aspirations.

The same succinct instruction given in another discourse in the *Saṃyutta-nikāya* and its parallels to the monk Māluṅkyaputta does not have the same effect right away, since Māluṅkyaputta does not become an arahant on the spot. Nevertheless, he does reach full liberation after sustained practice. This shows that the transformative potential of this brief instruction can also unfold for those who have not yet reached the high degree of inner maturity of someone like Bāhiya. In fact Māluṅkyaputta features elsewhere in the discourses as someone obsessed with irrelevant philosophical speculations and as someone with a weak understanding of the Dharma.[19] In short, the Bāhiya instruction is not only for those who are highly developed.

According to the *Saṃyukta-āgama* version of the discourse in question, the instruction Māluṅkyaputta received on this occasion was as follows:

> "See by limiting it to seeing, hear by limiting it to hearing, feel by limiting it to feeling, cognize by limiting it to cognizing."
>
> Then [the Buddha] spoke in verse:
>
> "If you are not in that,
> and [not being in] that you are also not in this,
> and you are also not in between the two,
> this then is the end of *dukkha* indeed."[20]

---

18 Ud 1.10 at Ud 8,13 (translated Ireland 1990: 20).

19 His obsession with what early Buddhist thought considers to be questions to be set aside is reported in MN 63 at MN I 427,6 (translated Ñāṇamoli 1995: 533) and its parallels MĀ 221 at T I 804b11, T 94 at T I 917c2, and T 1509 at T XXV 170a9. His weak understanding of the teachings, in particular of the nature of the underlying tendencies, emerges in MN 64 at MN I 432,11 (translated Ñāṇamoli 1995: 537) and its parallels MĀ 205 at T I 778c16, SHT V 1279V3–6, Sander and Waldschmidt 1985: 202, SHT IX 2155V3–5, Bechert and Wille 2004: 116, and D 4094 *ju* 260a1 or Q 5595 *thu* 2a1.

20 SĀ 312 at T II 90a12 to a16.

The formulation in the first part of the *Saṃyukta-āgama* version in a way helps to draw out the implications of the corresponding injunction in the *Saṃyutta-nikāya* parallel, which enjoins that in the seen there should just be what is seen, in the heard just what is heard, in the sensed just what is sensed, and in the cognized just what is cognized.[21]

The main implication of this instruction seems to be that one should remain aware of bare experience and limit one's mental processing to just that bare act of cognizing. Through such staying present with awareness of experience, the proliferations that usually arise can be avoided. One should just be aware of seeing forms, without all the mental chatter that such seeing normally arouses. In the same way one should just remain aware in relation to the other senses.

The *Saṃyutta-nikāya* version continues by indicating that once in the seen there is just the seen etc., one will not be by that. Not being by that, one will not be therein. Not being therein, one will not be here, or there, or in between the two. The formulation in the *Saṃyutta-nikāya* version helps to appreciate better the corresponding part in the *Saṃyukta-āgama* version, which takes the form of a poem spoken by the Buddha.

One way in which this injunction could be understood is that by just remaining aware at the sense-doors, one will not be carried away "by that", namely by the conditionality of the perceptual process and its potential to result in reactions by way of desire and aversion. Once this much has been achieved, one will also not be "therein", in the sense of not identifying with what is taking place, not even with the detachment achieved by staying free from desire and aversion.

Once defilements and patterns of identification are kept at bay, one will indeed not be here, or there, or in between. One does not take a stance on the senses, or on their objects, or on consciousness as what forms the middle between these. One also does not take a stance on the past, or on the future, or on the present moment as the middling ground between these two.[22] In short, the main point is simply that one does not take a stance on anything at all.

---

21 SN 35.95 at SN IV 73,5 (translated Bodhi 2000: 1175); a Tibetan version of this instruction can be found in D 4094 *ju* 241b3 or Q 5595 *tu* 276a2.

22 These approaches feature among several explanations offered in AN 6.61 at AN III 400,6 (translated Bodhi 2012: 951) and its parallel SĀ 1164 at T II 310c1 for the implications of a succinct reference in a stanza found at Sn 1042 (translated Norman 1992: 117) to the two ends and the middle.

In this way, by remaining with the consciousness side of experience without allowing name-and-form to thrive into elaborations that could lead to defilements, one does not react to or identify with any aspect of experience and one avoids taking a stance on anything.

That these are indeed central implications of this short instruction can be seen in the remainder of the discourse. Having received the above short instruction, Māluṅkyaputta claims to have understood it. The Buddha is quick to check and asks him to explain in what way he has understood it. In reply, Māluṅkyaputta expresses his inspiration, which the instruction evidently has aroused in him, by breaking out into a set of stanzas that elaborate on the significance of the short teaching he has received. His poem meets with the Buddha's approval, so it must capture the essential implications of the succinct instruction given by the Buddha. Here is the first part of Māluṅkyaputta's poetic explanation from the *Saṃyukta-āgama* version:

> On having seen a form with the eyes,
> if right mindfulness is lost,
> then in the form that is seen
> one grasps its characteristics (*nimitta*) with thoughts of craving.
> For one who grasps its characteristics with craving and delight
> the mind will constantly be in bondage to attachment,
> it will give rise to all kinds of craving
> for the countless forms that manifest.
> Thoughts of lustful sensual desire, ill will, and harm
> will bring about the mind's decline
> and foster a host of afflictions.
> One is forever far from Nirvāṇa.
>
> [If] on seeing a form one does not grasp its characteristics
> and the mind conforms to right mindfulness,
> [then] craving will not taint the mind with what is detrimental
> and the bondage of attachment will also not arise.
> Not giving rise to cravings
> for the countless forms that manifest,
> thoughts of lustful sensual desire, ill will, and harm
> will be unable to afflict the mind.[23]

23 SĀ 312 at T II 90a20 to a29.

The stanzas continue by making similar indications in regard to the other sense-doors. This confirms that the succinct instruction given to Bāhiya is indeed about remaining with awareness so that what is seen, heard, felt, or cognized is simply experienced as such, without giving rise to mental reactions related to craving and defilements.

This instruction offers a very practical way of working with dependent arising in the context of everyday activities. Based on having cultivated the step of infinite consciousness in the gradual entry into emptiness, the act of being conscious of things will naturally become a more prominent and better noticed part of one's experience. Remaining with this part of the mind without giving rise to reactions can become a powerful way of bringing emptiness to bear on challenging situations of various types. In actual practice, as soon as one turns attention directly to the mind as that which experiences any input through the senses, it naturally becomes silent and mental chatter vanishes. In this way, there will indeed be only the seen in what is seen, the heard in what is heard, etc. Instead of becoming mentally involved with what is experienced, one simply remains with that which experiences, with that which is aware.

Such meditative dwelling would also be a way of putting into practice the poem I took up in Chapter 4, which enjoins:

> In the present moment one should attend
> with mindfulness to the lack of stability
> of whatever phenomena there are;
> the wise awaken in this way.[24]

In the remainder of this chapter I continue to explore ways of relating emptiness to daily activities. At times there are situations when just remaining with bare sense data is simply not possible. Previous training in accordance with the Bāhiya instruction will sharpen one's awareness of the different mental evaluations that can set in after bare recognition. This will be of considerable assistance in such situations, by making one more clearly aware of what one adds on top of the bare sense data. In addition to this, however, there are several other and complementary ways in which one can bring emptiness to bear on daily-life situations. In what follows I will explore these, based on the exposition given of this topic in the

---

24 See above p.86.

*Mahāsuññata-sutta* and its parallels. I will return to studying the other steps in the gradual entry into emptiness in Chapter 6.

### V.5 EMPTINESS IN DAILY LIFE

The similar titles of the *Cūḷasuññata-sutta* and the *Mahāsuññata-sutta* point to a close relationship between the smaller (*Cūḷa°*) and the greater (*Mahā°*) discourse on emptiness (*°suññata-sutta*). This is also reflected in their location within the middle-length discourse collections, as the two discourses follow each other in the *Majjhima-nikāya* and in the *Madhyama-āgama*. Besides the titles and the locations, a close relationship between the *Cūḷasuññata-sutta* and the *Mahāsuññata-sutta* (and their respective parallels) is also evident from the fact that both start with the Buddha's own experience of emptiness and then show how others can cultivate the same.

In the case of the *Cūḷasuññata-sutta* and its parallels, Ānanda's enquiry about the Buddha's regular dwelling in emptiness leads to an exposition showing how such meditative dwelling can be undertaken. The *Mahāsuññata-sutta* and its parallels instead begin with the Buddha criticizing excessive socializing and putting an emphasis on the need to dwell in seclusion. Next the Buddha refers to his own dwelling in emptiness, after which he gives a description of dwelling in emptiness internally, externally, and internally and externally. A central theme in this description is the need for a strong foundation in mental tranquillity in order to be able to dwell in emptiness successfully.

The emphasis given to formal practice of tranquillity in a way complements the *Cūḷasuññata-sutta* and its parallels. These present a form of practice that involves the perceptions related to the immaterial spheres and which does not appear to be meant only for those who are able to attain these immaterial spheres, based on mastery of the four absorptions. Although this opens the door to practice undertaken with lower levels of concentration, the *Mahāsuññata-sutta* and its parallels make it clear that absorption, ideally the fourth absorption, is an important asset and provides a strong foundation for emptiness practice.

Lacking such foundation need not stop one from engaging in the gradual entry into emptiness, but alongside such practice the formal development of tranquillity should not be neglected if one's practice is to result in the realization of supreme emptiness with full awakening.

Here the cultivation of the divine abodes would recommend itself as a convenient option for building up a foundation in tranquillity alongside one's practice of the gradual entry into emptiness. In addition to the various advantages that the *brahmavihāra*s offer over other forms of concentration meditation, as discussed above,[25] another advantage relevant to the present context in particular is that their boundless nature offers an easy entry point into the boundless experiences of infinite space and infinite consciousness. I will explore this practical trajectory in Chapter 7, in which I present a form of meditation practice that proceeds from the *brahmavihāra*s to the gradual entry into emptiness.[26]

Besides highlighting the need for a strong basis in tranquillity, the exposition in the *Mahāsuññata-sutta* and its parallels confirms a point I made in Chapter 4,[27] namely that emptiness covers what is internal as well as what is external. In early Buddhist thought, there is nothing whatsoever that escapes from being empty.

After expounding how dwelling in internal and external emptiness should be combined with training in tranquillity, the *Mahāsuññata-sutta* and its parallels continue by surveying ways in which one's formal practice of emptiness meditation can be related to various aspects of everyday life. One such aspect concerns how to continue practice outside of formal sitting meditation. Here is the relevant part from the *Madhyama-āgama* parallel to the *Mahāsuññata-sutta*.

> Ānanda, if ... one who is dwelling in this abiding of the mind wishes to practise walking meditation, then ... one goes out of the meditation hut and practises walking meditation in the open, in the shade of the hut, with the faculties settled within, the mind not directed outwards or backwards, perceiving [only] what is in front. Having practised walking meditation like this, the mind does not give rise to covetousness, sadness, or [another] detrimental or unwholesome state – this is reckoned one's right comprehension.
>
> Ānanda, if ... one who is dwelling in this abiding of the mind wishes to sit in concentration, then ... one leaves the walking meditation, goes to the end of the walking meditation path, spreads the sitting mat, and sits down cross-legged. Having sat in concentration like this, the mind does not give rise to covetousness, sadness, or

25 See above pp.58 and 67.
26 See below p.151.
27 See above p.77.

[another] detrimental or unwholesome state – this is reckoned one's right comprehension.[28]

The *Mahāsuññata-sutta* mentions all four postures, but without detailed explanations comparable to the above instructions on how to undertake walking and sitting meditation.[29] In spite of such differences, the *Mahāsuññata-sutta* and its parallels agree that continuity of practice can be ensured by keeping the defilements at bay. In line with the indications provided in the Bāhiya instruction, a central component of emptiness meditation in early Buddhist thought is thus keeping the mind empty of desire and aversion. This is what makes for continuity of practice and this is how progress in the realization of emptiness manifests, namely when the mind becomes ever less prone to succumb to defilements.

The reference to the presence of right comprehension in the above passage, as well as in subsequent portions of the discourse I will take up below, makes it clear that some degree of conscious monitoring of the condition of aloofness from the defilements is required. At the same time, as the Bāhiya instruction shows, the actual effort to be made is to let go. Such letting go is an intelligent letting go. It takes place with mindfulness of one's present mental condition and thereby with the ability to discern when the letting go has not been successful and defilements begin to assert themselves.

Practice undertaken in the walking posture builds a firm foundation for sitting meditation, as shown in the excerpt above. Here, too, the central feature of proper practice is that the mind is emptied of defilements, which is what makes for continuity of emptiness in formal sitting as well as during other activities.

A complementary description can be found in the *Piṇḍapāta-pārisuddhi-sutta* and its *Saṃyukta-āgama* parallel. The *Piṇḍapāta-pārisuddhi-sutta* and its parallel also start off with a reference to someone who dwells in emptiness and then show how this can be achieved by others. Unlike the *Cūḷasuññata-sutta* and *Mahāsuññata-sutta* (as well as their parallels), however, in the present case the one whose dwelling in emptiness leads to an exposition is Sāriputta, instead of being the Buddha himself.

The *Piṇḍapātapārisuddhi-sutta* and its parallel report that Sāriputta,

---

28 MĀ 191 at T I 739a12 to a19.
29 MN 122 at MN III 112,31 (translated Ñāṇamoli 1995: 973).

who had been practising emptiness meditation, came to see the Buddha. The Buddha took this as the occasion for describing a mode of practice recommended for one who similarly wishes to dwell in emptiness. In what follows I translate the relevant part from the *Saṃyukta-āgama* parallel to the *Piṇḍapātapārisuddhi-sutta*.

> When entering the town, when walking for alms, when coming out of the town, one should reflect: "Seeing forms with the eye now, has sensual desire arisen in me, affection, thoughts of craving or attachment?"
>
> Sāriputta, if at the time when ... one examines [oneself] in this way there are thoughts of craving and one is defiled by attachment in relation to the forms cognized by the eye, then in order to eliminate such detrimental and unwholesome [states] ... one should be willing to make a strong effort enabling one to train in collected mindfulness.
>
> This is like a person whose turban is on fire. The person will arouse a superior effort in order to extinguish it completely and be diligent in trying to get it extinguished. In the same way ... one should arouse superior diligence and be willing to make an effort to train in collected mindfulness.
>
> If at the time when ... one examines [oneself] there are no thoughts of craving and being defiled by attachment in relation to forms cognized by the eye during the period of being on the road, being in the village walking for alms, or leaving the village, then ... one can be happy and delighted because of having this foundation in what is wholesome, and day and night one should make an effort to [continue] cultivating collected mindfulness.[30]

The relatively similar description in the *Piṇḍapātapārisuddhi-sutta* differs in so far as it does not explicitly mention the need for collected mindfulness.[31] Here the *Saṃyukta-āgama* version brings out with more clarity an aspect that is also evident in the Bāhiya instruction, in that mindfulness has a central role to play when it comes to bringing formal emptiness meditation to bear on daily activities. It is precisely through establishing mindfulness that one is able to remain just with the seen, heard, felt, and cognized. This is what makes it possible to avoid one's turban catching fire, that is, that one's mind starts

30 SĀ 236 at T II 57b13 to b24 (also translated Choong 2004/2010: 7–9).
31 MN 151 at MN III 294,29 (translated Ñāṇamoli 1995: 1143). The remainder of the two discourses, however, shows considerable differences; cf. Anālayo 2011a: 848.

burning with defilements. Although the passage above applies this in particular to the situation of a Buddhist monastic begging for alms in town, the same can similarly be applied to the case of any practitioner of emptiness who has to engage in various activities related to the need to gain one's livelihood.

The need to be wary of desire and aversion similarly stands in the foreground when it comes to applying the understanding of emptiness gained in silent meditation to thinking. The *Mahāsuññata-sutta* and its parallels describe how one who is devoted to dwelling in emptiness should handle the thinking activity of the mind. Here is a translation of this particular section from the *Madhyama-āgama* version.

> Ānanda, if ... one who is dwelling in this abiding of the mind wishes to think thoughts, then as regards the three detrimental and unwholesome thoughts – thoughts of sensual desire, thoughts of ill will, and thoughts of harming – ... one should not think these three detrimental and unwholesome thoughts. [Instead], as regards the three wholesome thoughts – thoughts of dispassion, thoughts without ill will, and thoughts without harming – one should think these three wholesome thoughts. Having thought like this, the mind does not give rise to covetousness, sadness, or [another] detrimental or unwholesome state – this is reckoned one's right comprehension.[32]

Here the same theme of staying aloof from mental defilements continues. So dwelling in emptiness does not necessarily require maintaining a non-conceptual mental condition in which any thought is inevitably a distraction and an obstacle to the practice. The eminently pragmatic stance in the *Mahāsuññata-sutta* and its parallels clearly approaches the thinking activity of the mind as yet another occasion for dwelling in emptiness. The point at stake is not just to avoid thought altogether, but rather to avoid certain types of thought, namely unwholesome thoughts. In this way emptiness can be practised even when the mind is crowded with thinking activity. Here, again, mindfulness has a key role to play. It is through establishing mindfulness that one learns to monitor the nature of one's thoughts and thereby becomes able to recognize whether they have started to move into the realm of what is unwholesome.

The pragmatic thrust of the *Mahāsuññata-sutta* and its parallels continues from thinking to speaking. This counterbalances the

---

32 MĀ 191 at T I 739a20 to a24.

indication made at the outset of the discourse regarding the importance of seclusion. Seclusion is a centrally important factor for meditative progress. Yet practice continues seamlessly from being in seclusion to situations where one is not in seclusion and has to engage in communication with others. How to do this is described in the *Madhyama-āgama* version as follows:

> Ānanda, if ... one who is dwelling in this abiding of the mind wishes to speak, then as regards talking ignoble talk related to what is not beneficial – talk such as talk about kings, talk about thieves, talk about battles and quarrels, talk about drinks and food, talk about clothes and bedding, talk about married women, talk about girls, talk about adulterous women, talk about the world, talk about wrong practices, talk about the contents of the ocean – ... one does not talk such types of irrelevant talk.
>
> [Instead], as regards talking noble talk that is related to what is beneficial, that makes the mind malleable, free of darkness and the hindrances – talk such as talk about generosity, talk about morality, talk about concentration, talk about wisdom, talk about liberation, talk about knowledge and vision of liberation, talk about self-effacement, talk about not socializing, talk about fewness of wishes, talk about contentment, talk about dispassion, talk about abandoning, talk about cessation, talk about sitting in meditation, talk about dependent arising, such talk [proper] for recluses – [one talks such talk]. Having talked like this, the mind does not give rise to covetousness, sadness, or [another] detrimental or unwholesome state – this is reckoned one's right comprehension.[33]

The parallels show a few variations in their listing of examples for the kind of talk that is inappropriate and the kind of talk that is appropriate for one who cultivates emptiness. The main point they make, however, is closely similar. Conversations should be meaningful, instead of chattering about this and that. The meaningfulness of conversations comes from their relation to one's practice of the path. The *Mahāsuññata-sutta* explicitly indicates

33 MĀ 191 at T I 739a25 to b5. MN 122 at MN III 113,12 (translated Ñāṇamoli 1995: 974) differs in so far as it turns first to talking and then to thinking, whereas the Tibetan version agrees with MĀ 191. As the general pattern in this part of the discourse moves from formal meditation to less formal activities, the progression in the Chinese and Tibetan versions from thoughts to conversation fits this pattern better.

that the conversations one should engage in are those that lead to detachment and Nirvāṇa. This is how even conversations can be pervaded by a flavour of emptiness.

Next the *Mahāsuññata-sutta* and its parallel turn to the topic of sensuality. This passage makes it unmistakeably clear that from an early Buddhist viewpoint engaging in sensuality is not compatible with genuine practice of emptiness. Here is the *Madhyama-āgama* version.

> Again, Ānanda, there are five strands of sensual pleasure that are pleasurable, that the mind thinks about, that are connected with craving and sensual desire: forms known by the eye, sounds known by the ear, odours known by the nose, flavours known by the tongue, and tangibles known by the body.
>
> If ... one's mind turns to contemplation and, in regard to these five strands of sensual pleasures, comes under the influence of these strands of sensual pleasures, then the mind will dwell among them. Why is that? Sooner or later, in regard to these five strands of sensual pleasures, [if] one comes under the influence of these strands of sensual pleasures, the mind dwells among them.
>
> Ānanda, if while contemplating ... one comes to know that in regard to these five strands of sensual pleasures one has come under the influence of these strands of sensual pleasures, that the mind is dwelling among them, then ... one should contemplate the impermanence of these various strands of sensual pleasures, contemplate their decay, contemplate their fading away, contemplate their abandoning, contemplate their cessation, contemplate abandoning and giving them up, becoming separated from them. Then, whatever one has of desire and defilement regarding these five strands of sensual pleasures will soon cease.
>
> Ānanda, if while contemplating like this ... one knows that whatever one had of desire and defilement in regard to these five strands of sensual pleasures has been abandoned – this is reckoned one's right comprehension.[34]

The *Mahāsuññata-sutta* differs from the above in so far as it does not provide instructions about what one should do when being overwhelmed by attraction towards the five types of sensual pleasures.[35] From a practical perspective, the indications given above

34 MĀ 191 at T I 739b5 to b15.
35 MN 122 at MN III 114,25 (translated Ñāṇamoli 1995: 975).

are quite helpful, since they show how one can strengthen one's practice of emptiness by relating it to insight into the impermanent nature of sensual pleasures.

As already mentioned in Chapter 4, a proper realization of the empty nature of material phenomena can go a long way in arousing detachment and dispassion.[36] This can take place by simply reminding oneself that, after all, these apparently so attractive and alluring material phenomena are truly empty. Yet this will not always suffice. Here the above passage offers another tool that can be employed for the same purpose of bringing about detachment and dispassion. The tool is attending to the impermanent nature of all phenomena. Awareness of impermanence and change brings about dispassion and naturally leads to an attitude of letting go.

Besides in this way encouraging an attitude of letting go in relation to sensually attractive things, the *Mahāsuññata-sutta* and its parallel also take up the need to let go of patterns of identification. They do so by bringing in the scheme of the five aggregates, whose empty nature the simile I took up in Chapter 4 illustratively compares to foam, a few bubbles, a mirage, some plantain sheaths, and a magical illusion. Here is the *Madhyama-āgama* parallel to the part of the *Mahāsuññata-sutta* that relates emptiness to a contemplation of the five aggregates:

> Again, Ānanda, there are the five aggregates [affected by] clinging. The form aggregate [affected by] clinging ... the feeling ... the perception ... the formations ... and the consciousness aggregate [affected by] clinging...
>
> One should contemplate their rise and fall thus: "This is bodily form, this is the arising of bodily form, this is the cessation of bodily form, this is feeling ... this is perception ... these are formations ... this is consciousness, this is the arising of consciousness, this is the cessation of consciousness." Then whatever conceit of an "I" one has in regard to these five aggregates [affected by] clinging, that will soon cease.
>
> Ānanda, if while contemplating like this ... one comes to know that whatever conceit of an "I" one had in regard to these five aggregates [affected by] clinging has ceased – this is reckoned one's right comprehension.[37]

36 See above p.93.
37 MĀ 191 at T I 739b16 to b21.

The *Mahāsuññata-sutta* similarly highlights the contribution that awareness of impermanence can make to the cultivation of emptiness. Becoming aware of the fact that all the different parts that make up oneself, from the physical body to consciousness, are impermanent and bound to cease, will indeed undermine all patterns of identification. The Tibetan parallel precedes its version of the above passage by describing how one first examines oneself to see if there is any conceit or tendency towards the notion "I" in relation to these five aggregates.[38] This offers another helpful indication for actual practice, in that for the contemplation of the five aggregates to unfold its full potential, one first needs to acknowledge honestly where and how one does have patterns of identification. Somewhat like a medical diagnosis providing the foundation for the administration of the cure, recognition of where one has invested one's sense of identity lays the foundation for being able to deconstruct this sense of identity.

In this way contemplation of the aggregates as described in the *Mahāsuññata-sutta* and its parallels provides a spotlight on the chief import of emptiness in early Buddhism, the giving up of all "I" and "me" and "mine", the letting go of any identifications as the path to supreme emptiness through full liberation.

### V.6 SUMMARY

The gradual entry into the realization of emptiness in the *Cūḷasuññata-sutta* and its parallels moves from deconstructing the solidity of matter to leaving behind even the notion of space with the experience of all-embracing consciousness. Such consciousness, although a constant given in all experience, is itself impermanent and conditioned.

A way of practice that avoids the conditioned arising of defilements in the mind is to remain aware of the cognizing part of the mind and thus stay with awareness of the input received through the senses, without allowing this to lead to proliferations in the mind. Other aspects of integrating emptiness in daily life involve walking, thinking, and speaking, all of which take place in a mental condition that remains as empty as possible of defilements. Successful cultivation of emptiness leaves behind all interest in sensuality and all forms of identification and conceit.

38 Skilling 1994: 236,7.

# VI

# EMPTY OF SELF

In the present chapter I examine the remainder of the gradual entry into emptiness described in the *Cūḷasuññata-sutta* and its parallels, before looking at the dynamics of the whole meditative progression.

## VI.1 NOTHINGNESS

The instructions in the *Madhyama-āgama* parallel to the *Cūḷasuññata-sutta* on the step that follows the perception of infinite consciousness are as follows.

> Again, Ānanda, if ... one wishes to dwell much in emptiness ... one should not give attention to the perception of the sphere of infinite space and not give attention to the perception of the sphere of infinite consciousness, but should frequently give attention to the unitary perception of the sphere of nothingness.
>
> In this way one knows that this is empty of the perception of the sphere of infinite space and empty of the perception of the sphere of infinite consciousness. Yet there is this non-emptiness: just the unitary perception of the sphere of nothingness.
>
> [One knows]: "Whatever weariness because of the perception of the sphere of infinite space there might be – that is not present for me; whatever weariness because of the perception of the sphere of infinite consciousness there might be – that is also not present for me. There is only the weariness because of the unitary perception of the sphere of nothingness."

> Whatever is not present, one therefore sees as empty; whatever else is present, one sees as truly present. Ānanda, this is called truly dwelling in emptiness, without distortion.[1]

With this step the gradual entry into emptiness continues along the trajectory of the immaterial spheres. At the present juncture, the infinite consciousness that had previously resulted from the experience of infinite space is replaced with the perception of nothingness. This replacement takes place through the realization that consciousness is insubstantial in every respect. This leads to the perception of "no-thing", in the sense that absence itself becomes the object, if one may so call it, of practice at this juncture.

Compared to the preceding steps in the gradual entry into emptiness, this involves a further degree of abstraction. The relinquishing of the already abstract notion of space had yielded an experience concerned entirely with the subjective, leaving behind any object. Now, even the subjective is let go of, being replaced by the notion of its absence.

In the present context this points squarely in the direction of not-self, although it needs to be kept in mind that mere attainment of the immaterial sphere of nothingness does not imply insight into not-self. The case of the Buddha's former teacher Āḷāra Kālāma shows that mastery of the sphere of nothingness was considered to be falling short of the final goal. This is why the Buddha-to-be left Āḷāra Kālāma to pursue his quest for total freedom. Nevertheless, having reached the final goal of his quest, the recently awakened Buddha wished to share his discovery first of all with his former teacher Āḷāra Kālāma.[2] Based on his high degree of mental maturity by having mastered the attainment of nothingness, Āḷāra Kālāma would have been able to progress easily and awaken to the not-self nature of the whole world. In sum, attaining the sphere of nothingness as such can serve as a preparation for, but at the same time falls short of awakening in the early Buddhist sense.

In the context of the gradual entry into emptiness, it can safely be assumed that cultivating insight into not-self would be a fitting way of going about the present step concerned with nothingness. In fact the discourses at times use the expression "nothingness" to refer to

1 MĀ 190 at T I 737b21 to b29.
2 MN 26 at MN I 165,10 (translated Ñāṇamoli 1995: 258), MĀ 204 at T I 776c1 (translated Anālayo 2012c: 28), and fragment 331v8 in Liu 2010: 155.

Nirvāṇa. A discourse in the *Saṃyutta-nikāya* and its *Saṃyukta-āgama* parallel indicate that lust, aversion, and delusion are a something.[3] One who has eradicated them has realized nothingness. According to a stanza in the *Dhammapada* and its parallels, by leaving behind anger, pride, and any fetter, one owns nothing (and thereby goes beyond *dukkha*).[4] In this way, although the instructions in the gradual entry into emptiness clearly refer to the perception of the sphere of nothingness, the connotations that the term "nothingness" itself carries elsewhere point to employing this perception to cultivate a profound level of insight.

For actual practice of the present step, the *Āneñjasappāya-sutta* and its parallels offer helpful information, to which I now turn.

## VI.2 IMPERTURBABILITY

The *Āneñjasappāya-sutta* and its parallels, preserved in Chinese and Tibetan translation, delineate different approaches to the gaining of mental imperturbability. In early Buddhist thought, "imperturbability" stands for deep concentration that has reached the strength of the fourth absorption, as well as for the imperturbable mental condition of one who has reached full awakening.[5] In keeping with this range of meanings of the term, the *Āneñjasappāya-sutta* and its parallels describe how to attain the imperturbability of the concentrative type, then how to move on to the sphere of nothingness and neither-perception-nor-non-perception, and eventually proceed to show how awakening can be reached.

In relation to the attainment of the sphere of nothingness, the *Āneñjasappāya-sutta* and its parallels offer three alternative routes that could be taken. Here is a translation of the second of these three approaches from the *Madhyama-āgama* parallel to the *Āneñjasappāya-sutta*:

> Again, a learned noble disciple contemplates in this way: "This world is empty, empty of a self, empty of what belongs to a self,

---

3 SN 41.7 at SN IV 297,18 (translated Bodhi 2000: 1326) and its parallel SĀ 567 at T II 150a8.

4 Dhp 221 (translated Norman 1997/2004: 34), with parallels in the Patna *Dharmapada* 238, Cone 1989: 164f, the Gāndhārī *Dharmapada* 274, Brough 1962/2001: 163, and in the *Udānavarga* 20.1, Bernhard 1965: 268.

5 For a more detailed discussion cf. Anālayo 2012c: 195–200.

> empty of what is permanent, empty of what is everlasting, empty of existing continuously, and empty of being unchanging."
>
> Practising and training in this way, developing [the mind] in this way in a broad and extensive manner, one easily attains purity of the mind in regard to that sphere. Having attained purity of the mind in regard to that sphere ... one will attain entry into the sphere of nothingness herein, or else employ wisdom for the sake of liberation. At a later time, when the body breaks up at death, because of that former mental disposition one will certainly reach the sphere of nothingness.[6]

The corresponding reflection in the *Āneñjasappāya-sutta* is shorter. It just reads "this is empty of a self and of what belongs to a self."[7] The Tibetan version, which has this particular approach as the third of the three alternative routes to be taken, describes the world as empty of being permanent etc., and thereby also brings in the topic of impermanence, similar to the *Madhyama-āgama* passage translated above.[8]

Important for my present purposes is that the *Āneñjasappāya-sutta* and its parallels agree that a meditative approach to nothingness can take place through the contemplation that this world of experience is empty of a self and of what belongs to a self. This is of eminent practical relevance for the gradual entry into emptiness in the *Cūḷasuññata-sutta* and its parallels. The presentation in the *Āneñjasappāya-sutta* and its parallels offers an approach to the perception of nothingness that is naturally in line with the overall dynamics of this gradual entry and brings out its insight potential in a particularly powerful manner. Understood in this way, progress from the perception of infinite consciousness to the next stage in the gradual entry into emptiness could take place by contemplating that in this experience of infinite consciousness there is nothing in the sense that there is nothing of a self and nothing that belongs to a self.

Besides this practical indication, the above passage also offers other helpful indications. One is that an emptiness contemplation – namely viewing the world as empty of a self – can function as a way to attain the immaterial sphere of nothingness. The *Āneñjasappāya-*

---

6 MĀ 75 at T I 542c18 to c29 (translated Anālayo 2012c: 210).
7 MN 106 at MN II 263,26 (translated Ñāṇamoli 1995: 871).
8 D 4094 *ju* 228b6 or Q 5595 *tu* 261a6.

*sutta* and its parallels clearly envisage this as one of two possible outcomes: attainment of the sphere of nothingness and rebirth in the corresponding realm. Wisdom leading to final liberation is an alternative outcome of the same practice.

In this way the *Āneñjasappāya-sutta* and its parallels show a contribution made by insight to the development of tranquillity. This contribution by insight is not just awareness of the factors of the mind that need to be overcome in order to reach a deeper level of concentration. Instead, it employs a theme that stands at the very heart of meditative wisdom, namely contemplation of the absence of a self. This very theme constitutes the path leading to the attainment of the immaterial sphere.

The *Āneñjasappāya-sutta* and its parallels thereby make a significant contribution to the topic of tranquillity and insight that I took up briefly in Chapter 3.[9] The *Yuganaddha-sutta* and its *Saṃyukta-āgama* parallel already showed that there are alternative ways in which these two central qualities of the early Buddhist path to awakening can be combined with each other. From their presentation it becomes clear that there is no need to assume that one of the two – tranquillity or insight – invariably has to be practised first, before being able to turn to the cultivation of the other one. Nor do the *Yuganaddha-sutta* and its parallel recommend developing only one out of the two, at the expense of the other. Instead, tranquillity and insight emerge as interrelated qualities that can be practised one after the other, or even both together.

In a way the *Āneñjasappāya-sutta* and its parallels draw out the practical implications of the close relationship between tranquillity and insight that is so clearly apparent in the *Yuganaddha-sutta* and its parallel. Once this close relationship is appreciated, it will no longer be surprising that one might use insight perceptions to cultivate tranquillity, as described in the *Āneñjasappāya-sutta* and its parallels. The complementary case then finds a practical illustration in the *Cūḷasuññata-sutta* and its parallels, which employ perceptions derived from tranquillity meditation for progress in insight. These two complementary perspectives corroborate that in early Buddhist thought tranquillity and insight are two qualities that in mutual collaboration lead to full liberation.

---

9 See above p.63.

Another significant aspect in the presentation in the *Āneñjasappāya-sutta* and its parallels is that the contemplation of not-self could merely lead to attaining the immaterial sphere of nothingness, instead of resulting in awakening. The discourse thereby reveals that profound experiences of emptiness need not invariably be of the liberating type, even if they have come about through contemplating that all this is empty of a self. Attaining the sphere of nothingness clearly falls short of being final liberation in the early Buddhist sense.

The same perspective also emerges from the *Cūḷasuññata-sutta* and its parallels, which depict a range of emptiness experiences. Although these have the potential to lead to awakening, if used properly, they fall short of being final liberation in themselves. What makes the difference is the eradication of defilements. Only when these are overcome for good is true liberation reached and therewith the supreme form of emptiness attained. This point comes up explicitly at the end of the *Āneñjasappāya-sutta*. In what follows I translate the relevant part from the *Madhyama-āgama* version:

> Ānanda, a learned noble disciple contemplates in this way: "Sensual pleasures now or in the future, forms now or in the future, sensual perceptions now or in the future, perceptions of forms now or in the future, the perception of imperturbability, the perception of the sphere of nothingness, and the perception of [neither-perception-nor]-non-perception – all these perceptions are of an impermanent nature, they are *dukkha* and [subject] to cessation – this is reckoned to be one's [notion of] identity (*sakkāya*). If there is one's [notion of] identity, there is birth, there is old age, there is disease, and there is death ... That which is Nirvāṇa without remainder, that is called the deathless."
>
> With such contemplation and such view one will certainly attain liberation of the mind from the influx of sensuality, [liberation of the mind] from the influx of existence, and liberation of the mind from the influx of ignorance. Being liberated, one knows that one is liberated: "Birth has been extinguished, the holy life has been established, what had to be done has been done, there will be no experiencing of a further existence", knowing this as it really is.[10]

10 MĀ 75 at T I 543b9 to b20.

The parallel exposition in the *Āneñjasappāya-sutta* does not refer to birth, old age, disease, and death.[11] Nevertheless, the basic contrast set in the parallel versions remains the same. On the one side of this contrast stand various modes of creating a sense of identity, which could be based on identifying with the experience of sensual perceptions, or on identifying with one's experience of the sublime perceptions of the immaterial spheres. On the other side of this contrast stands the deathless, Nirvāṇa, as the giving up of all identifications, whatever they may be.

The highlight placed in this way on the need to go beyond all types of identification fits in well with the main purpose of the gradual entry into emptiness depicted in the *Cūḷasuññata-sutta* and its parallels. This is what it all boils down to in the end, whether expressed in terms of highest imperturbability or supreme emptiness: giving up "I" making and "my" making.

### VI.3 NOT-SELF

For a better appreciation of the present step of practice, in what follows I examine the not-self teaching and the different ways in which, according to early Buddhist thought, a sense of identity can arise in relation to the five aggregates.

In Chapter 1 I briefly discussed the teaching of the four noble truths that according to tradition was the first instruction given by the Buddha to his five former companions.[12] Another discourse given subsequently to the same five is on record for leading to their full awakening. This discourse centres on the teaching of not-self. Here is the first part of this teaching according to the *Saṃyukta-āgama* version:

> Bodily form is not-self. If bodily form were the self, then it should not happen that disease and pain arise in relation to bodily form, and one should not get the wish for bodily form to be in this way and not in that way. Because bodily form is not-self, there is the arising of disease and pain in relation to bodily form and one gets the wish for bodily form to be in this way and not to be in that way. Feeling ... perception ... formations ... consciousness *is also like this*.[13]

11 MN 106 at MN II 265,30 (translated Ñāṇamoli 1995: 873). Birth, old age, disease, and death are also mentioned in the Tibetan version, D 4094 *ju* 230a5 or Q 5595 *tu* 263a1.

12 See above p.11.

13 SĀ 34 at T II 7c14 to c18 (translated Anālayo 2014e: 5f).

This passage clarifies the kind of self-notion that the not-self teaching addresses: a self that is in control and can therefore have everything as it wishes it to be. The above passage makes it amply clear that this is not the way things really are. One's body can get sick, feelings are at times painful, perceptions are not always enjoyable, one's decisions do not always lead to the desired result, and consciousness does not invariably experience only what one would wish. While one is able to influence things to some extent, they are nevertheless beyond one's complete control.

The discourse continues with a question-and-answer exchange, in the course of which the five first monk disciples of the Buddha confirm that each of the aggregates is impermanent and subject to change. Since the aggregates are impermanent, it follows that they are *dukkha*, in the sense of not being able to provide lasting satisfaction. Since the aggregates are *dukkha*, it follows that they are not really fit to be regarded as a self. This further explains what type of a self is being put into question, namely a self that is permanent and a source of unalloyed happiness. The Buddha then rounds off his exposition to the five monks as follows:

> Therefore, monks, whatever bodily form, whether past, future or present, internal or external, gross or subtle, sublime or repugnant, far or near, it is all not-self and does not belong to a self. In this way it should be examined as it really is. Feeling ... perception ... formations ... consciousness *is also like this*.
>
> Monks, a learned noble disciple sees these five aggregates of clinging as not-self and not belonging to a self. Examining them in this way, one does not cling to anything in the whole world. Because of not clinging to anything, one is not attached to anything. Because of not being attached to anything, one personally realizes Nirvāṇa, [knowing]: "Birth for me has been eradicated, the holy life has been established, what had to be done has been done, I myself know that there will be no receiving of further existence."[14]

According to the *Saṃyutta-nikāya* parallel, progress towards Nirvāṇa takes place by seeing the aggregates as they really are, which leads to becoming disenchanted, to becoming dispassionate, and to becoming liberated.[15] In short, not identifying with any aspect of experience —

---

14 SĀ 34 at T II 7c24 to 8a2.

15 SN 22.59 at SN III 68,20 (translated Bodhi 2000: 902); for a survey of the other parallels cf. Anālayo 2014e: 5 n.3.

be this body, feeling, perception, formations, or consciousness — is the path to freedom.

As the final part of the *Āneñjasappāya-sutta* and its parallels make amply clear, implementing insight into not-self requires avoiding identification with one's meditative experiences. Final liberation takes place when one does not turn meditation experience, however refined it may be, into a prop for creating a sense of identity (*sakkāya*).

The term *sakkāya* conveys the sense of something that makes up one's "identity" or "personality". The term occurs on its own, or else in combination with "view". Such "view of identity" (*sakkāyadiṭṭhi*) can according to the standard exposition in the early discourses arise in twenty different modes of positing a self in relation to the five aggregates. Here is an exposition of these twenty modes from the *Madhyama-āgama* parallel to the *Cūḷavedalla-sutta*:

> One sees bodily form as the self, or one sees the self as owning bodily form, or one sees bodily form as contained within the self, or one sees the self as contained within bodily form. One sees feeling ... perception ... formations ... consciousness as the self, or one sees the self as possessing consciousness, or one sees consciousness as contained within the self, or one sees the self as contained within consciousness. This is reckoned identity view.[16]

So the view of identity or personality comes about in these basic four patterns, with any of the aggregates represented by x:

- x is self,
- self possesses x,
- x is part of self,
- self is part of x.

The dictum in the *Āneñjasappāya-sutta* and its parallels that the world is "empty of a self and empty of what belongs to a self" covers all these possible notions.

The holding of a view of identity or personality (*sakkāyadiṭṭhi*) will be overcome with stream-entry. The task of fully penetrating the truth of not-self, however, is more demanding. It requires proceeding towards a complete integration of this truth in one's mental perceptions and reactions. Full penetration of the truth of not-

16 MĀ 210 at T I 788a28 to b2, an exposition found similarly in the parallels MN 44 at MN I 300,7 (translated Ñāṇamoli 1995: 397) and D 4094 *ju* 7a2 or Q 5595 *tu* 7b7 (translated Anālayo 2012c: 43).

self goes beyond any sense of identification with the aggregates and thereby beyond any trace of clinging to a sense of "identity" (*sakkāya*). The difference between these levels of realization reached with stream-entry and full awakening respectively finds an illustration in a simile in the *Khemaka-sutta* and its *Saṃyukta-āgama* parallel. In what follows I translate the Chinese version:

> It is just like a wet-nurse who gives a cloth [used as diaper] to the launderer. With various kinds of lye and soap he washes out the dirt, yet there is still a remainder of smell. By mixing it with various kinds of fragrance he makes that disappear.
>
> In the same way, although rightly contemplating these five aggregates of clinging as not-self and not belonging to a self, still the learned noble disciple has not yet abandoned the "I am" conceit in relation to these five aggregates of clinging, the desire [related to the notion] "I am" and the underlying tendency towards "I am", has not yet fully understood it, not yet become separated from it, not yet vomited it out.[17]

The *Saṃyutta-nikāya* parallel does not mention how the cloth became dirty.[18] In its version of the simile, the problem after washing is that the cloth still smells of the washing materials. To get rid of these smells, the owners then put the cloth into a scented casket.

The simile of the dirty cloth conveys that one not only needs to go beyond explicit views of the existence of a self – the dirt – but also needs to leave behind deeply ingrained patterns of identification in the mind – the smell that still hangs around the cloth when the dirt has already been removed. Just as the smell still hangs around, so the tendency to identify with things and cling to them as mine still hangs around even after it has become indubitably clear through stream-entry that no self exists.

To proceed further does not require, however, that from seeing that there is no permanent self one has to proceed to the notion that there is nothing at all. The task of complete de-identification only requires cutting through the bondage of attachment that expresses itself in the conceit "I am this" and in grasping things as "mine". As I already mentioned in Chapter 4 in relation to compassion,[19] according to

17 SĀ 103 at T II 30b24 to b29 (translated Anālayo 2014f: 9) – the translation is based on two emendations; cf. Anālayo 2014f: 9 n.16 and n.17.
18 SN 22.89 at SN III 131,8 (translated Bodhi 2000: 945).
19 See above p.97.

later tradition no living beings really exist that one could rightfully take as the object of one's compassion. In early Buddhist thought, however, not-self does not mean there are no living beings at all. It only means that living beings have no permanent self.

Applied to the present context of "nothingness", in spite of the connotations the term carries when taken on its own, the task is not to arrive at the notion that nothing exists at all. The very fact that nothingness is being experienced shows that something is still there, namely the conditioned and impermanent flow of awareness that experiences the perception of nothingness. What should be clear, however, is that this flow is not one's self. One should not identify even with this sublime experience, nor hold on to it with a sense of ownership as "mine".

### VI.4 NEITHER-PERCEPTION-NOR-NON-PERCEPTION

From the perception of nothingness, the *Cūḷasuññata-sutta* continues the gradual entry into emptiness with what corresponds to the fourth of the immaterial spheres, neither-perception-nor-non-perception. This is not mentioned at all in the two parallel versions.

When evaluating this difference, it needs to be kept in mind that the present depiction of a gradual entry into emptiness employs the perceptions that correspond to the immaterial spheres for the purpose of insight. The meditative progression is not just about attaining these immaterial spheres. Now the fact that elsewhere the early discourses regularly mention all four together could easily have resulted in an addition of the fourth to a passage that originally had only three. Such an addition would be a natural occurrence in an oral transmission. Conversely, it seems difficult to imagine, if originally there were indeed all four, why the fourth immaterial sphere would have been consciously deleted; and an accidental loss also seems unlikely.

In the case of another discourse, the *Mahāmāluṅkyaputta-sutta*, the Pāli and Chinese versions agree on relating insight contemplation only to the four absorptions and the first three immaterial attainments. They thus proceed up to nothingness, without continuing further to the attainment of neither-perception-nor-non-perception.[20]

---

20 MN 64 at MN I 436,28 (translated Ñāṇamoli 1995: 541) and its parallel MĀ 205 at T I 780a17.

The same is also the case for the *Aṭṭhakanāgara-sutta*, which describes different "doors to the deathless", that is, meditative approaches to full awakening. These can be based on the four absorptions, the four *brahmavihāra*s, and the first three of the immaterial spheres. The *Aṭṭhakanāgara-sutta* stops its exposition with the sphere of nothingness.[21] Its two Chinese parallels continue, however, and mention also the fourth immaterial sphere.[22]

According to a statement made in an *Aṅguttara-nikāya* discourse, penetration to liberating knowledge can take place only as far as an attainment involves perception.[23] Although no parallels to this discourse are known, a similar statement can be found as a discourse quotation in the *Dharmaskandha* and in the *Abhidharmasamuccaya*.[24] The *Yogācārabhūmi* somewhat similarly explains that, in contrast to the attainment of nothingness, neither-perception-nor-non-perception cannot be used to eradicate the influxes (*āsava*).[25] These sources agree that the fourth immaterial attainment, being neither fully a perception nor fully not a perception, is too subtle for insight purposes.

This in turn suggests the possibility that, in the case of the Chinese parallels to the *Aṭṭhakanāgara-sutta*, the reference to the fourth immaterial attainment was added mechanically, by way of conforming to the complete set of four immaterial attainments.[26]

In the case of the gradual entry into emptiness, the same possibility holds. On this assumption, the Chinese and Tibetan parallels to the *Cūḷasuññata-sutta* would have preserved a preferable version of the gradual entry into emptiness in this respect, in as much as they do not bring in neither-perception-nor-non-perception.

A similar problem comes up also with the next step, where the Pāli version brings up the signless concentration twice, whereas in the parallel versions it occurs only once. This part of the *Cūḷasuññata-sutta* thereby no longer conforms to the pattern observed throughout the rest of the discourse. In the rest of the discourse, each step involves overcoming a particular weariness, which then leads on to a different type of perception. This is not the case in the present passage.

21 MN 52 at MN I 352,18 (translated Ñāṇamoli 1995: 458).
22 MĀ 217 at T I 802b27 and T 92 at T I 916c8.
23 AN 9.36 at AN IV 426,9 (translated Bodhi 2012: 1301).
24 T 1537 at T XXVI 494b3 and Pradhan 1950: 69,15.
25 T 1579 at T XXX 859a13; cf. in more detail the discussion in Schmithausen 1981: 224 and 229.
26 Cf. also Maithrimurthi 1999: 97 n.136.

Moreover, already the first occurrence of the signless concentration in the *Cūḷasuññata-sutta* mentions the body and the six senses together with the life faculty as what still remains as a disturbance or weariness at this point.[27] In the parallel versions, such a reference occurs only when full liberation has been reached. This seems indeed the more meaningful placing. Once such liberation has been reached, sensory experience and the presence of the body are indeed the only forms of weariness or disturbance left.

Based on the above considerations, it seems to me preferable to follow the progression of the gradual entry into emptiness as described in the Chinese and Tibetan versions. This proceeds from nothingness to signlessness, and then onwards to realization. In what follows I examine these two steps.

## VI.5 SIGNLESSNESS

The instructions for signlessness in the *Madhyama-āgama* parallel to the *Cūḷasuññata-sutta* are as follows.

> Again, Ānanda, if ... one wishes to dwell much in emptiness ... one should not give attention to the perception of the sphere of infinite consciousness and not give attention to the perception of the sphere of nothingness, but should frequently give attention to the unitary <signless> concentration of the mind.
>
> In this way one knows that this is empty of the perception of the sphere of infinite consciousness and empty of the perception of the sphere of nothingness. Yet there is this non-emptiness: just the unitary <signless> concentration of the mind.
>
> [One knows]: "Whatever weariness because of the perception of the sphere of infinite consciousness there might be – that is not present for me; whatever weariness because of the perception of the sphere of nothingness there might be – that is also not present for me. There is only the weariness because of the unitary <signless> concentration of the mind."
>
> Whatever is not present, one therefore sees as empty; whatever else is present, one sees as truly present. Ānanda, this is called truly dwelling in emptiness, without distortion.[28]

27 MN 121 at MN III 108,4 (translated Ñāṇamoli 1995: 969).
28 MĀ 190 at T I 737c1 to c9.

In the passage above I have put the term "signless" in angle brackets. This is to mark it as an emendation on my part of what in the original is a reference to "non-perception". In Chinese texts in general there is a recurrent confusion between the characters for "sign" and for "perception".[29] The two Chinese characters look similar and are similarly pronounced. Since they also tend to occur in similar contexts, it is not surprising that they sometimes get mixed up with each other. This clearly seems to be the case here; in fact the Pāli and Tibetan parallels use the expression "signless".[30]

The term "sign" renders the Pāli word *nimitta*. A *nimitta* is a sign in the sense that it can refer to the outward characteristic mark of things. These characteristics are the signs, the sign-als, that make it possible to recognize things.

The sense of the *nimitta* as the characteristic mark of things occurs in the poem spoken by Māluṅkyaputta, for example, in which he explains the instruction also given to Bāhiya.[31] If in the seen there is only what is seen, if what is seen is limited just to seeing, then one does not grasp the *nimitta* of visible forms with thoughts of craving. That is, one does not grasp the outward characteristics of the form with craving.

The same term *nimitta* can also have a causal nuance. At times the Pāli discourses use *nimitta* on a par with terms like *nidāna*, *hetu*, and *paccaya*, all similarly standing for causes and conditions.[32] The same causal nuance also underlies the poem by Māluṅkyaputta, in as much as here the *nimitta*, on being grasped, causes the arising of craving and attachment. Another causal nuance of the term comes to the fore with the expressions *samathanimitta* or *samādhinimitta*, which refer to what causes one to gain tranquillity or concentration.

This causal nuance is also evident in the use of the term *nimitta* in modern-day meditation circles, where it often refers to an inner

---

29 For a survey of several cases where such confusion seems to have occurred cf. Anālayo 2011a: 274 n.54.

30 MN 121 at MN III 107,28 (translated Ñāṇamoli 1995: 968) refers to the "signless concentration of the mind", *animitta cetosamādhi*; the Tibetan version speaks of the "signless element", *mtshan ma med pa'i dbyings*, Skilling 1994: 172,5.

31 See above p.111.

32 An example for such usage can be found in AN 2.8 at AN I 82,17 (translated Bodhi 2012: 172).

experience of light or a mental vision of some meditation object.[33] Such a *nimitta* stands in a close conditional relationship to the deepening of concentration; attending to it can become the cause for gaining mental tranquillity.

In relation to the process of perception in general, the *nimitta* is what causes one to recognize something. An illustrative example for this function of the *nimitta* can be gathered from a situation depicted in the *Raṭṭhapāla-sutta*. Raṭṭhapāla had gone forth against the wish of his parents. After a long time had passed, he decided to visit his home town. Having arrived there, he approached his parental house while begging for alms. Seeing him from afar, his father did not recognize him and started abusing him, expressing his resentment towards these shaven-headed recluses who he felt had lured his only son away from him. Raṭṭhapāla turned around and left.

Here the father had not been able to recognize the characteristic marks, *nimitta*, of his own son, probably because he had never seen him dressed as a monk and with shaven head. In addition to the different outer attire, Raṭṭhapāla would also have been walking in a more self-restrained manner than earlier, when he was still living at home. All these differences, combined with the fact that the father only saw the monk from afar, would have made recognition difficult.

The story does not end here. A female servant left the house to throw away some stale food. Raṭṭhapāla approached her and asked that she give the food to him, instead of throwing it away. On coming close to Raṭṭhapāla to do that, the female servant recognized that this monk was the son of the head of her household. The *Raṭṭhapāla-sutta* and one of its parallels preserved in the *Madhyama-āgama* agree in using the term *nimitta* (and its Chinese equivalent) in this context, specifying that she recognized Raṭṭhapāla by the *nimitta* of his hands and feet, as well as by the *nimitta* of his voice.[34]

This shows the functioning of a *nimitta* as a central factor in the operational mechanics of memory and recognition. It is with the help of the *nimitta* that the perception aggregate is able to match information received through the senses with concepts, ideas, and memories.

33 See the detailed description in Vism 125,1 (translated Ñāṇamoli 1956/1991: 124).

34 MN 82 at MN II 62,10 (translated Ñāṇamoli 1995: 682) and MĀ 132 at T I 624c10.

From an early Buddhist viewpoint, the mere fact of using concepts is not necessarily problematic. Without some degree of conceptual recognition it would not be possible to develop wisdom and liberating insight. A problem does occur, however, when through the mirage-like ability of perception things are perceived with attachment. This happens precisely, as Māluṅkyaputta highlights in his poem, when the *nimitta* is grasped with craving.

The *nimitta* that one might grasp with craving during the perceptual process could be related to attraction or aversion. Giving attention to the *subhanimitta*, the sign of beauty or attraction, will encourage the arising of sensual desire. Giving attention to the *paṭighanimitta*, the sign of aversion or irritation, will foster the arising of anger. In order to nip both of these in the bud, the Bāhiya instruction can unfold its powerful potential.

Another problem that comes with the *nimitta* can also be illustrated with the Raṭṭhapāla story. The ability of the female servant to recognize him, although seen from afar he was not recognized even by his own father, relied on those *nimitta*s of Raṭṭhapāla that had not changed. His hairstyle, dress, and manner of walking would have been different. But the form of his hands and feet had not changed, nor had his voice.

So the ability to recognize relies in particular on those *nimitta*s that are least susceptible to change. Every successful act of recognition strengthens precisely this ability to discern those signs that are prone to remain stable. This inevitably leads to an emphasis on the most permanent aspects of experience in one's perceptual appraisal of the world. In this way, the *nimitta* as an indispensable ingredient in the basic ability to recognize can easily result in the mistaken notion that there is something permanent in things. This tendency needs to be counterbalanced by giving attention to the *nimitta* of impermanence, in the sense of intentionally directing attention to the characteristic of change.

The absence of any *nimitta* features as a form of concentration, *animitta cetosamādhi*. The basic procedure to arrive at such "signless concentration" is described in the *Mahāvedalla-sutta* and its *Madhyama-āgama* parallel. The instructions are that one should not give any attention to signs, and instead give attention to the signless element.[35]

35 MN 43 at MN I 296,33 (translated Ñāṇamoli 1995: 393) and its parallel MĀ 211 at T I 792b12 (this is another instance where the Chinese text confounds "sign" with "perception"). For a detailed study of signless concentrations cf. Harvey 1986.

Drawing out the implications of this succinct indication, the first part of the instruction to avoid giving attention to any sign seems to be similar to the Bāhiya instruction. When cultivating signless concentration, however, the absence of any mental proliferation and reaction is taken to such a level that this leads to a concentrated mental condition utterly devoid of any concept or notion whatsoever.

The second part, according to which attention should be given to the signless element, reflects a subtle but important difference between the experiences of signlessness and of neither-perception-nor-non-perception. In the latter case, perception itself has been subdued to such an extent that it becomes difficult to say whether it is there or not. In the case of signless concentration, however, perception is not subdued. But the object of perception is an absence, namely the absence of any sign.

In the context of the gradual entry into emptiness, attending to signless concentration thus continues the trajectory of abstraction already evident in the previous steps. From infinite space via infinite consciousness and nothingness to signlessness, the meditative progression at the present juncture involves a thorough degree of abstraction that dispenses with all concepts. Even the notion that the whole world is empty of a self and what belongs to a self has to be left behind at this point.

Such leaving behind finds an illustration in the famous parable of the raft.[36] Just as the raft is to be left behind, once it has fulfilled its purpose of allowing one to cross over a river, similarly even the core teaching of early Buddhism on not-self is only meant to lead over to the other shore. It is not something to be clung to and then carried around on one's head, so to speak. At this juncture, the gradual entry into emptiness arrives at an experience of emptiness that even dispenses with the concept of emptiness.

The absence of *nimitta*s is also characteristic of the experience of Nirvāṇa, together with the characteristics of desirelessness and emptiness. Contact with signlessness will also be experienced on emerging from the attainment of the cessation of perception and feeling.[37] In terms of the *Udānavarga* verse I took up in Chapter 4,

---

36 The parable of the raft is found in MN 22 at MN I 134,30 (translated Ñāṇamoli 1995: 228) and its parallels MĀ 200 at T I 764b19, EĀ 43.5 at T II 760a13, and D 4094 *nyu* 74b6 or Q *thu* 119b7.

37 MN 44 at MN I 302,22 (translated Ñāṇamoli 1995: 400) and its parallels MĀ 211 at T I 792a19 and D 4094 *ju* 9a6 or Q 5595 *tu* 10a8. The parallel versions

the range or pasture of those who are fully liberated is empty and signless.[38]

These indications make it clear that the signless concentration of the mind points to an experience that draws very close to the experience of Nirvāṇa. Understood in this way, in practical terms the present stage in the gradual entry into emptiness would require letting go of all signs and inclining the mind towards Nirvāṇa.

A simile in the *Mahāvacchagotta-sutta* and its parallels helps to appreciate the idea of inclining the mind towards Nirvāṇa. The simile expresses the conviction of a non-Buddhist wanderer that the Buddha's teaching is complete in all respects, after he found out that substantial numbers of monks and nuns, as well as male and female lay practitioners, had reached high levels of liberation. After delivering the simile, the wanderer went forth as a Buddhist monk and also became an arahant.

Here is the simile illustrating how the teachings given by the Buddha incline towards Nirvāṇa, translated from one of the *Saṃyukta-āgama* parallels:

> It is just as when a great rain falls from the sky and flowing downwards the water current pours into the great ocean. Your teaching is also like this. Male or female, young or old, even those very old, on receiving the rain of the Buddha's teaching for a long time completely incline towards Nirvāṇa.[39]

The *Majjhima-nikāya* version of this simile speaks more specifically of the river Gaṅges inclining towards the ocean.[40] Applying this simile to the present context of signlessness as a step in the gradual entry into emptiness, one lets go of all involvement with signs to allow the natural flow of this inclination towards the signless to lead one onwards to Nirvāṇa. Such inclining is a natural process that can begin like a small brook, after having received the great rain of the

---

of this discourse disagree on the other two contacts experienced, which according to MN 44 are empty contact and desireless contact, whereas the Chinese and Tibetan versions list imperturbable contact and nothingness contact.

38 See above p.96.

39 SĀ² 198 at T II 446c17 to c19.

40 MN 73 at MN I 493,24 (translated Ñāṇamoli 1995: 599). Another parallel, SĀ 964 at T II 247a15, describes just the water of a great rain flowing downwards, without explicitly mentioning either the river Gaṅges or the ocean.

teachings. In the course of time even the small brook will become a powerful river that irreversibly flows towards the great ocean of the realization of Nirvāṇa.

It needs pointing out, however, that experiencing concentration on the signless does not in itself imply having already reached final liberation. In terms of the simile from the *Mahāvacchagotta-sutta* and its parallels, even a mighty river is not yet the ocean. Another simile that employs various qualities of the ocean to illustrate the Buddha's teaching indicates that, just as all the water in the ocean is pervaded by salt, in the same way all the teachings are pervaded by the flavour of liberation.[41] Applied to the present context, signlessness inclining towards Nirvāṇa still lacks the salty quality of liberation. This will only manifest when the river has poured into the ocean and all its water becomes pervaded by the salty taste of sea water.

That concentration on the signless falls short of being in itself liberating also becomes clear from a discourse in the *Aṅguttara-nikāya* and its *Madhyama-āgama* parallel. In what follows I translate the relevant section from the *Madhyama-āgama*:

> Perhaps one person attains signless concentration of the mind. Having attained signless concentration of the mind, such a one dwells being at peace and does not strive further with a wish to attain what has not yet been attained, with a wish to gain what has not yet been gained, with a wish to realize what has not yet been realized.
>
> At a later time, such a one associates much with secular people, makes fun, becomes conceited, and engages in all sorts of boisterous talk. As such a one associates much with secular people, makes fun, becomes conceited, and engages in all sorts of boisterous talk, sensual desire arises in the mind. Sensual desire having arisen in such a one's mind, the body and the mind become heated up [with passion]. The body and the mind being heated up [with passion], such a one abandons the moral precepts and stops [practising] the path.[42]

---

41 AN 8.19 at AN IV 203,7 (translated Bodhi 2012: 1144). One parallel, MĀ 35 at T I 476c11 (translated Anālayo 2013c: 251), mentions the flavours of dispassion, realization, appeasement, and awakening; in another parallel, EĀ 42.4 at T II 753a28, the flavour of the ocean illustrates the noble eightfold path.

42 MĀ 82 at T I 559a21 to a27.

The parallel in the *Aṅguttara-nikāya* does not mention making fun and becoming conceited, or engaging in boisterous talk.[43] Alongside such minor differences, however, the two discourses agree in illustrating the predicament of this practitioner with a simile that takes up the chirping of crickets in a forest. If a king and his army come to stay overnight in the forest, there will be all kinds of sound and the crickets will no longer be heard. Yet it would be wrong to come to the conclusion that the chirping of crickets will never be heard again. When the king and his army have left and the place has become quiet, the chirping of crickets will again be audible.

The warning sounded in this passage is quite relevant for the gradual entry into emptiness. However profound a particular experience of emptiness may be, it is bound to change. Even if this experience was as powerful as the arrival of a king with his army, it does not follow that, because defilements do not manifest at that time, they could not emerge again afterwards. Even the most powerful experience of emptiness is bound to change, just as the king and his army are bound to move on. It is not the powerfulness of the experience of emptiness that really matters, but its effect in completely removing the chirping of the crickets in one's mind. How to make sure that the chirping of the crickets does not get a chance to manifest again in one's mind is the theme of the final step in the gradual entry into emptiness.

### VI.6 REALIZATION OF EMPTINESS

Here is the *Madhyama-āgama* version of the progression of practice after signless concentration has been attained, which provides the finishing touch to the gradual entry into emptiness:

> One thinks: "My [experience] of the <signless> concentration of the mind is rooted – it is rooted in formations, it is rooted in intentions. What is rooted in formations, rooted in intentions, I do not delight in that, I do not seek that, I should not become established in that."
>
> Knowing in this way, seeing in this way, one's mind is liberated from the influx of sensual desire, [one's mind is liberated] from the

43 AN 6.60 at AN III 397,13 (translated Bodhi 2012: 949). AN 6.60 gives more detailed information regarding the various persons such a practitioner of signless concentration associates with. These could be monks or nuns, male or female lay disciples, but also kings and ministers, as well as other teachers and their disciples.

> influx of existence, and one's mind is liberated from the influx of ignorance. Being liberated, one knows one is liberated. One knows as it really is that birth has been extinguished, the holy life has been established, what had to be done has been done, there will be no experiencing of further existence.
>
> In this way one knows that this is empty of the influx of sensual desire, empty of the influx of existence, and empty of the influx of ignorance. Yet there is this non-emptiness: just this body of mine with its six sense-spheres and the life faculty.
>
> [One knows]: "Whatever weariness because of the influx of sensual desire there might be – that is not present for me; whatever weariness because of the influx of existence [there might be – that is also not present for me; whatever weariness] because of the influx of ignorance there might be – that is also not present for me. There is only the weariness because of this body of mine with its six sense-spheres and the life faculty."
>
> Whatever is not present, one therefore sees as empty; whatever else is present, one sees as truly present.
>
> Ānanda, this is called truly dwelling in emptiness, without distortion, namely the eradication of the influxes, the influx-free and unconditioned liberation of the mind.[44]

The actual insight contemplation used for the breakthrough to full liberation in the *Cūḷasuññata-sutta* differs in so far as it involves directing attention to the conditioned and therefore impermanent nature of the signless concentration of the mind.[45] The Tibetan version is similar to the above-translated passage from the *Madhyama-āgama*.

The main point that emerges here is the realization that the experience of signlessness is still within the realm of what is conditioned. However much this experience is aloof from all involvement with any sign and free from any concepts, it nevertheless is still just something created by one's own mind. It is a product fabricated by one's own intentions.

This realization reveals that this experience is impermanent, as made explicitly clear in the Pāli version. What is conditioned and impermanent is not really fit for being clung to with delight, as noted

44 MĀ 190 at T I 737c9 to c21.
45 MN 121 at MN III 108,15 (translated Ñāṇamoli 1995: 969).

in the Chinese and Tibetan versions. The point made in different but complementary ways by the parallels could perhaps best be summarized with the term *virāga*. This term stands for "dispassion" (= absence of delight) as well as for "fading away" (= impermanence). From a practical perspective, impermanence and the absence of delight can be considered as two sides of the same coin.

Becoming dispassionate with what is impermanent and conditioned then enables the breakthrough to full liberation. At this point the only weariness left, if it can even be called such, is simply the continuity of life, symbolized by the body and the senses.

The *Cūḷasuññata-sutta* and its Tibetan parallel make a point of qualifying the destruction of the influxes as the "unsurpassable" manifestation of emptiness.[46] This is what emptiness is really about, namely voiding the mind of all defilements. With such unsurpassable emptiness reached, the chirping of the crickets has been silenced for good. The mind has become truly silent.

The three versions highlight that whoever in past, present, or future times have dwelled, now dwell, or will dwell in supreme emptiness, all dwell in this same type of emptiness. The discourse concludes with the Buddha encouraging Ānanda to put into practice this gradual entry into emptiness.

### VI.7 THE DYNAMICS OF EMPTINESS

By way of rounding off my study of the various steps of the gradual entry into emptiness, at this point I would like to summarize the entire meditative trajectory and the significance of each step.[47] Here are the main steps:

1) empty of animals and wealth, but not empty of the monastic community,

---

46 MN 121 at MN III 109,1 and Skilling 1994: 178,2. The same is implicit also in the presentation in MĀ 190 at T I 737c21 which, in agreement with its parallel, indicates that all those who truly realize emptiness do so by realizing the destruction of the influxes.

47 Skilling 2007: 240 points out that the gradual entry into emptiness "was fundamental to the development of emptiness in Yogācāra and Tathāgatagarbha thought". Although within the scope of my present study I am unable to follow up subsequent developments, it is noteworthy that a series of emptiness meditations described in Khenpo 1986/1988 shows considerable affinity with stages in the gradual entry into emptiness as delineated in MN 121 and its parallels.

2) empty of people (including monastics), but not empty of forest,
3) empty of forest, but not empty of earth,
4) empty of earth (as solidity), but not empty of infinite space,
5) empty of infinite space, but not empty of infinite consciousness,
6) empty of infinite consciousness, but not empty of nothingness,
7) empty of nothingness, but not empty of signlessness,
8) empty of influxes, but not empty of the body with the six senses and the life faculty.

1) The first of these steps directs attention to the present situation, taking this as a stepping stone for a gradual entry into emptiness. With this step, a unifying feature found in the monastic dwelling place receives attention, namely the presence of the other monks. With their shaven heads and similar robes the monks can be viewed to some degree as a unitary object. This unified vision stands in contrast to the variegated perceptions one would have when being in a village and seeing various animals etc.

2) With the second step, the unitary perception of the monks is replaced by a similarly unitary perception that is based on something more stable than the monks. The perception of the forest is also more encompassing, since the entirety of the landscape can be included under the heading of the perception of forest, whereas the earlier perception of monks took up a more limited object out of the present situation.

On a symbolic level, the perception of the forest brings in the theme of seclusion, an important foundation for cultivating the deeper levels of mental tranquillity and insight that the subsequent steps in the gradual entry into emptiness require. Overall, a shift towards a more comprehensive and stable perception appears to be a key aspect at this stage.

3) The third step proceeds from forest to earth. The progression takes place by disregarding any variation, such as different aspects of the vegetation or irregularities in the earth's surface. Instead one develops a perception of earth from a unitary viewpoint, as if the earth had been made completely straight like a stretched hide or like looking at the flat palm of one's hand. The task is to proceed to a

perception of earth as such, representative of the notion of solidity.

From this juncture onwards, the modes of viewing begin to employ abstraction. The employment of an abstract concept that to some extent goes beyond what is perceived by the eye – in the present case the notion of solidity – appears to be a distinct contribution of this particular step.

4) Next the notion of solidity is replaced by infinite space. This part of the gradual entry into emptiness follows the meditative trajectory of the immaterial spheres. The unitary perception of earth *qua* solidity is now replaced by attending to the space that had been taken up by this perception of earth, which by further development then results in the perception of infinite space.

In this way, the experience of matter is left behind and one's meditative experience is pervaded by a sense of there being no obstruction or limits anywhere. Cultivating this meditative step in the gradual entry into emptiness has the potential to deconstruct the mind's tendency to perceive material objects as if they were solid and independently existing in their own right, endowed with intrinsic qualities like beauty or ugliness, etc.

5) The next step follows the same dynamic that underlies a progression through the immaterial attainments, which now requires turning attention to the mind itself. Letting go of the notion of space and turning attention to the mind that has been aware of space enables the development of the perception of infinite consciousness.

With this step of practice, space is left behind and infinite consciousness becomes the pervasive theme of the meditative experience. This step reveals how consciousness functions as the very foundation of subjective experience. Its insight potential is to draw attention to the influence of mental projections and evaluations on one's experience, disclosing the degree to which much of it is merely mind-made.

6) With the sixth step the similarity with the immaterial attainments continues to hold, in that the experience of infinite consciousness is now attended to as something insubstantial in every respect, resulting in the notion that there is nothing. In this way, the perception of nothingness can be developed.

Following one of the options for entry into nothingness delineated in the *Āñenjasappāya-sutta* and its parallels, the reflection "this is empty of a self and what pertains to a self" could be employed to arouse the perception of nothingness. Undertaken in this way, attending to nothingness would involve the realization that there is nothing at all that could qualify as a self, nothing at all to be identified with, and nothing at all to be appropriated as one's own. A sense of disowning or dispossessing pervades this stage of the gradual entry into emptiness, whereby any notion of an "I" or "my", however subtle it may be, is left behind. The distinct feature of this step is to deepen insight into not-self.

7) The seventh step departs from the pattern set by the immaterial attainments. Instead of continuing abstraction to a point where the nature of perception itself is sublimated, the practice proceeds beyond the notion of nothingness by directing the mind to signlessness. Simply stated, attending to the signless means that those features and aspects of an object by which one recognizes things – their signs – are disregarded.

Although signlessness is one of the aspects of the experience of awakening, it can also occur in relation to various other levels of meditative experience in which the recognizing tendency of the mind has been transcended. The present stage completes the previous progression through ever more refined perceptions. The task is to let go of any notion or concept in the mind whatsoever. This is what marks this particular step.

8) With the eighth step in the gradual emptying of perception the practitioner becomes ready for the final touch of liberating insight. Central here is the recognition that the experience of signlessness is of a conditioned nature, therefore it is impermanent and one should avoid delighting in it. At this point, by giving up even the most subtle holding on to any experience of emptiness, the true realization of supreme emptiness dawns. For supreme emptiness, the preceding gradual emptying of perception formed the preparation.

Throughout this gradual progress, a crucial theme taken up at the present juncture – conditionality – was kept present in terms of the types of weariness overcome or still present because of one's meditative experience. This recurrent directing of the meditator's awareness to conditionality points to a close relationship between realization of emptiness and dependent arising.[48] With the present final step, the conditioned nature of all stages in the gradual entry into emptiness is left behind through realization of the unconditioned. What remains, after this supreme accomplishment in emptiness, is simply the continuity of life, exemplified by the body and its senses together with the life faculty.

1–8) In sum, with these different stages of transcendence a gradual refinement of experience takes place. Beginning with the present situation, the meditative progression leaves behind matter and then its complement of space. Next comes a letting go of one's identification with the experiencing mind, followed by leaving behind even the signs required for the formation of concepts. This then leads to a letting go of all emptiness experiences thus far. However sublime these may be, they are to be viewed as merely a conditioned product of the mind, so as to arrive at the supreme emptiness of liberating the mind from defilements. The previous steps require a progressive letting go within the realm of perceptual experience, and based on the dynamics cultivated in this way, the last step requires letting go of experience itself.

## VI.8 SUMMARY

The gradual entry into emptiness proceeds from infinite consciousness to the perception of nothingness, which could be implemented by contemplating that there is nothing of a self or what belongs to a self. The Chinese and Tibetan parallels to the *Cūḷasuññata-sutta* continue with signlessness, which refers to letting go of all those characteristic marks of experience with the help of which perception recognizes.

The resultant experience should be seen with insight as conditioned, and therefore as impermanent and not worth delighting in. This enables the breakthrough to supreme emptiness with full liberation, whereby the mind is forever voided of defilements.

The whole trajectory of the gradual entry into emptiness proceeds by way of a step-by-step deconstruction of the average way of experiencing the world. The gradual refinement of perception that

48 Based on a study of relevant early discourses, Shì Hùifēng 2013: 196 concludes that "emptiness and dependent origination were related as a key part of the *Dharma* from its inception."

ensues from this deconstruction proceeds by leaving behind matter, then space as a last vestige of an outer object, then the notion of a subject that experiences, and eventually any concept. The finishing touch comes through a stepping outside of perception and experience as such by realizing the supreme emptiness of full awakening.

# VII

# PRACTICAL INSTRUCTIONS

In this chapter I present one way of proceeding from the meditative practice of compassion to contemplation of emptiness. The mode of practice I describe sets compassion within the context of a cultivation of the four divine abodes, and then continues with the gradual entry into emptiness, starting with the experience of infinite space. Needless to say, my presentation is only meant to provide an inspiration for actual practice, without any claim to this being the only way one can go about it. Practitioners should feel free to adjust what I present to their personal requirements and inclinations.

## VII.1 LAYING THE FOUNDATION

The passage from the *Madhyama-āgama* parallel to the *Karajakāya-sutta*, which I translated in Chapter 1, makes it quite clear that moral conduct provides an indispensable foundation for successful meditation practice of the divine abodes.[1] Here compassion expresses itself in abstaining from activities that harm others. In combination with kindness through bodily, verbal, and mental activities, this sets the groundwork for formal practice, and at the same time is how meditation practice expresses itself outside of actual sitting.

The next level of foundation to be laid for meditation practice concerns the hindrances. The standard listing of these hindrances in the early discourses is as follows:

1 See above p.21.

1) sensual desire,
2) anger,
3) sloth-and-torpor,
4) restlessness-and-worry,
5) doubt.

The first step to be taken at this level of foundation building is honest recognition. For this purpose, I suggest to start actual meditation by briefly examining if any of these hindrances are present in the mind. At times such recognition can suffice for the hindrance to go into abeyance. If a particular hindrance manifests with some strength, however, measures need to be taken to overcome it. These could be: bringing to mind unattractive aspects of what arouses one's sensual desire (1); cultivating *mettā* to overcome anger (2); putting energy into the practice to emerge from sloth-and-torpor (3); calming the mind to leave behind restlessness-and-worry (4); and reflecting on what is wholesome and what is unwholesome to set aside doubt (5).[2]

In addition to these standard approaches for emerging from the hindrances, each of the four divine abodes can also make a contribution to keeping the hindrances at bay. Here equanimity is particularly helpful in the case of sensual desire (1), which often thrives based on a combination of visual images etc., experienced through the senses, and an inner building up of the energy of desire. Whereas giving attention to unattractive aspects of what arouses one's sensual desire can deal with the first of these two aspects, it has less impact on the second. Here the contribution made by equanimity would fall into place, as it can lead to an immediate sense of inner distancing and result in an energetic balancing that deprives sensual desire of its pushing force. Besides equanimity, which recommends itself when sensual desire has actually arisen, the other three divine abodes could also make their contribution, especially sympathetic joy. Generating wholesome forms of non-sensual joy provides a readily available source of happiness within, which deprives the search for happiness outside of its main wellspring in an inner feeling of want and discontent.

The first of the divine abodes is the standard remedy for the second hindrance of anger or ill will (2). Besides *mettā*, compassion could also be of similar assistance, since the wish for others to be free from

2 For a more detailed discussion of the five hindrances in the context of *satipaṭṭhāna* meditation cf. Anālayo 2003: 182–200 and 2013c: 177–194.

any harm or affliction directly opposes anger and ill will. Moreover, the compassionate wish for freedom from affliction for all living beings, including oneself, can become a powerful stimulation for emerging from the suffering that anger causes to oneself. As in the case of sensual desire, here, too, equanimity could lead to an inner distancing. This can be particularly useful as an immediate antidote when anger is just flaring up, a situation where the mind can come to be in a condition that would make it rather difficult to bring *mettā* or compassion into being right on the spot. Here, remaining equanimous could function as an initial buffer, to avoid reacting with anger. Once this has been achieved and the mind has become broad through radiation of equanimity as a divine abode, it will be easier to move on to radiating *mettā* or compassion.

One of the causes for the arising of sloth-and-torpor (3) is a lack of inspiration and some degree of boredom with the practice. In order to counter the resulting dullness of the mind, sympathetic joy would recommend itself due to its strong inspirational qualities. Such inspiration could gather additional support from compassion, by bringing to mind the altruistic dimension of one's own meditative practice undertaken for the sake of benefiting others. This leaves less scope for boredom to arise, compared to a form of practice that aims only at one's own benefit.

In the opposite case of restlessness-and-worry (4), the other two divine abodes of *mettā* and equanimity appear particularly apt. Here, *mettā* introduces a basic kindness towards oneself, which can go a long way in softening an attitude of excessive striving that can lead to restlessness. Equanimity would take care of worry as the other aspect of this hindrance, by introducing an inner distancing to whatever causes worry and by bringing about mental balance.

Doubt (5) can manifest in various ways, and some of its manifestations cannot be settled during the meditation session, but have to be set aside for clarification at a later time. Doubts about the meaningfulness of engaging in meditative practice, however, could be countered with compassion in particular, which, just as in the case of sloth-and-torpor, throws into relief the altruistic dimension of one's own meditative practice. As long as one's sincere intention is to benefit oneself as well as others, every step taken with such an intention is certainly meaningful and wholesome results will sooner or later naturally manifest.

## VII.2 COMPASSION AND THE OTHER DIVINE ABODES

Once no hindrance is present in the mind, it can be helpful to pause a moment with awareness of their absence and consciously rejoice in this mental condition. The discourses provide a set of similes explicitly meant for this purpose, which compare the presence of these five hindrances to being in debt, being sick, being in bondage, being a slave, and being on a dangerous journey.[3] The similes can be used as props for making the absence of the hindrances an occasion for joy. A mind free from the hindrances is comparable to having paid off a debt, having recovered from a disease, being released from bondage or slavery, and having safely completed a dangerous journey. Combining one's practice in this way with an intentional element of rejoicing in the wholesome condition of the mind makes it considerably more difficult for these hindrances to arise again later on. At the same time this offers an excellent basis for deepening concentration, which comes about naturally once a wholesome form of joy is present in the mind.

With wholesome joy present in a mind that is free from the hindrances, the arousing of the divine abodes can be undertaken in various ways. Two main approaches are based on either employing a particular phrase that expresses the sentiment of each of the *brahmavihāras*[4] or else using a mental image or picture, such as, for example, that of a baby, a puppy, a kitten, etc.[5] Whatever best arouses within oneself the mental attitude of the respective divine abode can become the starting point for the boundless radiation.

In case one decides to start with mental reflections in the form of phrases, then these are best kept short and concise right from the outset.[6] Both reflections and mental images can be skilful means to

3 DN 2 at DN I 71,31 (translated Walshe 1987: 101) and a parallel in the *Saṅghabhedavastu*, Gnoli 1978: 241,19 (translated with discussion Anālayo 2013c: 192f).

4 Salzberg 2002: 30 recommends phrases that express the wish to be free from danger, to have mental and physical happiness, and to experience the ease of well-being as a way into *mettā* meditation.

5 Brahm 2006: 66f describes using the mental image of a kitten as a starter for *mettā* meditation.

6 Indaka 2004: 7 emphasizes that "we should use as few words as possible, and the phrases or sentences should be short. The reason for this is that short clear [and] concise sentences will help to make metta powerful and strong ... if we use too many words and sentences, it will not be easy to develop strong potent metta because we will have to put a lot of effort into remembering and reciting these words ... and if the words are too seductive to fantasy, we might become entranced by the words themselves."

arouse the divine abodes; once they have fulfilled this task, however, they should be left behind. Such tools are supports meant to lead on to a stage of practice where they are no longer needed.

In the early discourses the use of phrases or images does not appear to be mentioned at all in relation to the divine abodes. Reflections do occur in relation to the practice of recollection,[7] for example, and mental images appear in relation to the cemetery contemplations as part of *satipaṭṭhāna* contemplation of the body.[8] Thus the fact that the discourses do not employ any such reflections or mental images in relation to the *brahmavihāra*s is not because such aids are not recommended at all, but rather is a characteristic of their description of the cultivation of the divine abodes. What the discourses do provide is indications of what mental states are opposed to the *brahmavihāra*s, a topic to which I return below.

A precedent for the use of phrases, however, can be found in the *Paṭisambhidāmagga*, a canonical path manual of the Theravāda tradition. In its description of *mettā*, the *Paṭisambhidāmagga* formulates a four-faceted wish directed to all living beings. Although the *Paṭisambhidāmagga* relates all of these to *mettā*, from a practical perspective it seems to me that they could be used to arouse all four *brahmavihāra*s. The four facets are wishing for all living beings to be:

- free from enmity,
- free from affliction,
- at ease,
- taking care of their own happiness.[9]

The first phrase wishes all living beings "to be free from enmity", *averā hontu*, which can refer both to harbouring enmity within and to being affected by the enmity of others. This effectively expresses the two aspects of *mettā* as protecting and being protected. Both spring from an attitude of kindness and benevolence that is ready to make friends with all those with whom one comes into contact.

The aspiration for all living beings "to be free from affliction", *avyāpajjhā hontu*, can also be taken in a twofold manner, namely as referring to the absence of being afflicted as well as of afflicting others. This allows the same interrelation of the internal and the external dimensions as in the previous case of *mettā*. The term

7 See above p.84 n.12.
8 See in more detail Anālayo 2013c: 97–116.
9 Paṭis II 130,23 (translated Ñāṇamoli 1982: 317).

*vyāpajjha* has in fact a close etymological relation to *vyāpāda*, which is precisely the mental state of ill will that wishes the affliction of others. The wish for freedom from affliction in this way succinctly expresses the main thrust of compassion.

The wish for all living beings "to be at ease", *anīghā hontu*, requires a little elaboration. Such a wish needs to be combined with an understanding of what leads to being truly at ease. Truly being at ease can only happen within the sphere of what is wholesome. Unwholesome deeds may yield momentary pleasure, but they are incapable of resulting in truly being mentally at ease. So the wish for others to be at ease best takes the form of wishing others to be at ease in wholesome ways, wanting them to find joy in doing and intending what is wholesome. This then has a close relationship to sympathetic joy.

The fourth divine abode of equanimity would find a suitable expression in the wish that all living beings "take care of their own happiness", *sukhī attānaṃ pariharantu*. The formulation makes it clear that the attitude evoked is not indifference, but rather a form of wholesome equanimity that allows others to take responsibility and do what they wish to do, without attempting to interfere. But at the same time one still wishes them happiness.

With these four phrases, which could be used in the original Pāli, in translation, or in whatever formulation best suits one's personal preferences, the mind could be stimulated to dwell in the corresponding *brahmavihāra*. As already mentioned above, eventually any phrase should be given up and one just dwells in the respective divine abode as such.

Alternatively, one might simply use the term of the *brahmavihāra* itself that one intends to cultivate. Briefly bringing to mind the word *mettā* could then become the basis for actually dwelling in the corresponding divine abode, and the same procedure can be used for *karuṇā*, *muditā*, and *upekkhā* respectively.

For progress on the path of mental purification, it can be quite helpful if the arousing of the divine abodes comes together with a reminder of those mental obstructions that each *brahmavihāra* is in particular opposed to. As mentioned above, indications regarding the mental states opposed to the divine abodes are already found in the discourses. In the case of *mettā*, this would mean paying attention to the fact that dwelling in this *brahmavihāra* one is without any ill will.

Compassion, *karuṇā*, implies having overcome any form of cruelty. Sympathetic joy, *muditā*, is to remain aloof from envy and discontent. Equanimity, *upekkhā*, entails being unmoved by any lust (as well as by any aversion). Paying attention to the mental obstructions that have been overcome can help to actualize the liberating potential of the *brahmavihāra*s and strengthen one's resolve to avoid succumbing to their opposites.

When due to prolonged distraction the divine abode has been completely lost, whatever aid one has used to arouse the *brahmavihāra* can be brought in again briefly to re-establish one's meditative dwelling. But the actual form of practice, when momentum has been established, is just to be with a mind that is imbued with *mettā*, compassion, sympathetic joy, and equanimity. With progressive practice, whatever tool one may have chosen will come to be used less and less, until it eventually becomes possible to arouse each *brahmavihāra* at will, without any need to formulate words or bring to mind images.

The actual experience of each divine abode has a distinct feel to it, and it is familiarity with this distinct feel that will eventually enable a practitioner to arouse each *brahmavihāra* without needing to rely on phrases or images. To illustrate this distinct quality of each divine abode and their radiation in all directions, I would like to propose a simile based on the sun. This simile is based on imagining that one is in a place that has a cool climate, where sunshine is experienced as something pleasant and agreeable rather than as something oppressive.

An aspect of the simile relevant to all four *brahmavihāra*s is based on the way sunlight originates. In the centre of the sun a constant process of thermonuclear fusion takes place. This fusion results in the release of photons whose motion out into space is responsible for the phenomenon of sunlight.

In actual meditation practice there is a similar combination of an inward fusion of the mind in concentration that results in the outward radiation of each of the *brahmavihāra*s. The more the mind is fused in deep concentration, the more powerful and pervasive the radiation of any *brahmavihāra* becomes.

Regarding the distinct quality of each divine abode in the context of the sun simile, *mettā* would be like the sun at midday in a cloudless sky, illuminating everything equally and providing warmth in all directions. Just as the sun shines on what is high and low, clean and dirty, so *mettā* shines on all without making distinctions. The sun keeps shining independently of how its rays are received. It does not shine more if people move out into the open to be warmed by its rays, nor does it shine less because people move back indoors. Similarly, *mettā* does not depend on reciprocation. Its rays of kindness shine on others out of an inner strength that pervades all bodily activities, words, and thoughts, without expecting a return. From the centre of one's heart *mettā* shines its rays on anyone encountered, just as the sun shines in all directions from its position in the midst of the sky.

Compassion in turn would be like the sun just before sunset. Darkness is close, almost palpably close, yet the sun keeps shining. In fact it shines all the more brilliantly, beautifully colouring the sky at sunset. Similarly, when being face to face with suffering and affliction, the mental attitude of compassion shines even more brilliantly, undeterred by all the darkness found in the world. At sunset the sun appears as if it were moving downwards. So, too, compassion is willing to reach out to those in a less fortunate position.

Continuing with the sun imagery, sympathetic joy would be comparable to sunrise in the early morning. The birds are singing merrily, the air is fresh, and the surroundings are illuminated by the rising sun and appear as if pervaded by joyful delight. At times the rays of the sun touch a dewdrop on a flower or tree and break into a myriad of colours. In the same way, the joy of others can become the source of a myriad of joyful rejoicings within oneself. At sunrise the sun appears as if it were moving on an upward trajectory. This mirrors the disposition of sympathetic joy to direct positive feelings towards those who are in a better position than oneself.

The fourth of the divine abodes, equanimity, is then like the full moon on a cloudless night. Just as the sun and moon are both up in the vast sky, in the same way the four *brahmavihāra*s share with each other the boundless nature of a mind that has become vast like the sky. The moon is not itself a source of sunlight, unlike the sun. So, too, equanimity is not actively involved with others in the way the other three *brahmavihāra*s are. At the same time, however, the moon does reflect the light of the sun, just as equanimity reflects within itself the positive disposition of the other divine abodes.

### VII.3 THE RADIATION PRACTICE

Proceeding from the initial arousing of the divine abodes to their boundless radiation, it may be advisable to engage with each of the *brahmavihāra*s for some time, until each is well established, before moving on to the next one. This will soon give place to a practice that effortlessly moves through all four divine abodes even in a short sitting.

The arising of *mettā* can be physically felt as a warm feeling of softness located somewhere in the centre of the chest.[10] So one simply allows the *mettā* that wells up from the heart to radiate in the different directions. Actual practice of the radiation begins by pervading the front, then the direction to the right, the back, and the left. Having in this way established pervasion of the four directions one radiates *mettā* upwards and then downwards. Here is the instruction again from the *Madhyama-āgama* parallel to the *Karajakāya-sutta*, for ease of reference:[11]

> One dwells having pervaded one direction with a mind imbued with *mettā*, and in the same way the second, third, and fourth directions, the four intermediate directions, above and below, completely and everywhere.

Such *mettā* radiation is something very soft and gentle, instead of being a forceful pushing out into these directions. The nature of the radiation could be compared to a source of light that is surrounded by a curtain on all sides. To allow the light to shine in all directions, one slowly and softly pulls away the curtain. It does not matter at all how far the light of *mettā* is able to shine right now. The task is only one of removing any boundary, of allowing it to be boundless. With continued practice, the inner light will shine with increasing strength and its illumination will spread further. However short or far it may spread, the basic condition of a temporary liberation of the mind is reached as soon as the radiation has become boundless in all directions.

Next one simply remains in the spaciousness of the mental liberation by *mettā*, without paying further attention to individual

---

10 Vimalaraṃsi 2012: 144 speaks of "radiating the warm-glowing feeling of Loving-kindness", which he indicates has its physical reference point "in the center of your chest".

11 See below p.172.

directions. In terms of my simile, the curtains having been gently pulled away, now the light just keeps shining in all directions. Here is the next part of the canonical instruction for ease of reference:

> Being without mental shackles, resentment, ill will, or contention, with a mind imbued with *mettā* that is supremely vast and great, boundless and well developed, one dwells having pervaded the entire world.

Within such spaciousness of the mind, any distraction, even the momentary arising of irritation or of any other hindrance, has no chance to remain. As soon as a distraction is noticed, one just allows the mind to return to its condition of spaciousness within which the mental narrowness that accompanies the defilement simply vanishes.

After long periods of dedicated practice, with increasing degrees of mental stillness, eventually entry into absorption can take place, based on the mental feeling of *mettā*.[12] The same procedure then applies to the other three divine abodes, where one similarly radiates compassion, sympathetic joy, and equanimity in all directions.

So the main steps in the meditative practice of the divine abodes described here are as follows:

1) arouse the divine abode, perhaps with the help of a reflection or a mental image,
2) allow the divine abode to well up from the heart,
3) allow the divine abode to radiate into the various directions,
4) rest in the condition of the boundless radiation of the divine abode.

Some may prefer to engage with all of the four divine abodes in an equal manner, dedicating roughly identical time periods to cultivating each of them. For those who wish to give predominance to compassion instead, it would nevertheless be advisable to devote some time also to the other three to ensure the best possible

---

12 Brahm 2006: 71 describes progress to absorption attainment with *mettā* based on the mind being "freed from the perception of separate beings. All that remains in your mind is what I call disembodied mettā ... you experience this as a blissful sphere of gorgeous golden light in your mind's eye. It is a nimitta. It's the mettā nimitta ... its nature is so alluring that you cannot resist hanging out with such intense bliss. Thus, in a short time the brilliant golden mettā nimitta becomes still and you fall into jhāna. This is how mettā meditation takes you into jhāna."

conditions for a flowering of compassion. In practical terms, in such a case I would recommend dedicating as much time of actual sitting practice to the other three *brahmavihāra*s together as one spends on compassion.

Those who wish to add a further insight component to this radiation practice can do so by combining this form of practice with a cultivation of the awakening factors. These are:

1) mindfulness,
2) investigation-of-dharmas,
3) energy,
4) joy,
5) tranquillity,
6) concentration,
7) equanimity.

In the context of such a cultivation of a divine abode, mindfulness (1) functions as the foundation through the presence of awareness during the actual arousing of the divine abode. The establishing of the divine abode in the mind will then be monitored with investigation (2), which stands for an attitude of interested observation. Such investigation needs to be sufficiently energized (3) so as to be continuous, able to alert one to any loss of the boundless radiation immediately. This energetic investigation then should be gentle so that it leads to joy (4), instead of resulting in mental tension. The wholesome joy arisen in this way should not become too exhilarating, but should remain a soothing type of joy that leads to tranquillity (5). Tranquillity of body and mind naturally lead onwards to a concentrated state of mind (6). The establishing of the awakening factors then culminates in mental equipoise (7).

In this way, one can cultivate the seven awakening factors while dwelling in a divine abode. At first it can appear somewhat demanding to keep monitoring seven mental factors alongside the actual radiation practice. In this case, just combining mindfulness with a sustained interest can suffice as a foundation. Once this becomes effortless, one might add to this an aiming at equipoise. With more familiarity in the cultivation of the awakening factors through repeated practice, it will eventually become possible to cultivate all seven effortlessly while doing one's *brahmavihāra* practice.

For these seven awakening factors to issue in liberating insight, they need to be combined with these four insight-related themes:

1) in dependence on seclusion,
2) in dependence on dispassion,
3) in dependence on cessation,
4) leading to letting go.

So once the time to dwell in the radiation comes close to its end, one remains in a condition of the mind that is secluded (1) from the hindrances and in which the awakening factors are still present. One then arouses dispassion (2) in regard to the sublime experience of temporary mental liberation just experienced, realizing that this beautiful mental experience of radiating a divine abode in all directions, however profound, concentrated, joyful, and balanced it may have been, is just as all other mental states: it is bound to cease (3). However peaceful any particular meditative experience may have been, one is willing to let go of it (4).

### VII.4 EMPTINESS MEDITATION

Instead of concluding the meditative cultivation of the divine abodes in this way, however, it is also possible to move on to the gradual entry into emptiness. Since with the practice of the divine abodes the mind has already been unified – a condition that in the gradual entry into emptiness takes place through the first steps up to the perception of earth – practice could directly move on to the perception of infinite space. As mentioned earlier, the gradual entry into emptiness seems to require only the cultivation of the perception of infinite space, not the full attainment of the sphere of infinite space.

In actual practice the transition from the boundless radiation of the fourth divine abode of equanimity to the perception of the infinite space that has been pervaded by this divine abode is surprisingly seamless – more so in fact than the transitions from one *brahmavihāra* to the next, or the transitions between the successive steps in the gradual entry into emptiness. All of these transitions involve a shift from one attitude or perception to another that is quite distinct. In the present transition, however, the difference is only that with the fourth divine abode the focus has been more on the attitude of equanimity that informs the boundlessness, whereas with infinite space the focus is more on the boundlessness that has been reached through dwelling in equanimity.

So the experience of infinite space can be aroused by directing attention to the boundless space that has been pervaded with the divine abode of equanimity. At times the transition may be so smooth that one is able to dwell immediately in the boundless condition of infinite space. At other times, in order to establish oneself firmly in the perception of infinite space, the same procedure could be used as employed previously with the divine abodes. In this way, one becomes aware of space in front, to the right, to the back, to the left, above and below. Similar to the pattern for the divine abodes, from becoming aware of space in the different directions, practice then proceeds to a stage where one just dwells in total spaciousness that is infinite and boundless, without any limit whatsoever.

When beginning with this type of practice, it might be easier to attend to these directions first, and only then turn attention to one's own body and allow that to dissolve as well. The reason is that actual space in front of oneself can more easily be experienced as space than the body, which one is so accustomed to viewing as solid. Once through repeated practice one has acquired some familiarity with the perception of infinite space, however, it will become easy to allow one's own body to dissolve into space as well.

The same procedure of starting with the body is also helpful when a distraction arises. In this way one first of all comes back to the body as a way of anchoring oneself in the present moment and then lets the body dissolve into space, after which one allows the resultant spaciousness to pervade all directions. By moving in this way from the internal to the external dimension of the perception of infinite space, it becomes easy to stabilize the mind and avoid it succumbing to another distraction.

With brief distractions it will be possible to return immediately to the experience of infinite space. The need to establish this experience through directional pervasion only arises when a distraction has been of the longer type and the mind does not naturally and effortlessly return to its spacious condition.

If a distraction has been long and intense, and the mind has really been taken for a long ride, it can be advisable to move briefly through the preceding step that one has taken to arrive at infinite space. In this way the mind is given something to do, which will keep it occupied and make it less probable that it reverts quickly to a distracted condition. Assuming one has taken the approach route via the divine abodes, one might just return to dwelling in equanimity. This can be swiftly built up in each direction until it reaches the boundless condition and from there one approaches the experience of infinite space afresh. If substantial distractions happen at subsequent levels of the gradual entry into emptiness, it would similarly be helpful to go back to the preceding step and build up practice from there in order to gather momentum.

Should this not prove enough to keep the mind from distraction, at times one might even decide to start right from the beginning in order to give the mind something to do. For a mind that really tends towards distraction, it can be helpful to be kept busy for some time by swiftly going through all four *brahmavihāra*s. One radiates each in the different directions and then moves through the steps in the gradual entry into emptiness that one had already been practising prior to getting completely lost in distraction.

For the actual experience of such spaciousness to become a step in the entry into emptiness, it needs to be accompanied by the understanding that in this way all the weariness of variety and of solidity has been left behind, that one's perceptual experience is empty of these. At first this would require the use of some degree of mental reflection to remind oneself of this aspect, at least just before entering into the actual experience and right after emerging from it. With continued practice, however, this type of understanding will come to inform the experience itself. The description of the practice in the *Cūḷasuññata-sutta* and its parallels in fact places reflections on the various types of weariness just before or right after one dwells in the actual step in the gradual entry into emptiness. Such reflections can then provide a direction to the practice even when the practice itself takes place in a condition of total mental silence.

Now the gradual entry into emptiness involves perceptual experiences that need to be handled well. Their profundity can trigger fear or else become seductive. If fear arises, the *brahmavihāra*s fall into place. If these experiences become seductive, however, the aspect of weariness needs to be more emphasized. The purpose of the gradual entry into emptiness is not to provide building blocks for the conceit of being an exceptional meditator; its purpose is to deconstruct any form of conceit and identification. As the final passage in the *Āneñjasappāya-sutta* indicates, it is only by letting go of all sense of identity that the deathless can be reached.[13] However profound the various experiences encountered during the gradual entry into emptiness may be, liberation is much more profound. This final goal of genuine practice needs at all times to be clearly held in mind.

Turning to the daily-life dimension, whereas in the case of the divine abodes the way to integrate their meditative cultivation in everyday life is predominantly through kindness in body, speech, and mind, in the case of emptiness each of the steps in the gradual approach has a specific relationship to everyday activities. These come in addition to the various aspects of integrating emptiness into daily life delineated in the *Mahāsuññata-sutta* and its parallels.[14]

In the case of the perception of infinite space, formal meditation practice can be complemented by becoming aware of space during periods outside of actual sitting practice. There is so much space surrounding the various things in the world, yet one usually only notices these things themselves, without paying any attention to the space between and around them.[15] Even right now one could notice the space between one's eyes and this text... The silence between sounds, the stillness between an inhalation and an exhalation are other pointers in the same direction, and of course looking up at the vastness of the sky, whenever possible.

Besides paying attention to visible space in this way, another dimension can be explored by reminding oneself of the ultimately insubstantial nature of all material things, which for the most part are just space. This can be helpful for remaining with mental balance in various challenging situations. Practised in this way, a taste of sameness comes to pervade one's experiences.

Training oneself to pay attention to space can also have a bearing on one's way of relating to others, in that it can express itself by giving space to others and their concerns. This relates back to the description given in the *Cūḷagosiṅga-sutta* and its parallels of a harmonious way of living together. Such harmony can be achieved

---

13 See above p.129.
14 See above p.115.
15 Catherine 2008: 196 suggests the following practical possibilities: "notice the space between things. Notice the pause between breaths. Notice the space between thoughts. Rest at ease with a spacious attention. Notice the aspect of space whenever and wherever you can."

by letting go of what one wants oneself and being willing to go along with others.[16] In relation to verbal activities, giving space to others can express itself in an increased willingness to listen, instead of feeling the need to break in and have one's own say or to dominate any discussion by the sheer quantity of one's verbal contribution to it. In this way, various aspects of the empty nature of space in everyday life can enhance one's understanding and actual practice of this particular step in the gradual entry into emptiness.

The best approach to be taken for the gradual entry into emptiness would probably not be one of trying to rush through the entire series in one go right from the outset. Rather, each single perception will need considerable time and practice to mature before becoming sufficiently well established and clear. In the present case, having well cultivated perception of infinite space with its insight implications will make it easier to progress to the next step in the gradual entry into emptiness, that of infinite consciousness. This requires directing attention to the spaciousness of the mind that has come about through paying attention to infinite space.[17]

Depending on the degree of mental stability achieved, it can at times be possible to shift directly to the boundless experience of consciousness. At other times, the same procedure could be used as employed with the divine abodes and infinite space. So one becomes aware of the front, the right, the back, and the left, above and below, all experienced as dimensions of consciousness that has become infinite.

For one not familiar with such a form of practice, this may at first seem difficult. So one might start by opening the eyes and looking at the space in front of the place where one is sitting. As one keeps gazing one mentally sort of moves back or inwards to become aware of that which knows the seeing, that which receives the visual information that enters through the eyes. Another approach could involve hearing. Ideal for that would be some sharp short sound, such as the clapping of hands. If one hears such sounds, ideally with closed eyes, instead of the natural tendency to locate the sound somewhere outside, one could allow the sound to come up to the

16 See above p.34.

17 Catherine 2008: 198f explains that "you turn attention around to perceive that which knows space ... this shift reveals an awareness that is ... without bounds."

ear. Then one in a way continues in the same inward direction by becoming aware of that which knows the sound. Once in this or any other way consciousness has been recognized, it will be possible to develop this in formal meditation, following the model of practice of the divine abodes and of infinite space, with which one is already familiar.

To turn the perception of infinite consciousness into a step in the gradual entry into emptiness, the meditative experience needs to be accompanied by the understanding that at this juncture the weariness of solidity and that of space have been left behind. One's experience is empty of these. What still remains is just the mind. At this point the external and the internal converge, and the subjective has become its own object.

In everyday life practice results in an increasing awareness of the role that the mind plays in the world. The experience of infinite consciousness will make it unmistakeably clear that mind by nature has no boundaries, unless we impose boundaries on it. As a result of directing attention to consciousness during formal meditation, in daily situations one more keenly notices one's own intentions and mental reactions as well as the influence exerted by mental evaluations on how one perceives what is experienced. One also becomes more sensitive to what motivates others, better able to notice and understand their concerns. The realization dawns that all that really matters is the mind.

Practice in any situation can take the Bāhiya instructions as a model.[18] Stopping short at just being aware in this way will reveal the potential of this succinct instruction to decondition the mind, directly counteracting the tendency to cling and grasp, and to project one's evaluations tinged by clinging and grasping onto the raw data of sense experience.

---

18 See above p.110. Another aid for such practice could be found in the injunction for Chan practice given by Sheng Yen 2008: 23, who explains that "a direct method is to let go of the past, not project into the future, not fixate in the 'space' between past and future, but maintain clarity and nonattachment of the present moment ... the mind will not 'abide' anywhere." Or else one might rely on a *gter ma* attributed to Guru Rinpoche (Longchenpa), translated in Schmidt 1990: 69, which enjoins: "do this towards all that you see: outside, inside, environment and beings, all things, while seeing them, without grasping, remain." Similarly, "do this towards all that you hear: all sounds, grasped as sweet or harsh, while hearing them, empty without judgment, remain."

Further progress in the gradual entry into emptiness then requires proceeding from infinite consciousness to nothingness.[19] As I suggested in Chapter 6, based on the *Āneñjasappāya-sutta* and its parallels, this step can be implemented in the present context through the contemplation that all is empty of a self and of what belongs to a self. There is nothing whatsoever to own, nothing whatsoever to possess, nothing whatsoever to identify with. At this point, the weariness of space and consciousness have been left behind and the resultant experience is thoroughly empty, except for this very last vestige of weariness, the notion of not-self.

In daily life, practice of this stage in the gradual entry into emptiness manifests in a lessening of identification and of the tendency to appropriate things as one's own. The burden of the sense of self gradually becomes less and a sense of ease and balance pervades one's experience, an ease that in turn positively shows itself whenever one comes in contact with others, in particular in one's increased ability to react to whatever happens with compassion or any of the other divine abodes.

Continuing the trajectory of the gradual entry into emptiness then leads to the signless. At this point, even the concept of not-self is allowed to vanish. Due to the momentum gathered with the previous steps in the gradual entry into emptiness, the mind has been so thoroughly emptied that it effortlessly remains in a condition without any reference point. In this way the mind has become empty of the notion of the cognizing subject as well as of the notion of not-self. All that remains is an inclination towards supreme emptiness.

The everyday-life dimension of signlessness as a step in the gradual entry into emptiness manifests in a profound sense of letting go that pervades all activities and experiences. Nothing can really agitate the mind, which has but one priority: progress to freedom.

Even the sublime stage of deep meditative signlessness, so utterly void, is not yet the final goal in the gradual entry into emptiness. This final goal requires insight into the impermanent nature of this

19 Catherine 2008: 201 enjoins: "drop the perception of infinite consciousness and notice what is left. No-thing remains! Directly perceive the absence of things ... the concept of absence will become the subtle object for attention."

and any other experience, together with the absence of any delight in it. Letting go in the most thorough way possible, relinquishing all and everything without any exception, enables the breakthrough to Nirvāṇa, the supreme in emptiness indeed.

Nirvāṇa is the theme of a succinct description in the discourses with which I conclude this chapter and my whole study, in the hope that it can serve as a practical stepping stone for cultivating the final step in the gradual entry into emptiness:[20]

This is peaceful, this is sublime, namely:
the calming of all constructions,
the letting go of all supports,
the extinguishing of craving,
dispassion,
cessation,
Nirvāṇa.

20 MN 64 at MN I 436,1 (also translated in Ñāṇamoli 1995: 540): *etaṃ santaṃ etaṃ paṇītaṃ, yadidaṃ sabbasaṅkhārasamatho sabbūpadhipaṭinissaggo taṇhakkhayo virāgo nirodho nibbānaṃ*. In my translation I have decided to render the term *saṅkhāra* as "construction", instead of following its usual translation as "formation", so as to combine an allusion to the unconstructed nature of Nirvāṇa with a pointer to the path of perceptual deconstruction that leads to it; regarding *upadhi*, which could alternatively be rendered as "asset" or "acquisition", with the translation "support" I intend to convey the nuance of not taking a stance on anything at all. For a detailed exegesis based on this passage cf. Ñāṇananda, 2003, 2004, 2005, 2006, 2007, 2010, and 2012.

# VIII

# TRANSLATIONS

## VIII.1 THE *MADHYAMA-ĀGAMA* PARALLEL TO THE *KARAJAKĀYA-SUTTA*

### DISCOURSE ON INTENTION[1]

Thus have I heard. At one time the Buddha was dwelling at Sāvatthī, staying in Jeta's Grove, Anāthapiṇḍika's Park. At that time, the Blessed One told the monks: "If [someone] performs deeds intentionally, I say that he will inevitably have to experience their fruits, either experiencing them in this life or experiencing them in a later life. If [someone] performs deeds unintentionally, I say that he will not necessarily have to experience their fruits.

"Herein, three are the [types] of intentionally performed bodily deeds that are unwholesome, that result in the experience of *dukkha* and that have *dukkha* as their fruit; four are the [types] of verbal deeds and three are the [types] of mental deeds that are unwholesome, [437c] that result in the experience of *dukkha* and that have *dukkha* as their fruit.

"What are the three [types] of intentionally performed bodily deeds that are unwholesome, that result in the experience of *dukkha* and that have *dukkha* as their fruit? Killing living beings is reckoned the first. [Someone is] supremely bad and blood-thirsty, having the wish to injure and being without compassion for living beings, including insects.

---

1 The translated text is MĀ 15 at T I 437b24 to 438b11 (translated Anālayo 2012c: 494–502).

"Taking what is not given is reckoned the second. Out of attachment he takes the possessions of others with the intention of stealing.

"Sexual misconduct is reckoned the third. He has intercourse with a woman that is protected by her father, or protected by her mother, or protected by both parents, or protected by her sister, or protected by her brother, or protected by her parents-in-law, or protected by relatives, or protected by the clan; or a woman protected by threat of corporal punishment, even one who has been garlanded in token of betrothal.

"These are reckoned the three types of intentionally performed bodily deeds that are unwholesome, that result in the experience of *dukkha*, and that have *dukkha* as their fruit.

"What are the four [types] of intentionally performed verbal deeds that are unwholesome, that result in the experience of *dukkha* and that have *dukkha* as their fruit? Speaking falsehood is reckoned the first. On being questioned in an assembly, or among family members, or in the king's palace thus: 'say what you know', he claims to know what he does not know, or claims not to know what he knows; claims to have seen what he has not seen, or claims not to have seen what he saw; he knowingly speaks falsehood either for his own sake or for the sake of others, or for the sake of wealth.

"Divisive speech is reckoned the second. Wishing to divide others, he tells those what he has heard from these, out of a wish to harm these, [or else] tells these what he has heard from those, out of a wish to harm those. Wishing to divide those who are united, and further to divide those who are already divided, he forms factions, delights in [the forming of] factions and praises [the forming of] factions.

"Harsh speech is reckoned the third. He employs a type of speech that is rough and rude in tone, which sounds offensive and grates on the ear, that living beings neither enjoy nor desire, which causes others suffering and vexation, and which does not lead to calmness, speaking such type of speech.

"Frivolous talk is reckoned the fourth. He speaks at the wrong time, speaks what is not true, what is not meaningful, what is contrary to the Dharma, what does not [lead] to appeasement, and also commends issues that do not [lead] to appeasement. Disregarding the [proper] timing, he does not teach or admonish properly.

"These are reckoned the four types of intentionally performed verbal deeds that are unwholesome, that result in the experience of *dukkha*, and that have *dukkha* as their fruit.

"What are the three [types] of intentionally performed mental deeds that are unwholesome, that result in the experience of *dukkha* and that have *dukkha* as their fruit? Covetousness is reckoned the first. On seeing another endowed with wealth and all the necessities of life, he constantly has the wish and desire: 'May I get it!'

"Irritation and ill will are reckoned the second. With a mind [full of] dislike and irritation, he has the thought: 'May those living beings be killed, be bound, be arrested, be removed, and be banished', having the wish that others experience infinite *dukkha*.

"Wrong view is reckoned the third. He has a view that is distorted, a view like this, declaring thus: 'There is no [efficacy in] giving, there is no [efficacy in] offerings [during a sacrifice], there is no [efficacy in] reciting hymns [during a sacrifice], there are no wholesome and bad deeds, there is no result of wholesome and bad deeds, there is neither this world nor another world, there is no [obligation towards one's] father and mother, in the world there are no worthy men who have reached a wholesome attainment, [438a] who are well gone and have progressed well, who by their own knowledge and experience abide in having themselves realized this world and the other world.'

"These are reckoned the three types of intentionally performed mental deeds that are unwholesome, that result in the experience of *dukkha* and that have *dukkha* as their fruit.

"The learned noble disciple leaves behind unwholesome bodily deeds and develops wholesome bodily deeds, leaves behind unwholesome verbal and mental deeds and develops wholesome verbal and mental deeds. Being endowed with diligence and virtue in this way, having accomplished purity of bodily deeds and purity of verbal and mental deeds, being free from ill will and contention, discarding sloth-and-torpor, being without restlessness or conceit, removing doubt and overcoming arrogance, with right mindfulness and right comprehension, being without bewilderment, the learned noble disciple dwells having pervaded one direction with a mind imbued with *mettā*, and in the same way the second, third, and fourth directions, the four intermediate directions, above and below, completely and everywhere. Being without mental shackles, resentment, ill will, or contention, with a mind imbued with *mettā* that is supremely vast and great, boundless and well developed, [the learned noble disciple] dwells having pervaded the entire world.

"Then [the learned noble disciple] reflects like this: 'Formerly my mind was narrow and not well developed; now my mind has become boundless and well developed.'

"When the mind of the learned noble disciple has in this way become boundless and well developed, if because of [associating with] bad friends he formerly dwelled in negligence and performed unwholesome deeds, those [deeds] cannot lead him along, cannot defile him, and will not come back to meet him.

"Suppose there is a small boy or girl, who since birth is able to dwell in the liberation of the mind through *mettā*. Later on, would [he or she] still perform unwholesome deeds by body, speech, or mind?" The monks answered: "Certainly not, Blessed One."

"Why is that? Not performing bad deeds themselves, how could bad deeds arise? Therefore, a man or woman, at home [or] gone forth, should constantly make an effort to develop liberation of the mind through *mettā*. If that man or woman, at home [or] gone forth, develops liberation of the mind through *mettā*, [since] when going towards the other world [he or she] will not take this body along, [he or she] will proceed [just] in accordance with [the developed quality of their] mind.

"Monks, you should reflect like this: 'Formerly I was negligent and performed unwholesome deeds. Let the fruits of these be experienced entirely now, not in a later world.' If liberation of the mind through *mettā* has become boundless and well developed like this, certainly non-returning will be attained, or else that which is even higher.

"[Again, the learned noble disciple dwells having pervaded one direction with a mind imbued with] compassion, [and in the same way the second, third, and fourth directions, the four intermediate directions, above and below, completely and everywhere. Being without mental shackles, resentment, ill will, or contention, with a mind imbued with compassion that is supremely vast and great, boundless and well developed, the learned noble disciple dwells having pervaded the entire world.]

"[Then the learned noble disciple reflects like this: 'Formerly my mind was narrow and not well developed; now my mind has become boundless and well developed.']

"[When the mind of the learned noble disciple has in this way become boundless and well developed, if because of associating with bad friends he formerly dwelled in negligence and performed unwholesome deeds, those deeds cannot lead him along, cannot defile him, and will not come back to meet him.]

"[Suppose there is a small boy or girl, who since birth is able to dwell in the liberation of the mind through compassion. Later on, would he or she still perform unwholesome deeds by body, speech, or mind?" The monks answered: "Certainly not, Blessed One."]

"[Why is that? Not performing bad deeds themselves, how could bad deeds arise? Therefore, a man or woman, at home or gone forth, should constantly make an effort to develop liberation of the mind through compassion. If that man or woman, at home or gone forth, develops liberation of the mind through compassion, since when going towards the other world he or she will not take this body along, he or she will proceed just in accordance with the developed quality of their mind.]

"[Monks, you should reflect like this: 'Formerly I was negligent and performed unwholesome deeds. Let the fruits of these be experienced entirely now, not in a later world.' If liberation of the mind through compassion has become boundless and well developed like this, certainly non-returning will be attained, or else that which is even higher.]

"[Again, the learned noble disciple dwells having pervaded one direction with a mind imbued with] sympathetic joy, [and in the same way the second, third, and fourth directions, the four intermediate directions, above and below, completely and everywhere. Being without mental shackles, resentment, ill will, or contention, with a mind imbued with sympathetic joy that is supremely vast and great, boundless and well developed, the learned noble disciple dwells having pervaded the entire world.]

"[Then the learned noble disciple reflects like this: 'Formerly my mind was narrow and not well developed; now my mind has become boundless and well developed.']

"[When the mind of the learned noble disciple has in this way become boundless and well developed, if because of associating with bad friends he formerly dwelled in negligence and performed unwholesome deeds, those deeds cannot lead him along, cannot defile him, and will not come back to meet him.]

"[Suppose there is a small boy or girl, who since birth is able to dwell in the liberation of the mind through sympathetic joy. Later on, would he or she still perform unwholesome deeds by body, speech, or mind?" The monks answered: "Certainly not, Blessed One."]

"[Why is that? Not performing bad deeds themselves, how could bad deeds arise? Therefore, a man or woman, at home or gone forth, should constantly make an effort to develop liberation of the mind through sympathetic joy. If that man or woman, at home or gone forth, develops liberation of the mind through sympathetic joy, since when going towards the other world he or she will not take this body along, he or she will proceed just in accordance with the developed quality of their mind.]

"[Monks, you should reflect like this: 'Formerly I was negligent and performed unwholesome deeds. Let the fruits of these be experienced entirely now, not in a later world.' If liberation of the mind through sympathetic joy has become boundless and well developed like this, certainly non-returning will be attained, or else that which is even higher.]

"[Again, the learned noble disciple dwells having pervaded one direction with a mind imbued with] equanimity, [and in the same way the second, third, and fourth directions, the four intermediate directions, above and below, completely and everywhere]. Being without mental shackles, resentment, ill will, or contention, [with a mind that is] supremely vast and great, boundless and well developed, [the learned noble disciple] dwells having pervaded the entire world.

"Then [the learned noble disciple] reflects like this: 'Formerly my mind was narrow and not well developed; now my mind has become boundless and well developed.

"When the mind of the learned noble disciple has in this way become boundless and well developed, if because of [associating with] bad friends he formerly dwelled in negligence and performed unwholesome deeds, those [deeds] cannot lead him along, cannot defile him, and will not come back to meet him. [438b]

"Suppose there is a small boy or girl, who since birth is able to dwell in the liberation of the mind through equanimity. Later on, would [he or she] still perform unwholesome deeds by body, speech, or mind?" The monks answered: "Certainly not, Blessed One."

"Why is that? Not performing bad deeds themselves, how could bad deeds arise? Therefore a man or woman, at home [or] gone forth, should constantly make an effort to develop liberation of the mind through equanimity. If that man or woman, at home [or] gone forth, develops liberation of the mind through equanimity, [since] when going towards the other world [he or she] will not take this body along, [he or she] will proceed [just] in accordance with [the developed quality of their] mind.

"Monks, you should reflect like this: 'Formerly I was negligent and performed unwholesome deeds. Let the fruits of these be experienced entirely now, not in a later world.' If liberation of the mind through equanimity has become boundless and well developed like this, certainly non-returning will be attained, or else that which is even higher."

The Buddha spoke like this. The monks, who had listened to what the Buddha said, were delighted and received it respectfully.

## VIII.2 THE *MADHYAMA-ĀGAMA* PARALLEL TO THE *CŪḶASUÑÑATA-SUTTA*

### SHORTER DISCOURSE ON EMPTINESS[2]

Thus have I heard. At one time the Buddha was dwelling at Sāvatthī, staying in the Eastern Park, in the Mansion of Migāra's Mother. [737a]

At that time, in the afternoon, the venerable Ānanda got up from sitting in meditation and approached the Buddha. Having paid homage at the Buddha's feet, he stepped back to stand to one side and said:

"At one time the Blessed One was dwelling among the Sakyans, in a town of the Sakyans named Nagaraka. At that time I heard the Blessed One speak like this: 'Ānanda, I often dwell in emptiness.' Did I understand well, receive well, and remember well that saying by the Blessed One?"

Then the Blessed One replied: "Ānanda, you truly understood well, received well, and remembered well that saying by me. Why is that? From then until now, I often dwell in emptiness.

"Ānanda, just as this Mansion of Migāra's Mother is empty of elephants, of horses, of cattle, of sheep, of wealth, of grain, and of

---

2 The translated text is MĀ 190 at T I 736c27 to 738a1 (translated Anālayo 2012c: 326–333).

male and female slaves; yet there is this non-emptiness: [the presence] of just the community of monks. Thus, Ānanda, whatever is not present, I therefore see as empty; and whatever else is present, I see as truly present. Ānanda, this is called truly dwelling in emptiness, without distortion.

"Ānanda, if a monk wishes to dwell much in emptiness, that monk should not give attention to the perception of village and not give attention to the perception of people, but should frequently give attention to the unitary perception of forest.

"In this way he knows that this is empty of the perception of village and empty of the perception of people. Yet there is this non-emptiness: just the unitary perception of forest. [He knows]: 'Whatever weariness because of the perception of village there might be – that is not present for me. Whatever weariness because of the perception of people there might be – that is also not present for me. There is only the weariness because of the unitary perception of forest.' Whatever is not present, he therefore sees as empty; whatever else is present, he sees as truly present. Ānanda, this is called truly dwelling in emptiness, without distortion.

"Again, Ānanda, if a monk wishes to dwell much in emptiness, that monk should not give attention to the perception of people and not give attention to the perception of forest, but should frequently give attention to the unitary perception of earth. If that monk sees this earth as having hills and hollows, with clusters of snakes, with clumps of thorn-bushes, with sand and rocks, steep mountains and deep rivers, he should not attend to it so. If [instead] he sees this earth as level and flat like the palm of a hand, then his manner of looking at it is beneficial and should be frequently attended to.

"Ānanda, it is just as a cow hide which, when stretched and fastened with a hundred pegs, being fully stretched, has no wrinkles and no creases. [Similarly], if he sees this earth as having hills and hollows, with clusters of snakes, with clumps of thorn-bushes, with sand and rocks, steep mountains and deep rivers, he should not attend to it so. If [instead] he sees this earth as level and flat like the palm of his hand, then his manner of looking at it is beneficial and should be frequently attended to.

"In this way he knows that this is empty of the perception of people and empty of the perception of forest. Yet there is this non-emptiness: just the unitary perception of earth. [He knows]: 'Whatever weariness because of the perception of people there might be [737b] – that is not present for me; whatever weariness because of the perception of forest there might be – that is also not present for me. There is only the weariness because of the unitary perception of earth.' Whatever is not present, he therefore sees as empty; whatever else is present, he sees as truly present. Ānanda, this is called truly dwelling in emptiness, without distortion.

"Again, Ānanda, if a monk wishes to dwell much in emptiness, that monk should not give attention to the perception of forest and not give attention to the perception of earth, but should frequently give attention to the unitary perception of the sphere of infinite space.

"In this way he knows that this is empty of the perception of forest and empty of the perception of earth. Yet there is this non-emptiness: just the unitary perception of the sphere of infinite space. [He knows]: 'Whatever weariness because of the perception of forest there might be – that is not present for me; whatever weariness because of the perception of earth there might be – that is also not present for me. There is only the weariness because of the unitary perception of the sphere of infinite space.' Whatever is not present, he therefore sees as empty; whatever else is present, he sees as truly present. Ānanda, this is called truly dwelling in emptiness, without distortion.

"Again, Ānanda, if a monk wishes to dwell much in emptiness, that monk should not give attention to the perception of earth and not give attention to the perception of the sphere of infinite space, but should frequently give attention to the unitary perception of the sphere of infinite consciousness.

"In this way he knows that this is empty of the perception of earth and empty of the perception of the sphere of infinite space. Yet there is this non-emptiness: just the unitary perception of the sphere of infinite consciousness. [He knows]: 'Whatever weariness because of the perception of earth there might be – that is not present for me; whatever weariness because of the perception of the sphere of infinite space there might be – that is also not present for me. There is only the weariness because of the unitary perception of the sphere of infinite consciousness.' Whatever is not present, he therefore sees as empty; whatever else is present, he sees as truly present. Ānanda, this is called truly dwelling in emptiness, without distortion.

"Again, Ānanda, if a monk wishes to dwell much in emptiness, that monk should not give attention to the perception of the sphere of infinite space and not give attention to the perception of the sphere of infinite consciousness, but should frequently give attention to the unitary perception of the sphere of nothingness.

"In this way he knows that this is empty of the perception of the sphere of infinite space and empty of the perception of the sphere of infinite consciousness. Yet there is this non-emptiness: just the unitary perception of the sphere of nothingness. [He knows]: 'Whatever weariness because of the perception of the sphere of infinite space there might be – that is not present for me; whatever weariness because of the perception of the sphere of infinite consciousness there might be – that is also not present for me. There is only the weariness because of the unitary perception of the sphere of nothingness.' Whatever is not present, he therefore sees as empty; whatever else is present, he sees as truly present. Ānanda, this is called truly dwelling in emptiness, without distortion. [737c]

"Again, Ānanda, if a monk wishes to dwell much in emptiness, that monk should not give attention to the perception of the sphere of infinite consciousness and not give attention to the perception of the sphere of nothingness, but should frequently give attention to the unitary <signless> concentration of the mind.[3]

"In this way he knows that this is empty of the perception of the sphere of infinite consciousness and empty of the perception of the sphere of nothingness. Yet there is this non-emptiness: just the unitary <signless> concentration of the mind. [He knows]: 'Whatever weariness because of the perception of the sphere of infinite consciousness there might be – that is not present for me; whatever weariness because of the perception of the sphere of nothingness there might be – that is also not present for me. There is only the weariness because of the unitary <signless> concentration of the mind.' Whatever is not present, he therefore sees as empty; whatever else is present, he sees as truly present. Ānanda, this is called truly dwelling in emptiness, without distortion.

"He thinks: 'My [experience] of the <signless> concentration of the mind is rooted – it is rooted in formations, it is rooted in intentions. What is rooted in formations, rooted in intentions, I do not delight in that, I do not seek that, I should not become established in that.' Knowing in this way, seeing in this way, his mind is liberated from

3 My translation is based on emending the text, which actually speaks of "unconscious concentration of the mind"; see the discussion above p.137.

the influx of sensual desire, [his mind is liberated] from the influx of existence, and his mind is liberated from the influx of ignorance. Being liberated, he knows he is liberated. He knows as it really is that birth has been extinguished, the holy life has been established, what had to be done has been done, there will be no experiencing of further existence.

"In this way he knows that this is empty of the influx of sensual desire, empty of the influx of existence, and empty of the influx of ignorance. Yet there is this non-emptiness: just this body of mine with its six sense-spheres and the life faculty.

[He knows]: "'Whatever weariness because of the influx of sensual desire there might be – that is not present for me; whatever weariness because of the influx of existence [there might be – that is also not present for me; whatever weariness] because of the influx of ignorance there might be – that is also not present for me. There is only the weariness because of this body of mine with its six sense-spheres and the life faculty.' Whatever is not present, he therefore sees as empty; whatever else is present, he sees as truly present. Ānanda, this is called truly dwelling in emptiness, without distortion, namely the eradication of the influxes, the influx-free and unconditioned liberation of the mind.

"Ānanda, whatever Tathāgatas, free from attachment and completely awakened, there have been in the past, they all truly dwelled in this emptiness, without distortion, namely in the eradication of the influxes, the influx-free and unconditioned liberation of the mind.

"Ānanda, whatever Tathāgatas, free from attachment and completely awakened, there will be in the future, they will all truly dwell in this emptiness, without distortion, namely in the eradication of the influxes, the influx-free and unconditioned liberation of the mind.

"Ānanda, I, who am the Tathāgata now, free from attachment and completely awakened, I also truly dwell in this emptiness, without distortion, namely in the eradication of the influxes, the influx-free and unconditioned liberation of the mind.

"Ānanda, you should train yourself like this: 'I shall also truly dwell in this emptiness, without distortion, namely in the eradication of the influxes, the influx-free and unconditioned liberation of the mind.' Ānanda, you should train yourself like this."

The Buddha spoke like this. [738a] The venerable Ānanda and the monks, who had listened to what the Buddha said, were delighted and received it respectfully.

### VIII.3 THE *MADHYAMA-ĀGAMA* PARALLEL TO THE *MAHĀSUÑÑATA-SUTTA*

#### GREATER DISCOURSE ON EMPTINESS[4]

Thus have I heard. At one time the Buddha was dwelling among the Sakyans at Kapilavatthu, staying in the Nigrodha Park.

At that time, when the night was over, at dawn, the Blessed One put on his [outer] robe, took his bowl and entered Kapilavatthu to collect almsfood. Having completed his meal, in the afternoon he went to the dwelling of Kāḷakhemaka the Sakyan. At that time, in the dwelling of Kāḷakhemaka the Sakyan numerous beds and seats had been set out, [indicating that] many monks were staying there. Then the Blessed One came out of the dwelling of Kāḷakhemaka the Sakyan and went to the dwelling of Ghāṭā the Sakyan.

At that time the venerable Ānanda and many monks had congregated in the dwelling of Ghāṭā the Sakyan to make robes. The venerable Ānanda saw from afar that the Buddha was coming. Having seen this, he came out to receive the Buddha, took the Buddha's [outer] robe and bowl, and returned to prepare a bed and seat and to draw water for washing his feet.

When the Buddha had washed his feet and had sat down on the seat prepared by the venerable Ānanda in the dwelling of Ghāṭā the Sakyan, he said: "Ānanda, in the dwelling of Kāḷakhemaka the Sakyan numerous beds and seats have been set out, [indicating that] many monks are staying there."

The venerable Ānanda said: "Yes, indeed, Blessed One, in the dwelling of Kāḷakhemaka the Sakyan numerous beds and seats have been set out, [indicating that] many monks are staying there. Why is that? We are now making robes."

Then, the Blessed One told Ānanda: "A monk should not desire vociferous talk, delight in vociferous talk, associate with vociferous talk, desire company, delight in company, associate with company,

---

4 The translated text is an excerpt from MĀ 191, ranging from the beginning of the discourse at T I 738a5 to 739b21 (translated Anālayo 2012c: 349–360).

not desiring to be separated from company, not delighting in dwelling alone in remote places.

"If a monk desires vociferous talk, delights in vociferous talk, associates with vociferous talk, desires company, delights in company, associates with company, not desiring to be separated from company, not delighting in dwelling alone in remote places, then it is impossible for him to attain, easily and without difficulty, that happiness which is called noble happiness, the happiness of dispassion, the happiness of separation, the happiness of stillness, the happiness [that leads to] full awakening, the non-worldly happiness, the happiness [that leads beyond] birth and death.

"Ānanda, if a monk does not desire vociferous talk, does not delight in vociferous talk, does not associate with vociferous talk, does not desire company, does not delight in company, does not associate with company, desiring to be separated from company, constantly delighting in dwelling alone in remote places, then it is certainly possible for him to attain, easily and without difficulty, that happiness which is called noble happiness, the happiness of dispassion, the happiness of separation, the happiness of stillness, the happiness [that leads to] full awakening, the non-worldly happiness, the happiness [that leads beyond] birth and death. [738b]

"Ānanda, a monk should not desire vociferous talk, delight in vociferous talk, associate with vociferous talk, desire company, delight in company, associate with company, not desiring to be separated from company, not delighting in dwelling alone in remote places. If a monk desires vociferous talk, delights in vociferous talk, associates with vociferous talk, desires company, delights in company, associates with company, not desiring to be separated from company, not delighting in dwelling alone in remote places, then it is impossible for him to attain either the temporary liberation of the mind that is delightful or the permanent liberation of the mind that is unshakeable.

"Ānanda, if a monk does not desire vociferous talk, does not delight in vociferous talk, does not associate with vociferous talk, does not desire company, does not delight in company, does not associate with company, desiring to be separated from company, constantly delighting in dwelling alone in remote places, then it is certainly possible for him to attain either the temporary liberation of the mind that is delightful or the permanent liberation of the mind that is unshakeable.

"Why is that? I do not see a single form that I might desire or delight in, [since] with the decay and change of that form there would at some time arise sorrow and lamentation, sadness, pain, and vexation.

"For this reason, I fully and completely awoke to this other abiding, namely dwelling in emptiness externally by transcending all perception of form. Ānanda, when I dwell in this abiding, there arises joy. I experience this joy throughout the whole body with right mindfulness and right comprehension.

"[When I dwell in this abiding], there arises rapture. [I experience this rapture throughout the whole body with right mindfulness and right comprehension. When I dwell in this abiding], there arises tranquillity. [I experience this tranquillity throughout the whole body with right mindfulness and right comprehension. When I dwell in this abiding], there arises happiness. [I experience this happiness throughout the whole body with right mindfulness and right comprehension. When I dwell in this abiding], there arises concentration. I experience this concentration throughout the whole body with right mindfulness and right comprehension.

"Ānanda, there may be monks, nuns, male lay followers, or female lay followers who together come to see me. Then, behaving in such a way towards them, being in such a mental state, secluded and delighting in dispassion, I teach them the Dharma, to encourage and help them.

"Ānanda, if a monk wishes to dwell much in emptiness, then that monk should keep the mind internally established in tranquillity so that it becomes unified and concentrated. Having kept the mind internally established in tranquillity so that it becomes unified and concentrated, he should attend to emptiness internally. Ānanda, if a monk speaks like this: 'Without keeping the mind internally established in tranquillity so that it becomes unified and concentrated, I attend to emptiness internally', you should know that that monk will [just] greatly trouble himself. Ānanda, how does a monk keep the mind internally established in tranquillity so that it becomes unified and concentrated?

"A monk completely drenches and pervades this body with rapture and pleasure born of seclusion [experienced in the first absorption], so that no part [of his body] is not pervaded by the rapture and pleasure born of seclusion. Ānanda, it is just as a person taking a bath, who has placed bath powder in a vessel, sprinkles it with water and kneads it into a ball, so that every bit of it, inside and out, is completely drenched and pervaded with the water, with none seeping out. In the same way, Ānanda, a monk completely drenches and pervades this body with rapture and pleasure born of seclusion, so that there is no part [of his body] that is not pervaded by rapture and pleasure born of seclusion. [738c] Ānanda, in this way a monk should keep the mind internally established in tranquillity so that it becomes unified and concentrated.

"Keeping the mind internally established in tranquillity so that it becomes unified and concentrated, he should attend to emptiness internally. Having attended to emptiness internally, his mind is perturbed, does not advance and progress, does not attain spotlessness, is not established, and is not released in regard to emptiness internally.

"Ānanda, if a monk, while he is contemplating, comes to know that on attending to emptiness internally his mind is perturbed, does not advance and progress, does not attain spotlessness, is not established, and is not released in regard to emptiness internally, then that monk should attend to emptiness externally. Having attended to emptiness externally, his mind is perturbed, does not advance and progress, does not attain spotlessness, is not established, and is not released in regard to emptiness externally.

"Ānanda, if a monk, while he is contemplating, comes to know that on attending to emptiness externally his mind is perturbed, does not advance and progress, does not attain spotlessness, is not established, and is not released in regard to emptiness externally, then that monk should attend to emptiness internally and externally. Having attended to emptiness internally and externally, his mind is perturbed, does not advance and progress, does not attain spotlessness, is not established, and is not released in regard to emptiness internally and externally.

"Ānanda, if a monk, while he is contemplating, comes to know that on attending to emptiness internally and externally his mind is perturbed, does not advance and progress, does not attain spotlessness, is not established, and not released in regard to emptiness internally and externally, then that monk should attend to imperturbability. Having attended to imperturbability, his mind is perturbed, does not advance and progress, does not attain spotlessness, is not established, and is not released in regard to imperturbability.

"Ānanda, if a monk, while he is contemplating, comes to know that on attending to imperturbability his mind is perturbed, does not advance and progress, does not attain spotlessness, is not established, and is not released through imperturbability, then that monk should repeatedly direct his mind to this or that concentration,[5] repeatedly practise it, repeatedly soften [the mind] so that it becomes joyful and tender, absorbed in the pleasure of seclusion.

"Repeatedly directing his mind to this or that concentration, repeatedly practising it, repeatedly softening [the mind], so that it becomes joyful and tender, absorbed in the pleasure of seclusion, he should accomplish dwelling in emptiness internally. Having accomplished dwelling in emptiness internally, the mind becomes imperturbable, advances and progresses, attains spotlessness, is established, and is released in regard to emptiness internally. Ānanda, if a monk, while he is contemplating, comes to know that he has accomplished dwelling in emptiness internally, that the mind has become imperturbable, advances and progresses, attains spotlessness, is established, and is released in regard to emptiness internally – then this is reckoned his right comprehension.

"Ānanda, the monk should then accomplish dwelling in emptiness externally. Having accomplished dwelling in emptiness externally, the mind becomes imperturbable, advances and progresses, attains spotlessness, is established, and is released in regard to emptiness externally. [739a] Ānanda, if a monk, while he is contemplating, comes to know that he has accomplished dwelling in emptiness externally, that the mind has become imperturbable, advances and progresses, attains spotlessness, is established, and is released in regard to emptiness externally – then this is reckoned his right comprehension.

"Ānanda, the monk should then accomplish dwelling in emptiness internally and externally. Having accomplished dwelling in emptiness internally and externally, the mind becomes imperturbable, advances and progresses, attains spotlessness, is established, and is released in regard to emptiness internally and externally. Ānanda, if a monk,

---

5 My translation is based on emending the present reading in conformity with a repetition of the phrase found two lines below in the Chinese text.

while he is contemplating, comes to know that he has accomplished dwelling in emptiness internally and externally, that the mind has become imperturbable, advances and progresses, attains spotlessness, is established, and is released in regard to emptiness internally and externally – then this is reckoned his right comprehension.

"Ānanda, he should then accomplish dwelling in imperturbability. Having accomplished dwelling in imperturbability, the mind becomes imperturbable, advances and progresses, attains spotlessness, is established, and is released in regard to imperturbability. Ānanda, if while contemplating a monk comes to know that he has accomplished dwelling in imperturbability, that the mind has become imperturbable, advances and progresses, attains spotlessness, is established, and is released in regard to imperturbability – then this is reckoned his right comprehension.

"Ānanda, if a monk who is dwelling in this abiding of the mind wishes to practise walking meditation, then that monk goes out of his meditation hut and practises walking meditation in the open, in the shade of the hut, with his faculties settled within, the mind not directed outwards or backwards, perceiving [only] what is in front. Having practised walking meditation like this, his mind does not give rise to covetousness, sadness, or [another] detrimental or unwholesome state – this is reckoned his right comprehension.

"Ānanda, if a monk who is dwelling in this abiding of the mind wishes to sit in concentration, then that monk leaves the walking meditation, goes to the end of the walking-meditation path, spreads his sitting mat, and sits down cross-legged. Having sat in concentration like this, his mind does not give rise to covetousness, sadness, or [another] detrimental or unwholesome state – this is reckoned his right comprehension.

"Ānanda, if a monk who is dwelling in this abiding of the mind wishes to think thoughts, then as regards the three detrimental and unwholesome thoughts – thoughts of sensual desire, thoughts of ill will, and thoughts of harming – that monk should not think these three detrimental and unwholesome thoughts. [Instead], as regards the three wholesome thoughts – thoughts of dispassion, thoughts without ill will, and thoughts without harming – he should think these three wholesome thoughts. Having thought like this, his mind does not give rise to covetousness, sadness, or [another] detrimental or unwholesome state – this is reckoned his right comprehension.

"Ānanda, if a monk who is dwelling in this abiding of the mind wishes to speak, then as regards talking ignoble talk related to what is not beneficial – talk such as talk about kings, talk about thieves, talk about battles and quarrels, talk about drink and food, talk about clothes and bedding, talk about married women, talk about girls, talk about adulterous women, talk about the world, talk about wrong practices, talk about the contents of the ocean – the monk does not talk such types of irrelevant talk.

"[Instead], as regards talking noble talk that is related to what is beneficial, that makes the mind malleable, [739b] free of darkness and the hindrances – talk such as talk about generosity, talk about morality, talk about concentration, talk about wisdom, talk about liberation, talk about knowledge and vision of liberation, talk about self-effacement, talk about not socializing, talk about fewness of wishes, talk about contentment, talk about dispassion, talk about abandoning, talk about cessation, talk about sitting in meditation, talk about dependent arising, such talk [proper] for recluses – [the monk talks such talk]. Having talked like this, his mind does not give rise to covetousness, sadness, or [another] detrimental or unwholesome state – this is reckoned his right comprehension.

"Again, Ānanda, there are five strands of sensual pleasure that are pleasurable, that the mind thinks about, that are connected with craving and sensual desire:[6] forms known by the eye, sounds known by the ear, odours known by the nose, flavours known by the tongue, and tangibles known by the body.

"If a monk's mind turns to contemplation and, in regard to these five strands of sensual pleasure, he comes under the influence of these strands of sensual pleasure, then his mind will dwell among them. Why is that? Sooner or later, in regard to these five strands of sensual pleasure, [if] one comes under the influence of these strands of sensual pleasure, the mind dwells among them.

"Ānanda, if a monk, while he is contemplating, comes to know that in regard to these five strands of sensual pleasure he has come under the influence of these strands of sensual pleasure, that his mind is dwelling among them, then that monk should contemplate the impermanence of these various strands of sensual pleasure, contemplate their decay, contemplate their fading away, contemplate

6 The translation is based on an emendation by deleting an additional reference to forms.

their abandoning, contemplate their cessation, contemplate abandoning and giving them up, becoming separated from them. Then, whatever he has of desire and defilement regarding these five strands of sensual pleasure will soon cease. Ānanda, if while contemplating like this a monk knows that whatever he had of desire and defilement in regard to these five strands of sensual pleasure has been abandoned – this is reckoned his right comprehension.

"Again, Ānanda, there are the five aggregates [affected by] clinging. The form aggregate [affected by] clinging, the feeling [aggregate affected by clinging], the perception [aggregate affected by clinging], the formations [aggregate affected by clinging], and the consciousness aggregate [affected by] clinging.

The monk should contemplate their rise and fall thus: "'This is bodily form, this is the arising of bodily form, this is the cessation of bodily form, this is feeling, [this is the arising of feeling, this is the cessation of feeling], this is perception, [this is the arising of perception, this is the cessation of perception], these are formations, [this is the arising of formations, this is the cessation of formations],[7] this is consciousness, this is the arising of consciousness, this is the cessation of consciousness.' Then whatever conceit of an 'I' he has in regard to these five aggregates [affected by] clinging, that will soon cease.

"Ānanda, if the monk, while he is contemplating like this, comes to know that whatever conceit of an 'I' he had in regard to these five aggregates [affected by] clinging has ceased – this is reckoned his right comprehension.

"Ānanda, these states are entirely desirable, entirely delightful, entirely [worth] thinking about. They are without influxes, without clinging, beyond the reach of Māra, beyond the reach of the Evil One, beyond the reach of all detrimental and unwholesome states that defile and are the root of future becoming, that result in vexation and *dukkha*, and that are the cause of birth, old age, disease, and death. This is reckoned accomplishment in diligence. Why is that? All Tathāgatas, who are without attachment and fully awakened, attained awakening through diligence. Through the faculty of

7 The translation is based on an emendation by deleting an additional reference to consciousness.

diligence, innumerable wholesome states arise that are in accordance with the requisites of awakening. Ānanda, for this reason you should train like this: 'I will also be accomplished in diligence' – you should train like this."

# REFERENCES


Anālayo, Bhikkhu 2003: *Satipaṭṭhāna, The Direct Path to Realization*, Birmingham: Windhorse Publications.

Anālayo, Bhikkhu 2008: "The Conversion of Aṅgulimāla in the Saṃyukta-āgama", *Buddhist Studies Review*, 25/2: 135–48.

Anālayo, Bhikkhu 2011a: *A Comparative Study of the Majjhima-nikāya*, Taipei: Dharma Drum Publishing Corporation.

Anālayo, Bhikkhu 2011b: "Living in Seclusion and Facing Fear – The Ekottarika-āgama Counterpart to the Bhayabherava-sutta", in *Buddhism as a Stronghold of Free Thinking? Social, Ethical and Philosophical Dimensions of Buddhism*, S.C.A. Fay and I.M. Bruckner (ed.), 203–31, Nuesttal: Edition Unbuntu.

Anālayo, Bhikkhu 2011c: "Right View and the Scheme of the Four Truths in Early Buddhism, The Saṃyukta-āgama Parallel to the Sammādiṭṭhi-sutta and the Simile of the Four Skills of a Physician", *Canadian Journal of Buddhist Studies*, 7: 11–44.

Anālayo, Bhikkhu 2012a: "The Chinese Parallels to the Dhamma-cakkappavattana-sutta (1)", *Journal of the Oxford Centre for Buddhist Studies*, 3: 12–46.

Anālayo, Bhikkhu 2012b: *Excursions into the Thought-world of the Pāli Discourses*, Onalaska, WA: Pariyatti.

Anālayo, Bhikkhu 2012c: *Madhyama-āgama Studies*, Taipei: Dharma Drum Publishing Corporation.

Anālayo, Bhikkhu 2013a: "The Chinese Parallels to the Dhamma-cakkappavattana-sutta (2)", *Journal of the Oxford Centre for Buddhist Studies*, 5: 9–41.

Anālayo, Bhikkhu 2013b: "On the Five Aggregates (2) – A Translation of Saṃyukta-āgama Discourses 256 to 272", *Dharma Drum Journal of Buddhist Studies*, 12: 1–69.

Anālayo, Bhikkhu 2013c: *Perspectives on Satipaṭṭhāna*, Cambridge: Windhorse Publications.

Anālayo, Bhikkhu 2014a: "The Buddha's Last Meditation in the Dīrgha-āgama", *Indian International Journal of Buddhist Studies*, 15: 1–43.

Anālayo, Bhikkhu 2014b: "Discourse Merger in the Ekottarika-āgama (1)", *Singaporean Journal of Buddhist Studies*, 2: 5–35.

Anālayo, Bhikkhu 2014c: "The First Absorption (Dhyāna) in Early Indian Buddhism – A Study of Source Material from the Madhyama-āgama", in *Cultural Histories of Meditation*, H. Eifring (ed.), 69–90, Oslo: Hermes Academic Publishing.

Anālayo, Bhikkhu 2014d: "The Hīnayāna Fallacy", *Journal of the Oxford Centre for Buddhist Studies*, 6: 9–31.

Anālayo, Bhikkhu 2014e: "On the Five Aggregates (4) – A Translation of Saṃyukta-āgama Discourses 33 to 58", *Dharma Drum Journal of Buddhist Studies*, 14: 1–72.

Anālayo, Bhikkhu 2014f: "On the Five Aggregates (5) – A Translation of Saṃyukta-āgama Discourses 103 to 110", *Dharma Drum Journal of Buddhist Studies*, 15: 1–64.

Anālayo, Bhikkhu 2015a: "Brahmavihāra and Awakening, The Dīrgha-āgama parallel to the Tevijja-sutta", *Asian Literature and Translation*, 3.4: 1–27.

Anālayo, Bhikkhu 2015b: "Compassion in the Āgamas and Nikāyas", *Dharma Drum Journal of Buddhist Studies*, 16: 1–31.

Anālayo, Bhikkhu 2015c: "Nāma-rūpa", in *Encyclopedia of Indian Religions*, A. Sharma (ed.), Dordrecht: Springer (forthcoming).

Anālayo, Bhikkhu 2015d: "The Second Absorption in Early Buddhist Discourse", in *Buddhist Meditation Traditions: An International Symposium*, Kuo-pin Chuang (ed.), Taiwan: Dharma Drum Publishing Corporation (forthcoming).

Ariyaratne, Iromi 2010: "Early Buddhist Environmental Philosophy and Ethics in Cūlagosiṅga Sutta", *Sri Lanka International Journal of Buddhist Studies*, 1: 239–49.

Aronson, Harvey B. 1979a: "Equanimity (Upekkhā) in Theravāda Buddhism", in *Studies in Pali and Buddhism, A Memorial Volume in Honor of Bhikkhu Jagdish Kashyap*, A.K. Narain (ed.), 1–18, Delhi: B.R. Publishing Corporation.

Aronson, Harvey B. 1979b: "The Relationship of the Karmic to the Nirvanic in Theravāda Buddhism", *Journal of Religious Ethics*, 7/1: 28–36.

Aronson, Harvey B. 1980/1986: *Love and Sympathy in Theravāda Buddhism*, Delhi: Motilal Banarsidass.

Aronson, Harvey B. 1984: "Buddhist and Non-buddhist Approaches to the Sublime Attitudes (Brahma-vihāra)", in *Buddhist Studies in Honor of Hammalava Saddhatissa*, Dhammapāla et al. (ed.), 16–24, Sri Lanka: University of Jayewardenepura.

Bechert, Heinz and K. Wille 2004: *Sanskrithandschriften aus den Turfanfunden, Teil 9*, Wiesbaden: Franz Steiner.

Bendall, Cecil 1902/1970. *Çikshāsamuccaya: A Compendium of Buddhist Teaching Compiled by Çāntideva, Chiefly from Earlier Mahāyāna-Sūtras*, Osnabrück: Biblio Verlag.

Bendall, Cecil and W.H.D. Rouse 1922/1990: *Śikṣā Samuccaya, A Compendium of Buddhist Doctrine*, Delhi: Motilal Banarsidass.

Bernhard, Franz 1965 (vol. 1): *Udānavarga*, Göttingen: Vandenhoeck & Ruprecht.

Bingenheimer, Marcus et al. (ed.) 2013: *The Madhyama Āgama (Middle Length Discourses), Volume I*, Berkeley: Numata Center for Buddhist Translation and Research.

Bodhi, Bhikkhu 2000: *The Connected Discourses of the Buddha, A New Translation of the Saṃyutta Nikāya*, Boston: Wisdom Publications.

Bodhi, Bhikkhu 2012: *The Numerical Discourses of the Buddha, A Translation of the Aṅguttara Nikāya*, Boston: Wisdom Publications.

Bodhi, Bhikkhu 2013: "Arahants, Buddhas and Bodhisattvas", in *The Bodhisattva Ideal, Essays on the Emergence of Mahāyāna*, Bhikkhu Ñāṇatusita (ed.), 1–30, Kandy: Buddhist Publication Society.

Brahm, Ajahn 2006: *Mindfulness, Bliss, and Beyond, A Meditator's Handbook*, Boston: Wisdom Publications.

Bronkhorst, Johannes 1993/2000: *The Two Traditions of Meditation in Ancient India*, Delhi: Motilal Banarsidass.

Brough, John 1962/2001: *The Gāndhārī Dharmapada, Edited with an Introduction and Commentary*, Delhi: Motilal Banarsidass.

Burbea, Rob 2014: *Seeing that Frees, Meditations on Emptiness and Dependent Arising*, West Ogwell: Hermes Amāra Publications.

Catherine, Shaila 2008: *Focused and Fearless, A Meditator's Guide to States of Deep Joy, Calm, and Clarity*, Boston: Wisdom Publications.

Choong, Mun-keat 2004/2010: *Annotated Translations of Sutras from the Chinese Saṃyuktāgama Relevant to the Early Buddhist Teachings on Emptiness and the Middle Way*, Songkhla and Nakhon Ratchasima: International Buddhist College.

Cleary, Thomas 1984/1993: *The Flower Ornament Scripture*, Boston: Shambala.

Collett, Alice and Anālayo 2014: "Bhikkhave and Bhikkhu as Gender-inclusive Terminology in Early Buddhist Texts", *Journal of Buddhist Ethics*, 21: 760–97.

Collins, Steven 1987: "Kalyāṇamitta and Kalyāṇamittatā", *Journal of the Pali Text Society*, 11: 51–72.

Cone, Margaret 1989: "Patna Dharmapada", *Journal of the Pali Text Society*, 13: 101–217.

Conze, Edward 1973/1994: *The Perfection of Wisdom in Eight Thousand Lines & Its Verse Summary*, Delhi: Sri Satguru.

Cowell, E.B. and R.A. Neil 1886: *The Divyāvadāna, A Collection of Early Buddhist Legends, Now First Edited from the Nepalese Sanskrit Mss. in Cambridge and Paris*, Cambridge: Cambridge University Press.

Cowell, E.B. and W.H.D. Rouse 1907 (vol. 6): *The Jātaka or Stories of the Buddha's Former Births, Translated from the Pāli by Various Hands*, Cambridge: Cambridge University Press.

de La Vallée Poussin, L. 1911: "Documents sanscrits de la seconde collection M.A. Stein", *Journal of the Royal Asiatic Society*, 759–77 and 1063–79.

Delhey, Martin 2009: *Samāhitā Bhūmiḥ, Das Kapitel über die meditative Versenkung im Grundteil der Yogācārabhūmi*, Vienna: Arbeitskreis für tibetische und buddhistische Studien, Universität Wien.

Dhammadinnā, Sāmaṇerī 2013: "A Translation of the Quotation in Śamathadeva's Abhidharmakośopāyikā-ṭīkā, Parallel to the Chinese Saṃyukta-āgama Discourse 265", *Dharma Drum Journal of Buddhist Studies*, 12: 71–84.

Dhammadinnā, Sāmaṇerī 2014a: "Semantics of Wholesomeness: Purification of Intention and the Soteriological Function of the Immeasurables (appamāṇas) in Early Buddhist Thought", in *Buddhist Meditative Traditions: Their Origin and Development*, Kuo-pin Chuang (ed.), 51–129, Taipei: Shin Wen Feng Print.

Dhammadinnā, Sāmaṇerī 2014b: "A Translation of a Discourse Quotation in the Tibetan Translation of the Mūlasarvāstivāda Vinaya Parallel to Chinese Saṃyukta-āgama Discourse 36 and of the Discourse Quotations in Śamathadeva's Abhidharmakośopāyikā-ṭīkā Parallel to Chinese Saṃyukta-āgama Discourses 39, 42, 45, 46, 55, 56, 57 and 58", *Dharma Drum Journal of Buddhist Studies*, 14: 73–127.

Dhammajothi Thero, Medawachchiye 2008: *The Concept of Emptiness in Pāli Literature*, Taipei: The Corporate Body of the Buddha Educational Foundation.

Engelmajer, Pascale 2003: "Perfect or Perfecting? Reflections on the Arahant in the Nikāyas", *Contemporary Buddhism*, 4/1: 33–54.

Gethin, Rupert 1992: *The Buddhist Path to Awakening: A Study of the Bodhi-Pakkhiyā Dhammā*, Leiden: E.J. Brill.

Gnoli, Raniero 1978 (part 2): *The Gilgit Manuscript of the Saṅghabhedavastu, Being the 17th and Last Section of the Vinaya of the Mūlasarvāstivādin*, Rome: Istituto Italiano per il Medio ed Estremo Oriente.

Gombrich, Richard F. 1988: *Theravāda Buddhism, A Social History from Ancient Benares to Modern Colombo*, London: Routledge & Kegan Paul.

Gonda, Jan 1973: "Mitra and Mitra: The Idea of 'Friendship' in Ancient India", *Indologica Taurinensia*, 1: 71–107.

Harrison, Paul 1997: "The Ekottarikāgama Translations of An Shigao", in *Bauddhavidyāsudhākaraḥ: Studies in Honour of Heinz Bechert on the Occasion of his 65th birthday*, P. Kieffer-Pülz and J.-U. Hartmann (ed.), 261–84, Swisstal-Odendorf: Indica et Tibetica.

Hartmann, Jens-Uwe 1989: "Fragmente aus dem Dīrghāgama der Sarvāstivādins", in *Sanskrit-Texte aus dem Buddhistischen Kanon: Neuentdeckungen und Neueditionen*, 37–67, Göttingen: Vandenhoeck & Ruprecht.

Harvey, Peter 1986: "'Signless' Meditations in Pāli Buddhism", *Journal of the International Association of Buddhist Studies*, 9/1: 25–52.

Hirabayashi, Jiro 2009: "The Sanskrit Fragments Or. 15009/91–100 in the Hoernle Collection", in *Buddhist Manuscripts from Central Asia, The British Library Sanskrit Fragments*, S. Karashima and K. Wille (ed.), 2: 160–8, Tokyo: International Research Institute for Advanced Buddhology, Soka University.

Hoernle, A.F. Rudolf 1897: *The Bower Manuscript, Facsimile Leaves, Nagari Transcript, Romanised Transliteration and English Translation with Notes, Parts III to VII*, Calcutta: Office of the Superintendent of Government Printing.

Hoernle, A.F. Rudolf 1916: *Manuscript Remains of Buddhist Literature Found in Eastern Turkestan, Facsimiles of Manuscripts in Sanskrit, Khotanese, Kuchean, Tibetan and Chinese with Transcripts, Translations and Notes, Edited in Conjunction with Other Scholars, with Critical Introduction and Vocabularies*, Amsterdam: St. Leonards Ad Orientem.

Horner, I.B. 1952/1975 (vol. 5): *The Book of the Discipline (Vinaya-Piṭaka), Volume V (Cullavagga)*, London: Pali Text Society.

Indaka, Sayadaw U 2004: *Metta, The Practice of Loving-Kindness as the Foundation for Insight Meditation Practice*, Ariya Ñani (trsl.), Myanmar: Chanmyay Yeiktha Meditation Centre.

Ireland, John D. 1990: *The Udāna, Inspired Utterances of the Buddha, Translated from the Pali*, Kandy: Buddhist Publication Society.

Ireland, John D. 1991: *The Itivuttaka, The Buddha's Sayings, Translated from the Pali*, Kandy: Buddhist Publication Society.

Jenkins, Stephen Lynn 1999: *The Circle of Compassion: An Interpretative Study of Karuṇā in Indian Buddhist Literature*, PhD thesis, Cambridge, MA: Harvard University.

Khenpo Tsultrim Gyamtso Rimpoche 1986/1988: *Progressive Stages of Meditation on Emptiness*, S. Hookham (trsl.), Oxford: Longchen Foundation.

King, Winston L. 1980/1992: *Theravāda Meditation: The Buddhist Transformation of Yoga*, Delhi: Motilal Banarsidass.

Kudara Kōgi and P. Zieme 1995: "Uigurische Āgama-Fragmente (3)", *Bulletin of [the] Institute of Buddhist Cultural Studies, Ryukoku University*, 34: 23–84.

Lévi, Sylvain 1907: *Mahāyāna-sūtrālaṃkāra, exposé de la doctrine du grand véhicule selon le système Yogācāra, édité et traduit d'après un manuscrit rapporté du Népal*, Paris: Librairie Honoré Champion Éditeur.

Lévi, Sylvain 1932: *Mahākarmavibhaṅga (La grande classification des actes) et Karmavibhaṅgopadeśa (Discussion sur le Mahā Karmavibhaṅga), textes sanscrits rapportés du Népal, édités et traduits avec les textes parallèles en sanscrit, en pali, en tibétain, en chinois et en koutchéen*, Paris: Ernest Leroux.

Liu, Zhen 2010: *Dhyānāni tapaś ca*, Shanghai: Guji chubanshe.

Longchenpa 2007: *Now That I Come to Die, Intimate Guidance from One of Tibet's Greatest Masters*, H.V. Guenther (trsl.), California: Dharma Press.

Mahāsi Sayādaw 1981/2006: *A Discourse on Sallekha Sutta*, U Aye Maung (trsl.), Malaysia: Selangor Buddhist Vipassanā Meditation Society.

Maithrimurthi, Mudagamuwe 1999: *Wohlwollen, Mitleid, Freude und Gleichmut, Eine ideengeschichtliche Untersuchung der vier apramāṇas in der buddhistischen Ethik und Spiritualität von den Anfängen bis hin zum frühen Yogācāra*, Stuttgart: Franz Steiner.

Martini, Giuliana 2011: "Meditative Dynamics of the Early Buddhist Appamāṇas", *Canadian Journal of Buddhist Studies*, 7: 137–80.

Matics, Marion L. 1971: *Entering the Path of Enlightenment, The Bodhicaryāvatāra of the Buddhist Poet Śāntideva*, London: George Allen & Unwin Ltd.

Mitra, Rajendralāla 1888: *Ashṭasáhasriká, A Collection of Discourses on the Metaphysics of the Maháyána School of the Buddhists, Now First Edited from Nepalese Sanskrit Mss.*, Calcutta: Asiatic Society.

Mittal, Kusum 1957: *Dogmatische Begriffsreihen im älteren Buddhismus, I, Fragmente des Daśottarasūtra aus zentralasiatischen Sanskrit-Handschriften*, Berlin: Akademie Verlag.

Nagashima, Jundo 2009: "The Sanskrit Fragments Or. 15009/251–290 in the Hoernle Collection", in *Buddhist Manuscripts from Central Asia, The British Library Sanskrit Fragments*, S. Karashima and K. Wille (ed.), 2: 258–86, Tokyo: International Research Institute for Advanced Buddhology, Soka University.

Namdol, Gyaltsen 1997: *Bhāvanākramaḥ of Ācārya Kamalaśīla*, Sarnath: Central Institute of Higher Tibetan Studies.

Ñāṇamoli, Bhikkhu 1956/1991: *The Path of Purification (Visuddhimagga) by Bhadantācariya Buddhaghosa*, Kandy: Buddhist Publication Society.

Ñāṇamoli, Bhikkhu 1982: *The Path of Discrimination (Paṭisambhidāmagga), Translated from the Pāli*, London: Pali Text Society.

Ñāṇamoli, Bhikkhu 1995: *The Middle Length Discourses of the Buddha, A Translation of the Majjhima Nikāya*, Bhikkhu Bodhi (ed.), Boston: Wisdom Publications.

Ñāṇananda, Bhikkhu 2003 (vol. 1), 2004 (vol. 2), 2005 (vol. 3), 2006 (vol. 4), 2007 (vol. 5), 2010 (vol. 6), 2012 (vol. 7): *Nibbāna – The Mind Stilled*, Sri Lanka: Dharma Grantha Mudrana Bhāraya.

Ñāṇaponika Thera 1966/1981: *The Greater Discourse on the Elephant-Footprint Simile, from the Majjhima Nikāya*, Kandy: Buddhist Publication Society.

Nattier, Jan 2003: *A Few Good Men, The Bodhisattva Path according to The Inquiry of Ugra (Ugraparipṛcchā)*, Honolulu: University of Hawai'i Press.

Norman, K.R. 1969: *The Elders' Verses I, Theragāthā, Translated with an Introduction and Notes*, Oxford: Pali Text Society.

Norman, K.R. 1991/1993: "Theravāda Buddhism and Brahmanical Hinduism", in *Collected Papers*, K.R. Norman (ed.), 4: 271–80, Oxford: Pali Text Society.

Norman, K.R. 1992: *The Group of Discourses (Sutta-nipāta), Revised Translation with Introduction and Notes*, Oxford: Pali Text Society.

Norman, K.R. 1997/2004: *The Word of the Doctrine (Dhammapada)*, Oxford: Pali Text Society.

Ohnuma, Reiko 2012: *Ties that Bind, Maternal Imagery and Discourse in Indian Buddhism*, Oxford: Oxford University Press.

Pradhan, Pralhad 1950: *Abhidharma Samuccaya of Asaṅga, Critically Edited and Studied*, Santiniketan: Visva-Bharati.

Pradhan, Pralhad 1967: *Abhidharmakośabhāṣya of Vasubandhu*, Patna: K.P. Jayaswal Research Institute.

Ricard, Matthieu and Trinh Xuan Thuan 2001: *The Quantum and the Lotus, A Journey to the Frontiers Where Science and Buddhism Meet*, New York: Three Rivers Press.

Salzberg, Sharon 2002: *Loving-kindness, The Revolutionary Art of Happiness*, Boston: Shambala.

Samtani, N.H. 1971: *The Arthaviniścaya-Sūtra & Its Commentary (Nibandhana) (Written by Bhikṣu Vīryaśrīdatta of Śrī-Nālandāvihāra), Critically Edited and Annotated for the First Time with Introduction and Several Indices*, Patna: K.P. Jayaswal Research Institute.

Sander, Lore and E. Waldschmidt 1985: *Sanskrithandschriften aus den Turfanfunden, Teil 5*, Stuttgart: Franz Steiner.

Schlingloff, Dieter 1967: Review [of *Sanskrithandschriften aus den Turfanfunden, Teil I*], *Zeitschrift der Deutschen Morgenländischen Gesellschaft*, 116: 419–25.

Schmidt, Erik Hein 1990: *Crystal Cave, A Compendium of Teachings by Masters of the Practice Lineage*, Kathmandu: Rangjung Yeshe.

Schmithausen, Lambert 1981: "On Some Aspects of Descriptions or Theories of 'Liberating Insight' and 'Enlightenment' in Early Buddhism", in *Studien zum Jainismus und Buddhismus, Gedenkschrift für Ludwig Alsdorf*, K. Bruhn and A. Wezler. (ed.), 199–250, Wiesbaden: Franz Steiner.

Schmithausen, Lambert 1997: *Maitrī and Magic: Aspects of the Buddhist Attitude towards the Dangerous in Nature*, Vienna: Verlag der Österreichischen Akademie der Wissenschaft.

Schmithausen, Lambert 2000: "Mitleid und Leerheit, zu Spiritualität und Heilsziel des Mahāyāna", in *Der Buddhismus als Anfrage an christliche Theologie und Philosophie*, A. Bsteh (ed.), 437–55, Mödling: St. Gabriel.

Schmithausen, Lambert 2004: "Benefiting Oneself and Benefiting Others: A Note on Aṅguttaranikāya 7.64", in *Gedenkschrift J.W. de Jong*, H.W. Bodewitz and M. Hara (ed.), 149–60, Tokyo: International Institute for Buddhist Studies.

Senart, Émile 1897 (vol. 3): *Le Mahāvastu, texte sanscrit publié pour la première fois et accompagné d'introductions et d'un commentaire*, Paris: Imprimerie Nationale.

Sharma, Parmananda 1997/2004: *Bhāvanākrama of Kamalaśīla*, Delhi: Aditya Prakashan.

Sheng Yen 2008: *The Method of No-Method, The Chan Practice of Silent Illumination*, Boston: Shambala.

Shì Hùifēng 2013: "'Dependent Origination = Emptiness' – Nāgārjuna's Innovation? An Examination of the Early and Mainstream Sectarian Textual Sources", *Journal of the Centre for Buddhist Studies, Sri Lanka*, 11: 175–227.

Skilling, Peter 1994 (vol. 1): *Mahāsūtras: Great Discourses of the Buddha*, Oxford: Pali Text Society.

Skilling, Peter 2007: "Mṛgāra's Mother's Mansion: Emptiness and the Śūnyatā Sūtras", *Journal of Indian and Tibetan Studies*, 11: 225–47.

Stoler Miller, Barbara 1979: "On Cultivating the Immeasurable Change of Heart: The Buddhist Brahma-vihāra Formula", *Journal of Indian Philosophy*, 7: 209–21.

Thiṭṭila, P.A. 1969: *The Book of Analysis (Vibhaṅga), The Second Book of the Abhidhammapiṭaka, Translated from the Pāḷi of the Burmese Chaṭṭasaṅgīti Edition*, London: Pali Text Society.

Trenckner, V. et al., 1924 (vol. 1): *A Critical Pāli Dictionary*, Copenhagen: Royal Danish Academy of Science.

Tripāṭhī, Chandrabhāl 1962: *Fünfundzwanzig Sūtras des Nidānasaṃyukta*, Berlin: Akademie Verlag.

Tripāṭhī, Sridhar 1988: *Bodhicaryāvatāra of Śāntideva with the Commentary Pañjikā of Prajñākaramati*, Darbhanga: Mithila Institute.

Vimalaraṃsi Mahāthera 2012: *The Breath of Love, A Simple Guide for Mindfulness of Breathing Meditation with Support Information for Loving-kindness Meditation, Forgiveness Meditation, and Walking Meditation*, Annapolis, MO: Dhamma Sukha Meditation Center.

Waldschmidt, Ernst 1951 (vol. 2): *Das Mahāparinirvāṇasūtra, Text in Sanskrit und Tibetisch, verglichen mit dem Pāli nebst einer Übersetzung der chinesischen Entsprechung im Vinaya der Mūlasarvāstivādins, auf Grund von Turfan-Handschriften herausgegeben und bearbeitet*, Berlin: Akademie Verlag.

Waldschmidt, Ernst 1957: "Das Upasenasūtra, ein Zauber gegen Schlangenbiss aus dem Saṃyuktāgama", *Nachrichten der Akademie der Wissenschaften in Göttingen*, 2: 27–46.

Waldschmidt, Ernst 1958: "Ein Zweites Daśabalasūtra", *Mitteilungen des Institutes für Orientforschung*, 6: 382–405.

Waldschmidt, Ernst 1979: "The Varṇaśatam, An Eulogy of One Hundred Epitheta of Lord Buddha Spoken by the Gṛhapati Upāli", *Nachrichten der Akademie der Wissenschaften in Göttingen, Philologisch-Historische Klasse, Jahrgang 1979 Nr. 1*, 3–19.

Waldschmidt, Ernst et al. 1965: *Sanskrithandschriften aus den Turfanfunden, Teil I*, Wiesbaden: Franz Steiner.

Walshe, Maurice 1987: *Thus Have I Heard: The Long Discourses of the Buddha*, London: Wisdom Publications.

Weller, Friedrich 1934: *Brahmajālasūtra, Tibetischer und Mongolischer Text*, Leipzig: Otto Harrassowitz.

Wille, Klaus 2008: *Sanskrithandschriften aus den Turfanfunden Teil 10*, Stuttgart: Franz Steiner.

Wogihara, Unrai 1930/1936: *Bodhisattvabhūmi, A Statement of Whole Course of the Bodhisattva (Being Fifteenth Section of Yogācārabhūmi)*, Tokyo: Sankibo.

Wogihara, Unrai 1936: *Sphuṭârthā Abhidharmakośavyākhyā by Yaśomitra, Part II*, Tokyo: The Publishing Association of Abhidharmakośavyākhyā.

Woodward, F.L. 1936/1955 (vol. 5): *The Book of the Gradual Sayings (Aṅguttara-Nikāya) or More-numbered Suttas*, London: Pali Text Society.

Woolner, Alfred C. 1924/1993: *Asoka Text and Glossary (Panjab University Oriental Publications)*, Delhi: Low Price Publications.

# LIST OF ABBREVIATIONS

| | |
|---|---|
| AN | *Aṅguttara-nikāya* |
| D | Derge ed. |
| DĀ | *Dīrgha-āgama* (T 1) |
| Dhp | *Dhammapada* |
| DN | *Dīgha-nikāya* |
| EĀ | *Ekottarika-āgama* (T 125) |
| It | *Itivuttaka* |
| Jā | *Jātaka* |
| MĀ | *Madhyama-āgama* (T 26) |
| MN | *Majjhima-nikāya* |
| Mp | *Manorathapūraṇī* |
| Paṭis | *Paṭisambhidāmagga* |
| Pj I | *Paramatthajotikā* |
| Ps | *Papañcasūdanī* |
| Ps-pṭ | *Papañcasūdanī-purāṇaṭīkā* |
| Q | *Peking ed.* |
| SĀ | *Saṃyukta-āgama* (T 99) |
| SĀ² | *Saṃyukta-āgama* (T 100) |
| SHT | *Sanskrithandschriften aus den Turfanfunden* |
| Sn | *Sutta-nipāta* |
| SN | *Saṃyutta-nikāya* |
| T | Taishō ed. (CBETA) |
| Th | *Theragāthā* |
| Ud | *Udāna* |
| Vibh | *Vibhaṅga* |
| Vin | *Vinayapiṭaka* |
| Vism | *Visuddhimagga* |

# SUBJECT INDEX

INTRODUCTORY NOTE

References such as '178–9' indicate (not necessarily continuous) discussion of a topic across a range of pages. Wherever possible in the case of topics with many references, these have either been divided into sub-topics or only the most significant discussions of the topic are listed.

# INDEX LOCORUM

## WINDHORSE PUBLICATIONS

Windhorse Publications is a Buddhist charitable company based in the UK. We place great emphasis on producing books of high quality that are accessible and relevant to those interested in Buddhism at whatever level. We are the main publisher of the works of Sangharakshita, the founder of the Triratna Buddhist Order and Community. Our books draw on the whole range of the Buddhist tradition, including translations of traditional texts, commentaries, books that make links with contemporary culture and ways of life, biographies of Buddhists, and works on meditation.

As a not-for-profit enterprise, we ensure that all surplus income is invested in new books and improved production methods, to better communicate Buddhism in the 21st century. We welcome donations to help us continue our work – to find out more, go to www.windhorsepublications.com.

The Windhorse is a mythical animal that flies over the earth carrying on its back three precious jewels, bringing these invaluable gifts to all humanity: the Buddha (the 'awakened one'), his teaching, and the community of all his followers.

Windhorse Publications
17e Sturton Street
Cambridge
CB1 2SN
UK
info@windhorsepublications.com

Perseus Distribution
210 American Drive
Jackson TN 38301
USA

Windhorse Books
PO Box 574
Newtown NSW 2042
Australia

## THE TRIRATNA BUDDHIST COMMUNITY

Windhorse Publications is a part of the Triratna Buddhist Community, an international movement with centres in Europe, India, North and South America and Australasia. At these centres, members of the Triratna Buddhist Order offer classes in meditation and Buddhism. Activities of the Triratna Community also include retreat centres, residential spiritual communities, ethical Right Livelihood businesses, and the Karuna Trust, a UK fundraising charity that supports social welfare projects in the slums and villages of India.

Through these and other activities, Triratna is developing a unique approach to Buddhism, not simply as a philosophy and a set of techniques, but as a creatively directed way of life for all people living in the conditions of the modern world.

If you would like more information about Triratna please visit thebuddhistcentre.com or write to:

London Buddhist Centre
51 Roman Road
London E2 0HU
UK

Aryaloka
14 Heartwood Circle
Newmarket NH 03857
USA

Sydney Buddhist Centre
24 Enmore Road
Sydney NSW 2042
Australia

**Satipaṭṭhāna**
**The Direct Path to Realization**

by Bhikkhu Anālayo

This best-selling book offers a unique and detailed textual study of the Satipaṭṭhāna Sutta, a foundational Buddhist discourse on meditation practice.

*This book should prove to be of value both to scholars of Early Buddhism and to serious meditators alike.* – Bhikku Bodhi

*. . . a gem . . . I learned a lot from this wonderful book and highly recommend it.* – Joseph Goldstein

*An indispensible guide . . . surely destined to become the classic commentary on the Satipaṭṭhāna.* – Christopher Titmuss

*Very impressive and useful, with its blend of strong scholarship and attunement to practice issues.* – Prof. Peter Harvey, author of *An Introduction to Buddhist Ethics*

ISBN 9781 899579 54 9
£15.99 / $24.95 / €19.95
336 pages

**Perspectives on Satipaṭṭhāna**

by Bhikkhu Anālayo

As mindfulness is increasingly embraced in the contemporary world as a practice that brings peace and self-awareness, Bhikkhu Anālayo casts fresh light on the earliest sources of mindfulness in the Buddhist tradition.

The Satipaṭṭhāna Sutta is well known as the main source for Buddhist teachings on mindfulness and its place in the Buddhist path. Ten years after Anālayo's acclaimed study of the Sutta, his current work, *Perspectives on Satipaṭṭhāna*, brings a new dimension to our understanding by comparing the Pali text with versions that have survived in Chinese. Anālayo also draws on the presentation of mindfulness in a number of other discourses as they survive in Chinese and Tibetan translations as well as in Pali.

The result is a wide-ranging exploration of what mindfulness meant in early Buddhism. Informed by Anālayo's outstanding scholarship, depth of understanding and experience as a practitioner, this book sheds fresh light on material that is central to our understanding of Buddhist practice, bringing us as close as we can come to the mindfulness teachings of the Buddha himself.

*'Anālayo builds on his earlier ground-breaking work,* Satipaṭṭhāna: The Direct Path to Realization. *The brilliance of his scholarly research, combined with the depth of his meditative understanding, provides an invaluable guide to these liberating practices.'* – Joseph Goldstein

*'He offers us a work of great scholarship and wisdom that will be of immense benefit to anyone who wants to seriously study or to establish a practice of mindfulness.'* – Sharon Salzberg

*'A treasury of impeccable scholarship and practice, offering a wise, open-minded and deep understanding of the Buddha's original teaching.'* – Jack Kornfield

ISBN: 9781 909314 03 0
£15.99 / $24.95 / €19.95
336 pages

**Mind in Harmony: The Psychology of Buddhist Ethics**

by Subhuti

*'It's not our bank balance, looks, social status or popularity that determines how happy, free and fulfilled we are in life. Finally, what really counts is our state of mind. Subhuti helps us to identify what's going on in our mind, including our moods and emotions, and see clearly what's helpful and what will end in tears.'* – Vessantara, author of *The Breath* and *A Guide to the Buddhas*

*'This is a refreshing approach to the classical Abhidharma material, relentlessly experiential and eminently practical. It offers a way of engaging directly with the sophisticated elements of Buddhist psychology that is immediately accessible and offers a real prospect of transformation. I heartily recommend it to anyone who wants to use Buddhist wisdom to explore and clarify their minds.'* – Andrew Olendzki, author of *Unlimiting Mind*, senior scholar at Barre Center for Buddhist Studies

'What exactly should I be working on in my spiritual life?'

This is the question that Subhuti sets before us, along with what we most need to answer it for ourselves.

Long before the discoveries of contemporary neuroscience and psychology, the Buddha gained insight into the nature of mind. In early Buddhism this profound insight informed the Abhidharma – a 'training manual' to help us understand and transform our own minds. Subhuti brings this manual to life, and shows us the ways in which it illuminates our mind's patterns.

Outlining the processes whereby the mind attends to the world, and explaining how mindfulness fits into the pattern of spiritual development from the perspective of the Abhidharma, Subhuti guides us expertly to an appreciation of how mental states arise, and how to distinguish between skilful mental states and their opposites. In this way, we are given the means to live a happier and more fruitful life, and ultimately a pathway to liberation from all suffering. We are also offered a glimpse of how the enlightened mind of a Buddha works – the mind in its ultimate harmony.

Subhuti has led retreats in Europe, the United States and India on the Buddhist texts of the Yogacara Abhidharma, the source of this system of mind training. This book is the fruit of that teaching experience.

ISBN 978 1 909314 08 5
£12.99 / $19.95 / €12.95
272 pages

**Buddhist Meditation**
**Tranquillity, Imagination & Insight**

by Kamalashila

First published in 1991, this book is a comprehensive and practical guide to Buddhist meditation, providing a complete introduction for beginners, as well as detailed advice for experienced meditators seeking to deepen their practice. Kamalashila explores the primary aims of Buddhist meditation: enhanced awareness, true happiness, and – ultimately – liberating insight into the nature of reality. This third edition includes new sections on the importance of the imagination, on Just Sitting, and on reflection on the Buddha. Kamalashila has been teaching meditation since becoming a member of the Triratna Buddhist Order in 1974. He has developed approaches to meditation practice that are accessible to people in the contemporary world, whilst being firmly grounded in the Buddhist tradition.

*A wonderfully practical and accessible introduction to the important forms of Buddhist meditation. From his years of meditation practice, Kamalashila has written a book useful for both beginners and longtime practitioners.* – Gil Fronsdal, author of *A Monastery Within*, founder of the Insight Meditation Center, California, USA.

*This enhanced new edition guides readers more clearly into the meditations and draws out their significance more fully, now explicitly oriented around the 'system of meditation'. This system provides a fine framework both for understanding where various practices fit in and for reflecting on the nature of our own spiritual experiences. Kamalashila has also woven in an appreciation of a view of the nature of mind that in the Western tradition is known as the imagination, helping make an accessible link to our own philosophical and cultural traditions.* – Lama Surya Das, author of *Awakening the Buddha Within*, founder of Dzogchen Center and Dzogchen Meditation Retreats, USA.

*His approach is a clear, thorough, honest, and, above all, open-ended exploration of the practical problems for those new to and even quite experienced in meditation.* – Lama Shenpen Hookham, author of *There Is More to Dying Than Death*, founder of the Awakened Heart Sangha, UK.

ISBN 9781 907314 09 4
£14.99 / $27.95 / €19.95
272 pages